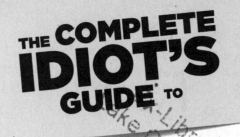

THE **COMPLETE IDIOT'S GUIDE** TO

Running

Third Edition

by Bill Rodgers and Scott Douglas

ALPHA

A member of Penguin Group (USA) Inc.

ALPHA BOOKS

Published by the Penguin Group

Penguin Group (USA) Inc., 375 Hudson Street, New York, New York 10014, USA

Penguin Group (Canada), 90 Eglinton Avenue East, Suite 700, Toronto, Ontario M4P 2Y3, Canada (a division of Pearson Penguin Canada Inc.)

Penguin Books Ltd., 80 Strand, London WC2R 0RL, England

Penguin Ireland, 25 St. Stephen's Green, Dublin 2, Ireland (a division of Penguin Books Ltd.)

Penguin Group (Australia), 250 Camberwell Road, Camberwell, Victoria 3124, Australia (a division of Pearson Australia Group Pty. Ltd.)

Penguin Books India Pvt. Ltd., 11 Community Centre, Panchsheel Park, New Delhi—110 017, India

Penguin Group (NZ), 67 Apollo Drive, Rosedale, North Shore, Auckland 1311, New Zealand (a division of Pearson New Zealand Ltd.)

Penguin Books (South Africa) (Pty.) Ltd., 24 Sturdee Avenue, Rosebank, Johannesburg 2196, South Africa

Penguin Books Ltd., Registered Offices: 80 Strand, London WC2R 0RL, England

Copyright © 2010 by Bill Rodgers

International Standard Book Number: 978-1-61564-028-7
Library of Congress Catalog Card Number: 2009937008

12   11   10   8   7   6   5   4   3   2   1

Interpretation of the printing code: The rightmost number of the first series of numbers is the year of the book's printing; the rightmost number of the second series of numbers is the number of the book's printing. For example, a printing code of 10-1 shows that the first printing occurred in 2010.

Printed in the United States of America

Most Alpha books are available at special quantity discounts for bulk purchases for sales promotions, premiums, fund-raising, or educational use. Special books, or book excerpts, can also be created to fit specific needs.

For details, write: Special Markets, Alpha Books, 375 Hudson Street, New York, NY 10014.

Publisher: *Marie Butler-Knight*
Associate Publisher: *Mike Sanders*
Senior Managing Editor: *Billy Fields*
Acquisitions Editor: *Tom Stevens*
Development Editor: *Nancy D. Lewis*
Production Editor: *Kayla Dugger*

Copy Editor: *Amy Borrelli*
Cover Designer: *Rebecca Batchelor*
Book Designers: *William Thomas, Rebecca Batchelor*
Indexer: *Heather McNeill*
Layout: *Brian Massey*
Proofreader: *Laura Caddell*

Contents

Introduction

Ask a group of regular runners if they hope to run for the rest of their lives, and they'll all tell you yes. Me? I've been a runner for more than 35 years, and I hope to still be one 35 years from now.

Running is great exercise—in fact, it's one of the simplest, most effective, and most convenient forms of exercise around. Keep running, and you'll do some incredible things for your health. But running is also a way of life. It's about having more energy, feeling good about yourself, making new friends, challenging yourself, enjoying nature, and a million other things that I want to tell you about. As you might have guessed, I love running. In this book, I hope to pass on that passion to you.

How to Use This Book

This book is divided into five parts. Think of them as five different runs, all interesting and enjoyable enough on their own, but even more so when combined with the others.

Part 1, In the Beginning, tells you what you need to know to start a running program. I'll explain why so many people run and how running helps your health. I'll give you a training plan that will take you from no running to 30 minutes at a time in just a month. Also, I'll give you tips about how to find the time to run, where to run, and how to stay motivated.

Part 2, The Right Stuff, deals with the main equipment that runners use. The most important thing here is a good pair of running shoes. I'll show you how to pick a pair that's right for you. I'll also list what running apparel you need to run comfortably. And I'll highlight some of the best running gadgets. At the end of this section, you'll know how to look the part.

Part 3, Body Shop, is all about the most important part of your running—your body. I'll show you how to prevent injuries with the right stretching and strengthening exercises. I'll also tell you how to treat common injuries, describe the runners' diet, highlight what's special about running for women, and explain how to run comfortably in different kinds of weather. Your legs will thank you once you're armed with this info.

Part 4, Join the Human Race, deals with my favorite aspect of this sport—racing. I'll explain why racing is so much fun and how to prepare for everything from your local 5K to the marathon, and all distances in between.

Part 5, Running Through the Ages, has special advice for younger and older runners. Regardless of how old you are now, it tells you how to stay a runner for the rest of your life. Isn't that what it's all about?

Extras

Every chapter in this book contains helpful and informative sidebars that show you how to run better and understand running a little bit more:

DEFINITION

What is a split, DNF, and fartlek? Look for these sidebars to learn today's running lingo.

TRAINING TIP

The information in this sidebar is a tidbit of how-to knowledge. Follow the advice here to supplement your running knowledge and training.

RULES OF THE ROAD

It takes more than proper form and training to become a good runner. These sidebars teach you about running safety and etiquette for when you're ready to put your best feet forward.

FOOTNOTES

You never know when someone might ask you who won the Boston Marathon in 1975 (yes, it was Bill Rodgers). These sidebars include bits of running lore, running history, and running facts and figures.

Acknowledgments

Although running is primarily an individual sport, you need the support and guidance of family and friends, coaches, and training partners to do your best. So thanks most of all to my parents, my brother Charlie, and sisters Linda and Martha for all of their support over the years as I've continued to aim for excellence in competitive running.

For showing me how to stay on the road, sincere thanks to Frank O'Rourke, who guided my best friend, Jason Kehoe, Charlie, and me through our first year of running in 1963. He must have done something right, because we're all still at it! My Wesleyan University coach, Elmer Swanson, taught me commitment and how to keep running fun, and Billy Squires, America's finest marathon coach, guided me and many others to the top of the marathon world.

Thanks also to my co-author, Scott Douglas, for joining me and successfully completing this marathon challenge.

Trademarks

All terms mentioned in this book that are known to be or are suspected of being trademarks or service marks have been appropriately capitalized. Alpha Books and Penguin Group (USA) Inc. cannot attest to the accuracy of this information. Use of a term in this book should not be regarded as affecting the validity of any trademark or service mark.

In the Beginning

Everywhere you look these days, you see runners. Your neighbor is a runner. Your co-worker is a runner. Heck, Oprah Winfrey, Will Ferrell, and Sarah Palin have run marathons. What's going on? What's so great about running?

In the first part of this book, I'll tell you some of the myriad reasons why people run. You'll learn that running, among other things, gives you more energy, helps you lose weight, and allows you to reclaim your youth. If you've always used the "I don't have the time" excuse, I'll show you how you can fit running into your busy life and still be gainfully employed. Once I've got you up and running, so to speak, I'll do my part to keep you going with special motivational strategies that longtime runners use.

Hit the Road, Jack and Jill

In This Chapter

- Why to start running
- How many runners there are in the United States
- The kinder, gentler face of running in the twenty-first century
- The difference between running and jogging
- Common myths about running

Thirty-five years ago, when I started training seriously for marathons, most people who saw someone running down the street thought that person was either a crook or a kook. That's no longer the case. During the last three decades, running has become a regular part of American life. Most people now know that running a few times a week on a regular basis is one of the best things you can do to take control of your health. In this chapter, I'll show you other reasons to start running, as well as give you a sense of how many other runners there are and what they're like so that you'll know whom you'll be sharing the roads with.

Reasons to Run

How do I love running? Let me count the ways. There are as many reasons to run as there are runners, and that's a lot of reasons! Most people, of course, run for physical reasons (or at least that's why they start to run); they want to lose weight, fight a family history of heart disease, or just feel better.

Other people run for different reasons. A lot of runners, especially young ones, get into it for the competition. They want to see how fast they can run a mile or whether they can beat their next-door neighbor in the local 5K. Other people run primarily for psychological reasons. They like the stress relief, reflection time, and sense of being in control that running brings.

Here's a baker's dozen of some of the most popular reasons to run:

1. Running is a great way to lose weight.

2. Regular *aerobic exercise,* such as running, decreases the risk of heart disease.

3. Running is one of the most effective ways to improve *cardiovascular fitness.*

4. Running is a great way to quit smoking.

5. Regular aerobic exercise reduces the risk of some cancers.

6. When you become fitter by running, you're more likely to improve other aspects of your lifestyle, such as your diet.

7. Running is the most convenient of sports; you can do it almost anytime, anywhere.

8. People who have a high level of physical fitness usually have a positive self-image.

9. Running is cheap; all you need are a good pair of running shoes and a few pieces of running apparel.

10. Fitter people are more productive on the job.

11. Running with others is a great way to build friendships.

12. Being fit increases mental sharpness; regular exercisers are able to concentrate longer and are better problem solvers.

13. Running is one of the best stress relievers around.

DEFINITION

Aerobic exercise means working out at a moderate level so that you're not out of breath for at least 20 minutes at a time. **Aerobic** means "with oxygen"; examples of aerobic exercises are distance running, swimming, cycling, and walking.

Cardiovascular fitness is the ability to sustain comfortably a moderate level of aerobic exercise. It's what people mean when they talk about stamina or endurance—being fit enough to keep up a decent level of activity. Of the main components of fitness, cardiovascular fitness is the most important and directly relates to your risk of heart disease and some cancers.

You might have noticed that some of these reasons can apply to other forms of exercise, such as cycling or walking. I have nothing against these sports, but you might have also noticed that some of these reasons only pertain to running. The combination of what running has in common with other ways to work out and its unique features is what, in my humble opinion, makes it the best exercise choice for the greatest number of people. You might not believe me now, but here are two more important reasons to run that you'll discover if you stick with it for just a bit: running feels good while you're doing it and after you've done it, and it's tons of fun!

The next chapter looks in depth at how running helps to improve your health. I'm guessing that if you've picked up this book, you already know about some of running's health benefits and that those all-important health reasons are among your strongest reasons for having an interest in running. So indulge me a bit here while I go off on a slightly different tack and tell you a little bit about why I started running. My point in doing so is to show you that, like you probably do, I had a lot of different motivations. One of the great things about running is that with so many compelling reasons to do it, these reasons tend to reinforce each other (at least that was the case with me).

Like a lot of kids, I started running as a member of a high school team. I ran a 1-mile race put on by the Newington, Connecticut, Parks and Recreation Department when I was in my mid-teens. I was able to win in a time of 5:20. I liked being good at something (and being better than the other kids), so I went out for the high school cross-country and track teams. I won the state championship in cross-country, and I got my mile time down to 4:28. I was drawn to running as a racer, but I also discovered that I simply liked to run. I liked how it felt when I did it. I liked the sense of being outside and exploring nature with my friends on the team. People usually don't think of these reasons for running right off the bat.

One of my goals in college had been to break 9:00 for 2 miles, and I achieved it. But when I got out of college in 1970, I stopped running. With so much else going on in my life at the time, I figured, what was the point of continuing to run? I drifted for a couple of years, working menial jobs to fulfill the requirements of being a conscientious objector. I started drinking a little too much, a little too often. And I became a smoker.

In 1972, Frank Shorter, an American, won the Olympic *Marathon*. I didn't know Frank then, but he's my age. I remember watching him win that race on television. Something in the back of my mind tugged at me to become a runner again.

DEFINITION

A **marathon** is a race that's 26 miles, 385 yards long. It's the farthest that most runners ever go. It's not accurate to call any long race a marathon because the name refers to the specific distance of 26.2 miles.

I can recall from around this time sitting in a bar and thinking, "This can't be it. This just can't be it. There has to be something more to life than drinking and smoking." Gradually, in fits and starts, I started to run again, for a whole new set of reasons. Competition wasn't my driving goal. Something more important was taking control of my life. When I was at my depths, running gave me back my self-esteem.

Running helped me to quit smoking, because as I became fitter, smoking became that much less enjoyable. Eventually, I got excited about competition again and ran the first race of my comeback in 1973. Two years later, I won the first of four Boston Marathons.

TRAINING TIP

If you're trying to quit smoking, one of the best ways to fight the urge to light up is to get outside and move around for a bit. The fresh air makes all that tar and nicotine that much more distasteful. I used this method to kick my two-pack-a-day habit.

Why am I telling you all this? Because I want you to see that every runner, even someone like me who you might think was born running a million miles a day at an ungodly speed, was at some point a confused, unsure beginner. But like me, every runner also soon discovers his or her own endless reasons for sticking with it. Ask any group of regular runners if they want to run for the rest of their lives, and the answer will be a unanimous yes. That is perhaps the single best reason to run: when you're a runner, life is better.

10,000,000 Runners Can't Be Wrong

How many runners are there in the United States? According to the National Sporting Goods Association, in 2008, 7.7 million Americans ran at least 110 times that year. If you run 110 times in a year, that means you're averaging almost 3 runs per week. I think that level of frequency is a good marker of someone being a regular runner. Run three times a week, and you'll be able to progress in terms of endurance, distance, and so on.

Running in the Twenty-First Century

Just who are these millions of runners who are so dedicated that they're out there more than 100 days a year? For the most part, they're otherwise average Americans. Subscribers to the largest running magazine, *Runner's World*, are split almost evenly between women and men. In American road races in 2008, 56 percent of the women were age 20 to 39, and another 34 percent were age 40 or older. That year, 45 percent of the men at road races were age 40 or older. So throw away your image of running being only for that 25-year-old guy down the street who looks as though he could break 4:00 for the mile.

Some of the misconceptions about who runners are stem from the first running boom, which took place in the mid- to late 1970s. At that time, a lot of runners were motivated primarily by competition and running high mileage. In some circles, your time for the marathon was the be-all and end-all of your existence. I certainly never thought this way; I've always been for people exploring all that running has to offer and finding the level that they're comfortable with. Yet I'm associated with what some people see as the extremes of the first running boom.

When the boom hit, I was at my peak. I won the Boston Marathon four times between 1975 and 1980. During those years, I also won the New York City Marathon four times. This was just as interest in large-scale running events was taking off. Marathons were held up to be the pinnacle of running achievement.

For a while, running was kind of chic. Even Hunter S. Thompson, the famous "gonzo journalist" for *Rolling Stone*, once covered the Honolulu Marathon. We baby boomers have been pretty good at being the center of the media's attention for most of our lives. During this time, in the late 1970s, we were around 30 years old—just about the age at which a marathoner peaks. Getting those peak performances in the marathon requires logging a lot of miles. So in the public's view, running was all about putting in more than 10 miles a day, eating funny, being really thin, and making all these sacrifices to better your time in this strange race called the marathon.

As with most other things, the media eventually got bored with running and moved on to something else. People didn't hear about some of the fundamental changes in running, both in terms of who participates and in their attitudes, for a long time. A lot of those baby boomers who were hard-core marathoners in the first running boom kept right on running. But like everyone else, they had to make adjustments as the years passed. Some of them learned that they just weren't cut out for constant high-mileage training. As their career and family responsibilities increased, their time and energy for running decreased. But the important thing is that most of them kept at it, and are still going.

Some people have said that American running is undergoing a second boom, but they say that because the media has started to pay attention again, not because participation numbers have skyrocketed out of nowhere in just the last few years. In 2008, there were 425,000 marathon finishers in the United States. That's more than double the number from 1986 and almost four times as many as in 1980, during the supposed "boom."

If there is a second boom going on, what marks it is a difference in participants and their attitudes and motivation. Running in the twenty-first century is said to be kinder and gentler. No longer do you see many people going around trying to flout their status by boasting about their marathon *PR*. The average runner today runs less than the average runner of the first boom and is drawn to running for health and social reasons more so than for hard-core competition reasons.

DEFINITION

PR stands for personal record, your best time for a distance. Runners cherish and talk about their PRs the way that new parents talk about their babies. When you're in the company of other runners, it's common runner's etiquette to talk about your PRs only if you're asked.

But wait a minute. Aren't I contradicting myself by saying that marathon participation has doubled in the last decade, and then saying that running these days is kinder and gentler? No, because even the marathon, which was once taken to be the holy grail of running for which runners had to sacrifice endlessly, is today seen as a solid, but conquerable, challenge for almost any runner.

What that means is that more marathoners are drawn to the event by the challenge of finishing, not seeing how quickly they can do so. "Completing, not competing" is how some people put it. People run marathons to raise money for charity, mark a significant turning point in their lives, and other reasons that have nothing to do with their finishing times. This more relaxed attitude has had the following effect: in the last 25 years, the median finish time at marathons has gotten a lot slower. The median finish time for a man is now 4:16, compared to 3:32 in 1980. For women, the median time is 4:43, compared to 4:03 in 1980.

Still think that running is only for skinny, fast, always-training competitive athletes? Still think that running isn't embraced by millions of Americans of all ages and shapes and backgrounds as an inclusive, healthful way to lead their lives? Then I'll leave you with this tidbit: in 1994, Oprah Winfrey finished the Marine Corps Marathon. She then appeared on the cover of *Runner's World*. Oprah later said that of all the magazine covers she's ever been on, being on *Runner's World*'s was the biggest thrill. That issue of *Runner's World* is still the biggest seller in the magazine's 40-year history.

FOOTNOTES

Runner's World is the most popular running magazine in the world, with a circulation of about 600,000. The other major American running magazine is *Running Times*.

Running vs. Jogging

What is the difference between jogging and running? There are lots of ways to make the distinction—how far you run, how fast you run, why you run, how often you run, and so on, ad infinitum. No, make that ad nauseum. The debates about who's a jogger and who's a runner are endless and fierce, but they're also pointless.

Usually, the distinction is made in a condescending way, with running taken to be superior to jogging. Some runners like to puff themselves up by noting others' speed and saying, "Oh, he's just jogging." Well, we're all slower than someone else. The best runners in the world cover 5 kilometers (3.1 miles; the distance is also called 5K) at just a bit slower than 4:00 per mile. The best marathoners in the world run sub-5:00 miles for 26.2 miles. By their standards, I guess we're all joggers, huh? So let's scratch pace as what makes one person a jogger and another person a runner.

Is the difference the distance run? As I said, 425,000 Americans completed a marathon in 2008. Ethiopia's Kenenisa Bekele doesn't run farther than 15 miles at a time in his training, but he holds the world records for 5K and 10K. Think any of those marathoners would call him a jogger?

And what about why you run? One old saw is that the difference between a jogger and a runner is an entry form. This saying was supposed to mean that by entering races, you somehow graduated from the vile level of jogger to the promised land of being a runner. I know plenty of people who faithfully put in their miles, but for a variety of reasons choose not to race. Yet many of these people are more dedicated and run faster and longer than the average person at a race. Another distinction along these lines that I've heard is that joggers are in it for the exercise, runners for the sport. This distinction is just plain silly. Runners can no more single out the one reason that they run any more than they can name the quality that they love most about their spouse. In both cases, there are many thrilling aspects, and each aspect plays off of all the others.

> **FOOTNOTES**
>
> Ron Hill, who won the Boston Marathon in 1970, is generally considered to have the longest running streak (not having missed a day of running) in the world. The last day that Hill didn't run was in 1964.

Okay, so what *is* the difference? There isn't any. Jogging, running—call it what you want. You'll know when you're doing more than walking. Why have I spent all this time making this point? Because it's easy for beginning runners to feel that what they're doing isn't important. Often, the people who make them feel that way the most are veteran runners, who forget what it's like to take those first tentative steps. Their attitude can cause a lot of beginners to feel that there's some standard they have to measure up to. There isn't; the only one that matters is your own satisfaction.

Mythical Contortions

While I'm disposing of stale arguments, I'll go ahead and discuss some of the myths you've probably heard about running. Maybe these myths have made you hesitant about starting a running program. Maybe they'll be thrown at you once your Uncle Zeke, that opinionated old cur whom you have to see every Thanksgiving, learns that you've started to run. Whatever the case, the following are a few myths you'll hear about running.

"You never see runners smile."

I guess this statement is supposed to mean that running isn't fun. Apparently, some people think that people should be smiling all the time; to them, if you're not smiling, you're not having a good time. But who would want to live in a world where everyone is always smiling? Sounds too much like *Brave New World*, filled with happy idiots.

More important, these people are just plain wrong. How often do they see runners? Do they see me out running with my friends, talking away for an hour, cracking jokes, telling stories, and sometimes even having to slow down a little because we're laughing so hard? Look around the next time you see people running together. Watch them long enough, and I guarantee you'll see some smiles.

The nonsmiling runner Uncle Zeke has seen is probably on a solo run. Where does it say that the only sign of enjoying yourself is a smile? I bet that Uncle Zeke doesn't grin his way through dinner or sex, but he'd probably like to repeat those experiences.

"You'll ruin your knees."

I hear some version of this statement about once a week. I worry more about injuring myself rolling my eyes in reaction than I do about my knees becoming arthritic because of running. Yes, people get injured running. As explained in Chapter 12, however, most of those injuries are predictable and preventable. They're usually caused by trying to do too much too soon at too quick a pace and by ignoring the body's warning signs.

What the ruin-your-knees naysayers usually mean is that running is going to do long-term damage to your body, especially in the form of arthritis. I don't mean to be mean here, and I know that this statement is often made with good intentions, but did you ever notice that the people making it don't exactly look like they view their bodies as temples? Instead, they're using the myth about ruining your knees to justify their own inactivity and to make themselves feel better about that by trying to make you feel worse.

I seriously doubt that the people making this prediction know that several studies comparing longtime runners to sedentary people have shown no difference in the rate at which people got arthritis. Also, studies comparing 55-and-older arthritis sufferers have found that over a five-year period, both the runners' and the nonrunners' arthritis got worse at the same rate. In other words, even in people who already had arthritis (which is often inherited), running didn't make it worse.

In fact, most experts agree that running can help against arthritis. First, weight-bearing exercise such as running strengthens bones and keeps joints better lubricated; "Use it or lose it" doesn't apply just to muscles. Second, you'll probably lose weight once you become a runner, and weighing less places less of a strain on your skeletal system than does forcing it to cart around an extra 30 pounds.

So with those myths out of the way, let's get running!

The Least You Need to Know

- Among the leading reasons to run regularly are to lose weight, prevent disease, and have more energy and self-esteem.
- Running is the most convenient form of vigorous exercise.
- By one measure, there are more than 10 million regular runners in the United States.
- Runners come in all shapes, sizes, and ages.
- There's no real difference between running and jogging.
- Running doesn't cause arthritis.

Run for the Health of It

In This Chapter

- Losing weight by running
- Preventing heart disease and other illnesses by running
- The mental benefits of running
- Increasing the quantity and quality of your years

Most people start running for health reasons. They want to lose weight, have more energy, protect themselves against heart disease, or they just want to feel better. Any one of these reasons is powerful enough not only to start running, but to stay motivated enough to keep at it.

The great thing about the health benefits of running is how they work together to reinforce each other. For example, running to lose weight also helps your heart and bones, and feeling better physically also improves your psychological health. This chapter details some of the main health benefits of running and points out how they work together to make your life better.

Lose the Fat

Everyone knows that it's bad to be overweight. Obese people (people who weigh at least 20 percent more than their ideal weight) are three times as likely as people of normal weight to develop high blood pressure and five times as likely to develop diabetes. The Centers for Disease Control and Prevention estimate that obesity causes more than 400,000 early deaths a year in the United States. Look around the next time you're at a mall or an airport, where you can see a good cross-section of

Americans, and you'll see that this problem is getting worse, not better, despite the fitness boom of the last 30 years. In 2008, two thirds of Americans (66.7 percent, to be precise) were overweight, up from 45 percent in 1991, and just more than a third (34 percent) were obese, compared to 12 percent in 1991.

You don't have to be obese to have a reason to shed some pounds, however. Those millions of Americans who are overweight but not obese are still placing additional stress on their hearts, bones, and joints. Maybe you have an extra 10 pounds that seems to have tacked itself on to your middle sometime in the last few years. What you want to know is whether running can help you to trim down. The short answer: you bet it can!

Weight for It

Running to lose weight is one of the single most popular reasons that people take up the sport, for good reason. Look around the next time you find yourself at a road race. See many overweight people finishing the race? That's not meant to imply that only runners who finish races lose weight. I just wanted to reinforce what most people know intuitively—regular runners are less likely to have problems with their weight than most people. That fact is important to remember if losing weight is one of your main motivations to start running. Why? Because although weight loss through running can be dramatic, it takes time.

FOOTNOTES

Who knows what might be hiding under that extra layer of flab? Canada's Peter Maher went from being a 210-pound smoker to a 2:11 marathoner who ran in the Olympics.

Nearly all of our society is based on quick results and instant gratification. Need cash? There's an ATM around the corner. Congress irritating you? Rant about it on Facebook. Dying to know the temperature in Outer Mongolia? Go to Weather.com. Can't place that song you hear waiting in line at the coffee shop? Fire up Shazam on your iPhone.

I'm all in favor of convenience. Unfortunately, though, the notion that everything can and should happen quickly has crept into areas of our lives where that's just not how things happen. Those areas include weight loss.

Although seemingly half the magazines in the world carry the line, "Lose 10 pounds before breakfast!" on their covers, that's just not how it works. If losing weight were that easy, then two thirds of Americans wouldn't be overweight (not to mention that the articles wouldn't keep appearing because everyone would have slimmed down by now). Taking off your extra flab takes time and patience. After all, you didn't gain your spare tire overnight, so you shouldn't expect to lose it overnight.

Depressed yet? Don't be. As I said, most people know that regular runners are less likely to be overweight. I'll spend pretty much the rest of this book showing you various ways to become and remain a regular runner. Do that and some (if not all) of the extra weight that you may be carrying around will disappear.

The Math of Losing Weight

So how do you lose weight by running? A pound of body fat contains 3,500 *calories*. Covering a mile on foot, either by walking or running, burns approximately 100 calories. The exact number depends on your weight, the terrain you cover, your fitness, and other factors, but the difference is small enough that 100 calories per mile is an applicable figure for all people. At the most basic level, you lose 1 pound of body fat for every 35 miles you run.

> **DEFINITION**
>
> A **calorie** is a measurement of heat. Only food and drinks containing calories can be burned for energy by your body. A pound is equal to 3,500 calories. Walking and running burn roughly 100 calories per mile.

I know what you're thinking: that's a lot of running just to lose 1 pound! Isn't there anything you can do to speed the process? Yes, there is. Let's look at the math more carefully. Okay, so you burn 100 calories per mile. Say you're running 10 miles per week. You're creating a calorie deficit of 1,000 calories per week, so it will take you about three and a half weeks to burn a pound of body fat through running alone.

But what if you make a few changes in your diet at the same time? What if you cut out that sugar-laden soda? There's 150 calories right there. What if you eat a banana instead of a chocolate chip cookie at lunch? There's another couple hundred calories saved. Yes, you've probably tried dieting before, and it didn't work for you. That's not what I'm recommending here. Diets alone don't work. Continually denying yourself is too hard, and it's also not a healthy way to live. But combine a few small changes a day in your diet with exercise, and things are different.

Suppose you combine running 10 miles a week with making good "food trades" that save you 300 calories a day. Suddenly, you're at a calorie deficit of more than 3,000 per week, or nearly enough to lose 1 pound a week. That's a safe level of weight loss. If you lose 4 to 5 pounds per month, it starts adding up.

TRAINING TIP

Don't weigh yourself more than once a week. Your weight varies from day to day because of water retention and other factors, so daily weighings can be misleading and frustrating. Try to weigh yourself under similar conditions each week, such as naked on Monday mornings.

Making running, not dieting, the main focus of your weight-loss program works in part because you're doing something positive (running) to shed the pounds rather than doing something unenjoyable (not eating). If you follow my advice in this book, then you'll come to enjoy your running, and the lost weight will be just one of the many things that you value it for.

In addition, exercise, not diet, is the way to go because after you work out, your metabolism remains elevated for hours. One study found that after an easy hour run, subjects were still burning calories at an accelerated rate more than seven hours later! Even after a 30-minute run, their metabolism was revved up for 2 hours after finishing. So by running, you're burning extra calories even when you're at rest. That doesn't happen with dieting. In fact, the opposite does. Also, every bit of muscle that you gain with your running helps you to lose weight. Muscles burn more calories at rest than fat does.

Just Run

You may have heard about special "fat-burning" workouts that draw exclusively from your fat stores and speed your weight loss. Runners are often told that running at a lower intensity will burn more fat than running faster. That's true, but incomplete and misleading.

DEFINITION

Glycogen is your body's main source of fuel during aerobic exercise. It's stored in your muscles and liver, and then burned when you work out. With training, you increase your body's capacity to store glycogen, but even well-trained runners can usually store only enough for 20 or so miles of running.

Here's the deal: when you're sitting in a chair, you're burning almost nothing but fat. As your activity level increases, your muscles start to burn *glycogen*, which is how your body stores most of the carbohydrates you eat. Glycogen is your muscles' preferred fuel source for exercise. The harder you work out toward a maximal effort, the higher the percentage of the calories burned from glycogen, and the lower the percentage that comes from fat. When you're sprinting all out, you're burning no fat at all.

Based on that information, some people will say to work out at a very easy pace to burn more fat. Technically, that's true. But as the previous example shows, if you want to do nothing but burn fat, sit down. You'll be burning almost nothing else!

What matters is not where the calories come from that you burn, but how many you burn. As I said, whether you walk or run, you burn about 100 calories per mile. So if you walk 3 miles, you'll burn 300 calories, and more of those calories will come from your fat stores than if you run 3 miles. But think about the time involved. Walking 3 miles is going to take close to an hour for most people. In the same amount of time, you could probably run twice as far. The result? You'll have burned twice as many calories, and that's what matters in taking and keeping the pounds off.

That's why running is so great for losing weight. In just half an hour, you can burn as many calories as you would doing many other exercises for an hour or more. Running's convenience and the short time each day that you need to allot for it mean that it's easy to do regularly, meaning that you're more likely to burn more calories more often.

 TRAINING TIP

Are you carrying too much fat? Try this quick test. While standing with erect posture, grab a section of flesh between your thumb and fingers, about 1 to 2 inches to the side of your navel. If the fold of skin is less than an inch thick, then you probably don't need to worry about excess body fat.

Composition Exercise

How do you know if you need to lose weight? This question is tricky, with everyone's situation being different. But ask yourself this: Were you a healthy, active person in your early 20s? If so, what did you weigh then? Do you weigh more now? You shouldn't. By your early 20s, you're pretty much done growing (at least vertically!). Unless you've spent most days in the gym since then lifting weights, it's probably not an extra 20 pounds of muscle you've gained.

Overall, it's better to focus on your *body composition* than exclusively on your weight. Your body composition is what percentage of your weight is lean body mass (muscles, bones, and everything else that isn't fat) and what percentage is fat (both the fat stored in and around organs of your body and what you can see or feel beneath your skin). Concentrating on body composition recognizes that you can be very fit but still be "overweight" by common standards.

DEFINITION

Your **body composition** is a measure of how much fat you're carrying compared to lean tissue. Generally, the lower your level of body fat, the less you are at risk for disease, the better you feel moving around, and the better you look!

Measurements of body composition get people to realize that you can be at what the weight charts would tell you is a "desirable" weight but still not be fit or even healthy. Think about how many people keep smoking because they don't want to gain 10 pounds. You can starve yourself and be at a "desirable" weight but be doing major damage to your body. It's how your body is constructed, not just how many pounds it weighs, that's important.

A good way to determine whether you have a decent body composition is by calculating your body mass index. This involves some math, so get out the calculator and follow these steps:

1. Determine your weight in kilograms by multiplying your weight in pounds by 0.454.

2. Determine your height in meters by multiplying your height in inches by 0.0254.

3. Square your height in meters (multiply it by itself).

4. Divide your weight in kilograms by the square of your height in meters.

The result is your body mass index. For example, if you are 5'10" and weigh 150 pounds, you would multiply 150 by 0.454, for a weight in kilograms of 68.1. Your height in inches is 70; multiply that by 0.0254 for a height in meters of 1.778. Square that number to get 3.16. Finally, divide 68.1 (weight in kilograms) by 3.16 (square of height in meters) to get a body mass index of 21.5. Desirable body mass index ranges are 19 to 25 for both men and women. If your index is above 25, you probably are carrying too much fat.

Of course, you may not need to do this test. For many people, a look in the mirror while naked does the trick. Is the waist in your jeans a few inches more than when you were in your early 20s? Has your shirt or dress size increased? As I said, unless you've been training with Mr. Universe, your clothes probably fit differently because of gaining fat, not muscle. Running can help you to lose the extra fat.

Disease Flees

Many runners are perfectly content with their weight but keep running for other health reasons. When you run regularly, your aerobic capacity increases. The exercise scientists refer to this capacity as maximal oxygen uptake, or VO_2 max. Whatever you call it, it refers to your body's plumbing for aerobic exercise. Runners with a high VO_2 max have a plumbing system that allows them to pump large amounts of oxygen-rich blood to working muscles. With training, you can maximize the size of your pump and the quantity of blood that it transports.

With six months to a year of training, previously sedentary people can expect to increase their aerobic capacity by 20 to 30 percent. That's a large part of why you're able to run substantially farther and faster after a few months of regular running than before you started. For racers, working to improve their VO_2 max is one of the most important parts of their training. For our purposes here, though, what's significant is that as your aerobic capacity increases, your risk for some of the most common debilitating diseases of modern society decreases.

Handling Heart Disease

The American Heart Association (AHA) lists six controllable major risk factors for developing coronary artery disease: smoking, high blood pressure, high blood cholesterol levels, lack of regular exercise, obesity, and diabetes mellitus. In other words, even if you don't smoke, aren't diabetic or overweight, and have acceptable blood pressure and cholesterol levels, you're still at an increased risk for heart disease if you're sedentary.

The reason why running and other aerobic exercise dramatically reduce your risk for heart disease isn't difficult to discern. As your aerobic capacity increases, your heart becomes more efficient and powerful. By stressing it for a short time at least a few times a week, you lessen the stress on it all the rest of the time.

Running also works to lower your other risk factors. In addition to helping you lose weight (which lowers your risk of developing noninsulin-dependent diabetes), running helps to prevent or delay the development of high blood pressure, and it helps to control it in people who have a genetic predisposition to the condition. Running also helps to lower your overall blood cholesterol level, and running is one of the greatest ways to quit smoking.

FOOTNOTES

The strongest link between aerobic exercise and lower cancer risk is in colon cancer. Studies have found that regular exercisers have about half the incidence of colon cancer as sedentary people do. There's also increasing evidence to suggest a lower risk of breast cancer among active women.

In other words, if you start running, you not only remove one of the major risks for developing heart disease (being sedentary), but you also go a long way toward eliminating the others. No wonder that one famous study of Harvard alumni, led by Ralph Paffenbarger, Ph.D., found that those who burned at least 2,000 calories a week in vigorous exercise (about 20 miles a week) were 64 percent less likely to suffer a heart attack than their sedentary contemporaries.

Better Bones

Studies show a direct link between regular weight-bearing exercise, such as running, and bone thickness. The stronger a bone, the more stress it can handle before it breaks. This health benefit is especially important for women runners. Everyone starts losing bone mineral density after the age of 30. When women are past menopause, their estrogen levels drop, and their bones lose even more density. But running, along with a diet rich in calcium, can halt this loss. The upshot is that runners are less likely to suffer from osteoporosis, a disease in which bones become brittle and break easily.

Breathe Easy

A key component of increased aerobic capacity is better lung function. Just as your heart becomes stronger with regular running, so do your lungs. They're able to sustain a higher workload for a longer period of time. As your lungs become more efficient, you can take in more oxygen with each breath. That's one of the reasons why you don't breathe as hard climbing stairs when you're fit—your lungs are better able to get oxygen to working muscles.

In terms of medical conditions, this better lung function means that people who have asthma not only can run, but should do some form of regular exercise. After all, when you improve your body's capacity to take in and use oxygen, then what it considers stressful occurs at a much higher level of exertion. So an activity that previously might have triggered an asthma attack doesn't as you become fitter. Also, because your breathing becomes smoother as you get fit, there's less chance that your airways will become irritated.

The other big breathing-related benefit of running is one that I've mentioned before: it can help you to stop smoking. Remember what I said about how most people know that regular runners don't have as many weight problems as sedentary people? Well, the same is true with respect to running and smoking. You just don't see the two mix after a while.

I know from my experience that when I started running again, smoking became increasingly less attractive. Yes, I still smoked when I started running again in the early 1970s. Nicotine is addictive, after all. But I knew that if I stuck with the running, my body would eventually get so fed up with me continuing to poison it that I would eventually be able to kick my habit. Take my word on it: as your system becomes cleaner and more efficient, it becomes more sensitive to things that damage it. Few things are more damaging to it than cigarettes.

Head Games

You've probably heard about "the runner's high." The definitions are never all that precise, but it's supposed to be some sort of transcendent state that you enter into after running for half an hour or so. Many beginning runners have been told about the runner's high and figure that they must be doing things wrong, because they've certainly never felt like the Dalai Lama on a run.

I'm here to tell you that the runner's high is an overblown concept. There's no such thing as a quantifiable, yes-or-no transcendent state that X amount of running induces, any more than listening to 3.4 of your favorite songs causes a definitive change in your mental condition. So don't belittle or doubt yourself because you're not achieving the runner's high—in one sense, there's no such thing to achieve.

But like music, running does have a dramatic effect on your mood. Let me be the first to tell you that if you don't finish most of your runs feeling calmer, more content and relaxed, and less tense and angst-ridden, then you're doing something wrong. If you want to call that a runner's high, I'm not going to argue. Short-term stress relief is one of the main things that gets busy runners out the door. Studies have found that people score much lower on tests of anxiety immediately after finishing a run, compared to how they scored before their run. As one knowledgeable running doctor has noted, even as little as 15 minutes of moderate walking reduces muscular tension more than a standard dose of a tranquilizer.

Over the long haul, those psychological benefits accrue. Indeed, aerobic exercise, such as running, is a common prescription for mild depression. Less dramatically, but just as important, runners consistently rate higher than average on these important personality characteristics:

- Emotional stability
- Optimism
- Self-sufficiency
- Self-esteem

Compared to sedentary people, runners have also been found to have an increased ability to concentrate and above-average organizational and problem-solving skills. They also report feeling content and mentally vigorous more often than do nonexercisers. In other words, running clears your brain along with your arteries.

 FOOTNOTES

The International Society of Sport Psychology says the following in a position statement, "Physical Activity and Psychological Benefits": "Individual psychological benefits of physical activity are: positive changes in self-perception and well-being, improvement in self-confidence and awareness, positive changes in mood, relief of tension, relief of feelings such as depression and anxiety, influence on premenstrual tension, increased sense of mental well-being, increased alertness and clear thinking, increased energy and ability to cope with daily activity, increased enjoyment of exercise and social contacts, and developing positive coping strategies."

Why does running put you in a better mood? The answer is endorphins. These chemicals, which act like morphine, are released by your brain when you're under stress. Studies have found that the level of endorphins circulating in your system can be more than twice as high after a run compared to when you're at rest.

In the long term, there's less of a chemical explanation for why running is so good for you psychologically. Nonetheless, the reasons seem pretty clear to me. For starters, as you become more fit, you're going to have a better self-image. You'll feel better about how you look and about your health. By being less absorbed with self-loathing, you can turn your attention toward having a brighter outlook toward the world.

 TRAINING TIP

When you're under a lot of stress, be more diligent than usual about making time to run. Those endorphins that flood your body will go a long way toward keeping you calm enough to work through your problems.

In addition, setting and achieving goals on a regular basis is tremendously satisfying. After almost every run, you'll have a feeling of accomplishment—you overcame inertia, got out the door, and did something good for yourself. Being able to remind yourself that you wanted to work out four times last week and did so can bring a boost when events seem to be directing you, rather than you directing them.

Adding Life to Your Years

If you've been paying attention during this chapter, you've probably already concluded what I'm about to say: one of the greatest health benefits of running is how all of the many wonderful things it does for your body and mind work together. You feel more at home in your body, you don't get as tired doing normal activities, you feel better about yourself, you're more regularly in a better mood—these aren't the kinds of things that can necessarily be quantified in medical terms, but I defy anyone to tell me that they don't go a long way toward improving your health.

Some people refer to this snowball effect of running's benefits as putting more life in your years. When you're a runner, you're more able to use your body as you want to, which makes you feel more alive. Life might not be any easier, but living it sure is. Any longtime runner will tell you that his or her quality of life is significantly higher since becoming a runner. That's what vitality is all about.

So running adds life to your years. But does running add years to your life? The answer is yes. As a surgeon general's report has put it, "Higher levels of regular physical activity are associated with lower mortality rates for both older and younger adults." In other words, when you compare runners and other exercisers to sedentary people, the active ones are more likely to outlive the couch potatoes.

Remember that study of Harvard grads that I mentioned previously in "Handling Heart Disease"? In that section, I explained that burning at least 2,000 calories a week in vigorous activity, which is the rough equivalent of running 20 miles a week, significantly lowers your risk for having heart disease. The same study found that the 20 miles per week threshold also coincides with longer lives. Participants in the study who maintained that level of activity from age 35 onward outlived the less active subjects by two and a half years.

And it's never too late: even those who waited until after the age of 50 to start that seemingly magic 2,000 calories a week level of exercise gained an extra 1 to 2 years. Put all of these benefits together, and you not only have extra years of life, but you also feel great during more years of that life. Can you believe that some people *don't* run?

The Least You Need to Know

- Running is a better way to lose weight and keep it off than dieting.
- You burn the equivalent of 1 pound of body fat for every 35 miles you run.
- Running can cut your risk of heart disease in half.
- Runners have stronger bones and lungs than sedentary people.
- Runners have more self-esteem, self-confidence, and mental alertness than sedentary people.
- Running at least 20 miles a week can increase your life span by more than 2 years.

Taking Your First Steps

In This Chapter

- What to do before you start running
- How to get started
- How to increase your endurance
- Running at the right pace
- Running with good form

Who said that the journey of a lifetime begins with a single step? Whoever it was understood what it's like to be a new runner. After all, at one point even the most experienced marathoners took their first running step. I certainly remember how momentous my first ones seemed when I started running again in the early 1970s after being a sedentary smoker.

So don't worry; we were all beginners once. Try not to let fear of the unknown deter you from running. Follow what I say in this chapter, and you'll be able to progress safely and satisfactorily from your current state of activity to being a regular runner.

Doctor's Orders?

I'm not a doctor; I don't even play one on TV. So I'm not going to claim to be qualified to dole out medical advice. Unfortunately, when it comes to running, a lot of doctors aren't experts, either. It's become almost reflexive to say that anyone thinking about starting a running program should get medical clearance first. Well, I'm going to be a bit different and not take cover under that blanket statement.

Why? A few reasons, none of which are meant to put down the medical profession. But consider this statistic: even after the last three decades of the fitness boom, less than 30 percent of doctors advise their patients about exercise and nutrition. Doctors are trained to fight disease, not prescribe health. I've had more than one doctor ask me if I'm amazed that my knees haven't given out yet.

There's a kind of philosophical basis to my argument. To me, it seems that saying that everyone has to get medical clearance before starting to run implies that running is some dangerous activity, not one of the best things you can do to take control of your health. You're preparing to go outside and use your body as it's meant to be used, not preparing to be sent to battle.

Why do so many people say that you should run only with a note from your doctor? In part, the reason is because running is portrayed so inaccurately in the general media. Every year, about 40,000 people run the New York City Marathon. Every few years, one of those runners has a heart attack during the race. Sadly, sometimes the runner dies. This tragedy is what gets play in the papers.

But did you know that at the University of Michigan's home football games, the medical teams expect to treat two heart attack patients per game from the stands? That's what the law of averages would tell you is going to happen when you have 100,000 people together in one place. Do you then see the media warning about the risks of watching football games?

RULES OF THE ROAD

Be honest with yourself when you're assessing whether you should see a doctor before starting to run. Running doesn't cause heart problems, but if you have an underlying one, it can aggravate it.

If I sound a little sensitive here, it's partly because of the attention the media gave when Jim Fixx died of a heart attack while running in 1984. Because Fixx was the author of the best-selling *The Complete Book of Running*, he was a spokesperson for the sport. I know a lot of people who subsequently quit running, because they figured that if running killed Jim Fixx, who wasn't at risk?

I knew Jim Fixx. What was not reported was that heart disease ran in his family and that even with dying at age 52, Fixx had already outlived his father by nine years. More important—and here I might win back some of the doctors I've just angered— is that Fixx thought that his marathon running made him immune and so ignored his medical history. He had been a heavy smoker before he started running, and his cholesterol levels were way above normal. He also ignored chest pains that he sometimes got while running, as well as pleas from Kenneth Cooper, M.D. (sometimes called the father of aerobics), to get regular check-ups.

Am I contradicting myself here? Not at all. Everyone should know their medical history, as well as that of their family. I'm assuming that you get regular physicals, know your blood pressure and cholesterol level, and so on. If you don't, and if starting a running program inspires you to see a doctor, then by all means go. I just worry sometimes that getting a doctor's "permission" to run keeps a lot of people from ever starting.

So besides those who don't know their basic health information, who should see a doctor before starting a running program? The National Heart, Lung, and Blood Institute has issued the following guidelines, and they seem reasonable to me. If one of these statements applies to you, discuss your desire to start a running program with a doctor, preferably one who is used to treating active patients.

- You're over the age of 60 and aren't used to regular exercise.
- You have family members who have had coronary artery disease before the age of 55.
- You frequently have pain or feel pressure in the left or midchest area, the left side of your neck, the left shoulder, or left arm during or immediately after exercise.
- You often feel faint, dizzy, or unaccountably out of breath after mild exertion.
- You have high blood pressure that isn't under control.
- You've had heart trouble, a heart murmur, or a heart attack.
- You have arthritis.
- You have a medical condition that might need special attention once you start exercising, such as diabetes.

If none of these statements applies to you, you can proceed to learning how to get going.

From 0 to 30 Minutes in a Month

There's no universally applicable program for starting a running program. As I stress again and again in this book, regardless of whether I'm talking about how to build endurance or why to run or even what shoes to wear, running is an individual sport.

As the old saying goes, every runner is an experiment of one. What works for one runner might be a disaster for another. All runners are going to progress at different rates.

Still, there are a few basic guidelines that all runners should follow. In telling you how to get going, I'll give these guidelines to you. You might find what I recommend either too easy or too hard. If either of these conditions is the case, that's fine. The guiding principle in your running should always be to stay in tune with what you feel comfortable with.

Walk, Don't Run

This advice might sound strange, but the best way to start a running program for a lot of people is to walk. That's especially the case if you haven't been active for the last few years or are overweight. I know, you bought a book on running. You want to run! But when it comes to starting a regular running routine, slow and steady is always going to win the race.

Now I'm not going to lie to you: when you're new to running, especially if you've been sedentary, running is going to hurt for a while. Later I'll explain how it should and shouldn't hurt, but I wanted to get that out on the table from the get-go. You're asking your body to do something that it's not accustomed to. Initially, your body is going to protest. You're going to be a little sore and, at first, a little more tired.

Your body is going to protest really loudly if you overload it too much right off the bat. If you try to do too much too soon, the soreness and fatigue are going to be so great that you're going to have to stop for several days at a time. When you start again, you'll be starting from scratch. Then you might feel as if you're behind schedule and might overdo it that much more. Bad idea!

 FOOTNOTES

Don't try this at home: when Patti Catalano, who eventually held the American record in the marathon, decided to start a running program, her first run was 7 miles. She could barely walk, much less run, for more than a week afterward.

A better idea is acknowledging that you're going to be sore and a little fatigued at first and doing what you can to minimize those inevitabilities. For a lot of people, that's going to mean walking at first, then gradually introducing some bouts of easy running, and then gradually increasing the length of those bouts.

The biggest battle that all runners face is sticking with it. Even longtime runners can find it tough to find a routine that works for them. What's most important at first is getting in the habit of exercising regularly. Erring on the side of caution when you start is going to help you to feel good enough to stick with it. As you become fitter, you'll already have your exercise routine down and can progress toward more running. So get out the door and start walking. When doing so is comfortable for you, report back, and I'll get going on making you a runner.

 TRAINING TIP

Start all of your workouts at a little slower pace than you think you need to. This slower pace gives your muscles and your heart and breathing rates a chance to warm up and increase gradually. You'll feel better if you ease into your workouts.

When to Run, When to Rest

What's a good routine to get into? I recommend that beginners shoot for half an hour, four days a week. Mind you, I don't mean half an hour of running four times a week right off the bat. In the schedule at the end of this section, I'll show you how to gradually build to being able to run 30 minutes at a time.

What I'm assuming in this chart is that at the start of the first week, you can handle walking at a brisk pace for half an hour at a time, four times a week. If you can't, then don't start the running portions of the schedule yet. Keep walking until you have that basic level of fitness that will allow you to walk for half an hour, four times a week.

If you've been doing a little running already, it's okay to jump into the chart at the level you're at. For example, if you know that you can run a mile, then it's okay to enter the schedule at the point where I have you running for 10 minutes straight at a stretch. But if you're going to do that, you have to promise to be honest with yourself. There's a big difference between knowing that you can run a mile because you did it once a few weeks ago and doing so four times in a week. If you don't run regularly, be conservative and enter the schedule at about half the level that you know you can handle in one run. So if you know that you can run a mile but haven't been doing so a few times a week, start where the schedule has you running for five minutes at a time.

 TRAINING TIP

Getting fit is hard enough on its own. Make doing so easier by doing your early walking and running on terrain as flat as you can find.

The reason behind this advice is an important principle that applies to all runners, from the most out-of-shape beginner to the fastest runners in the world. It's the *progression principle*. What it says is that the way to improve your fitness is gradually, in small, consistent steps, rather than in great leaps.

Consistency is the single-most important factor in determining whether you'll improve as a runner. Becoming a runner is like saving for retirement. The best way is to start small, but be consistent, and then build on your earlier progress. As you accumulate money for retirement or improve your fitness level, you can see the progress that you're making and will be motivated to keep at it. No one day is a great transformative event, where you suddenly have a lot more money or can suddenly run three times farther than usual. You chip away at it, and what once seemed impossible—setting aside $10,000, or running for 15 minutes without stopping—becomes just another signpost on the way to your next goal.

DEFINITION

The **progression principle** says that individual gains in fitness are small, but accumulate with consistency. That's why you can't go from being inactive to running a marathon; you have to gradually increase your endurance.

In retirement savings, progress happens because of interest. In running, progress happens because of how your body works. You give it this new task of running just a bit. Your body is a little shocked and thinks, "Hmm, I haven't really experienced that before. This crazy person just might ask me to do that again. I had better be ready." So it prepares itself in order to be just a little more capable of handling what you did to it recently.

Gain Through Pain

You're sore when you start working out regularly because you've done microscopic damage to your muscles, and they're irritated. But give them the chance to recover from that short-term damage, and they'll rebuild themselves to be a little bit stronger and better able to work at the level that they think you're going to ask them to again. The same goes for other body parts, such as your heart and lungs.

When you make another little progression in effort, the same thing happens again. This process is never too great a stress, but a stress nonetheless. After a few rounds of this, your body catches on that this is going to become a regular process. The result is that it fortifies itself, and you become fitter.

Now if you've been paying attention during this extended narrative, you'll have noted a crucial fact: the important gains in fitness come not while you're running, but after you run. That's an example of the *stress/recovery principle*. To put this principle into practice, you stress your body, which tears it down a little. Then you give your body a chance to recover, and while recovering, you body rebuilds itself to be just a little more capable of handling the next bout of similar stress.

In other words, providing adequate recovery is the key to progressing. That's why you can't hurry your way from being sedentary to fit. You have to allow your body time between workouts to become stronger. If you don't allow time, you're going to plateau. That's why I think you should start with four days a week—you're going often enough to make progress, but not so much that you can't recover between workouts.

DEFINITION

The **stress/recovery principle** says that you become fitter by subjecting your body to a stress, and then allowing recovery time before you stress it again. During the recovery time, the body rebuilds itself to be better able to handle that stress. In the case of running, this principle means that your heart, lungs, and muscles become stronger between running sessions.

But don't some runners run every day? What about their need for recovery time? One of the benefits of becoming fit is that your recovery time between workouts shortens dramatically. Most top runners train twice a day. Their bodies have become so accustomed to the stress/recovery process that they can do two runs within the space of eight hours and feel fine on both. But even they're not immune to the same principles that beginners are. When they do more than they're used to and don't allow enough time between hard efforts, they get sore and tired, just like you.

A Beginner's Schedule

A word about the following schedule: I don't know what your usual week is like, so it would be silly for me to say that you have to start your workout week on Sunday, then go again on Tuesday, Wednesday, and Saturday. When you go is going to depend on when the workout meshes best with the rest of your life. So in the schedule, I've marked workouts as the first one of the week rather than noting on which days to do them. What's important is following the progression and planning your workouts so that you have that crucial recovery time between workouts. In other words, try not to do the four workouts for a week on four consecutive days.

And now, at last, what follows is a schedule of how to progress from 0 to running for 30 minutes in 1 month. Remember, before starting workout 1 of week 1, you should already be able to walk for 30 minutes, 4 times a week. If you can't do a given workout, don't worry. Stay with that one until you can and move on to the next one only after you've mastered the prior one.

 TRAINING TIP

Before—and especially after—your workout, it's a good idea to do some gentle stretching. See Chapter 10 for more details.

WEEK 1

Workout 1: Walk 10 minutes. Then for the next 10 minutes, alternate running for 1 minute with walking for 1 minute. Walk 10 minutes.

Workout 2: Walk 10 minutes. Then for the next 15 minutes, alternate running for 1 minute with walking for 1 minute. Walk 5 minutes.

Workout 3: Walk 10 minutes. Then for the next 15 minutes, alternate running for 2 minutes with walking for 1 minute. Walk 5 minutes.

Workout 4: Walk 5 minutes. Then for 21 minutes, alternate running for 2 minutes with walking for 1 minute. Walk 4 minutes.

WEEK 2

Workout 1: Walk 5 minutes. Then for the next 20 minutes, alternate running for 3 minutes with walking for 1 minute. Walk 5 minutes.

Workout 2: Walk 5 minutes. Then for the next 21 minutes, alternate running for 5 minutes with walking for 2 minutes. Walk 4 minutes.

Workout 3: Walk 4 minutes. Then for the next 24 minutes, alternate running for 5 minutes with walking for 1 minute. Walk 2 minutes.

Workout 4: Walk 5 minutes. Then for the next 22 minutes, alternate running for 8 minutes with walking for 3 minutes. Walk 3 minutes.

WEEK 3

Workout 1: Walk 5 minutes. Run 10 minutes. Walk 5 minutes. Run 5 minutes. Walk 5 minutes.

Workout 2: Walk 5 minutes. Run 12 minutes. Walk 3 minutes. Run 5 minutes. Walk 5 minutes.

Workout 3: Walk 10 minutes. Run 15 minutes. Walk 5 minutes.

Workout 4: Walk 6 minutes. Run 18 minutes. Walk 6 minutes.

WEEK 4

Workout 1: Walk 5 minutes. Run 20 minutes. Walk 5 minutes.

Workout 2: Walk 5 minutes. Run 22 minutes. Walk 3 minutes.

Workout 3: Walk 3 minutes. Run 25 minutes. Walk 2 minutes.

Workout 4: Run 30 minutes.

Running on at the Mouth: The Talk Test

Most people think that running means being constantly out of breath. Most beginners contribute to this misconception because, believe it or not, they run too fast. They think that running is always supposed to be hard work, so the more difficult it feels, the more correctly they're doing it, and the more they're benefiting; but that's not the case.

Most runners should run at a relaxed, moderate pace just this side of being out of breath for most of their running sessions. That's certainly always been the case for me, even when I was training to be the best in the world. At this pace, you train, but don't strain. You're providing that slight stress to your body that's going to prompt it to get stronger, but you're running within yourself rather than going all out.

How do you know what this pace is? In scientific terms, it corresponds to getting your heart rate up to about 70 percent of its maximum. In Chapter 9, I'll tell you more about the benefits of monitoring your training based on tracking your heart rate.

Of course, most runners, especially most beginners, don't know what these figures are to begin with, much less use them for training. But that's not a problem. You don't need a battery of tests and a heart rate monitor to find your optimal training pace; you don't even need to check how fast per mile you're running. All you need to do is strike up a conversation. When you can do so while running, but still feel as though you're putting in a solid effort, you're training at the right pace. This is known as passing the *talk test*.

DEFINITION

The **talk test** is a way to know whether you're running at the proper pace to boost your endurance. You should be able to carry on a conversation while you run. If you can only say one or two words at a time, you're running too fast for a beginner.

Passing the talk test means that you should be able to speak in complete sentences while you're running at a moderate training level. If you can only offer one-word grunts in response to another runner's questions, then you're going too fast for how hard you should be running during the first few months of your running program. As I said, this is the level of effort that I maintain on most of my runs. (The exceptions are when I've planned to do some running at race pace or faster to prepare for competition.)

FOOTNOTES

When I used to race marathons, I would use a version of the talk test to evaluate my competition. If runners were still with me past the 15-mile mark, and I couldn't tell how tired they were by their breathing or form, I would ask them questions that required more than a word or two to answer. If they responded in complete sentences, I knew I had a race to the finish on my hands.

The next time you see a group of experienced runners, watch closely. I bet you that you're more than likely to see them carrying on a conversation, even at what might appear to be a startlingly quick pace. You should follow their example. On the other hand, if you can reel off a soliloquy from *Hamlet* without breaking stride, you might want to pick it up a bit.

Going too fast might seem like a good way to get past a more moderate progression, but you can't trick your body into getting fitter than it's ready to. When you run too fast, you're not going to be able to extend your distance as easily; when you're starting out, it's how far you can run, not how fast, that's more important in building your endurance. Also, when you run too hard all the time, you're more likely to get injured, and you're less likely to enjoy your running and want to stick with it.

Of course, a lot of beginners don't always have someone to run with, so it's tough to know if they can pass the talk test. After all, you're probably self-conscious enough as it is when you start a running program; you don't need to have your neighbors see you trotting down the street carrying on a conversation with yourself to add to things. An alternative to the talk test is to check to see whether you can hum a familiar tune to yourself for a line or two at a time.

Another good way to gauge your effort is by judging it against a scale called rating of perceived effort. Research has shown that once runners learn the scale, they can accurately say where they are on it. Here's one version of the scale:

Rating	Perception of Effort
0	Nothing at all
0.5	Very, very weak (just noticeable)
1	Very weak
2	Weak
3	Moderate
4	Somewhat strong
5	Strong
6	Strong
7	Very strong
8	Very strong
9	Very strong
10	Very, very strong (almost maximal)
>10	Maximal

When you're gradually building your endurance, you should be in the 3 to 4 range. That's a similar level of effort to being able to pass the talk test.

A Stitch in Time

A problem that many beginning runners encounter is side stitches. If you've ever had one, you know what I'm talking about; it's a sharp, sudden pain just below your rib cage that can double you over and make continuing to run a chore.

There are a lot of theories about what causes side stitches. Many people think they're caused by your diaphragm muscles cramping, either because those muscles, which help with breathing, aren't used to working hard or because someone has started a run too quickly. This theory sounds right to me because beginners get stitches more often than do longtime runners. Veterans' muscles are obviously more accustomed to regular exertion, and experienced runners know to ease into their runs. In contrast, as I said previously, beginners often start their runs too quickly.

Sharp pains in your stomach might also be from something as simple as eating too soon before a run. This is another reason that beginners might experience stitches more than veterans—because new runners often haven't learned how long they need to wait to eat after running or what foods don't mix well with their running.

FOOTNOTES

Beginners aren't the only ones who are occasionally plagued by side stitches. Todd Williams, who holds the American record for 15 kilometers, got such a bad side stitch in a road race once that he had to drop out of the race while leading.

The good news is that side stitches aren't a serious sort of problem, unlike if your foot starts throbbing a mile into most runs. If you get a side stitch, stop and walk. Concentrate on taking deep breaths. Exhale forcibly with your lips pursed. The stitch will usually go away in a minute or two. Then review how long ago you ate before your run and what you ate. Also, assess whether you began your run at an easy pace and increased your speed gradually only after you felt warmed up.

Running the Right Way

People worry too much about running form. Some books get so detailed in telling you how to run that you'd almost have to carry them with you when you run to make sure you're getting it right. How your feet should land, where they should land, how long your stride should be, what to do with your hands, how to hold your arms—I'd trip after a few hundred yards if I spent my runs thinking about this stuff. I'm not saying that good running form isn't important or that you can't or shouldn't try to improve yours. But running isn't a technique sport like golf. It's a lot easier to tell people how to have as sweet a stroke as Tiger Woods's than it is to say that all runners should run in one precise way.

We all run like we do for a reason, namely, according to how our bodies are put together. Look around, and you'll notice that no two bodies are put together the same. Some people's legs are bowed. Some people's feet are flatter than others. Some people have wider hips than others, or leg muscles that are stronger, or back muscles that are weaker. All of these factors determine what kind of running form you have.

Remember, each runner is an experiment of one. One of my legs is longer than the other. As a result, I land on the extreme outside edge of my left forefoot, and my right arm often swings across my body. This is not textbook form, but it's what works for me and what feels comfortable.

That last point is crucial. The best running form for you is the one that you feel most comfortable with. As you become fitter, your running form is going to become more natural to you, and you'll think about it less. Remember when you started driving a car? You were so concerned with how you were holding the wheel, the position of your feet, and so forth, that you could barely pay attention to the road. Now driving is second nature to you. Same thing for longtime runners. They just get out there and run and don't really think about how they're doing it all that much.

That's not to say that you should ignore your running form. Some basic points can help make running feel smoother and make you less susceptible to injury. Here are the most important ones:

- Upright posture, with your head, shoulders, torso, and pelvis aligned and your head held up and looking ahead, not down

- Arms carried low, with your shoulders relaxed

- Hands relaxed, cupped loosely, and passing your body at about waist level

- Arms moving in sync with your legs, driving forward, rather than from side to side

- Feet landing gently under your center of gravity

And that's just for starters. I told you it was a lot to think about.

 TRAINING TIP

Don't try to change your form all at once or overnight. Pick an element that you want to work on. On some runs, think about how to improve that element, and concentrate on running slightly differently for five minutes at a time. For example, if your shoulders are usually hunched forward, try pulling them back and see how that feels while running.

Is it worth it to try to improve your form? It can be if running doesn't feel comfortable once you attain a basic level of fitness. If you notice that you're often straining one body part, or that a certain body part, such as your shoulders, tires as you run, then it can be worth it to try to make a few adjustments.

Notice how Bill's posture is upright and aligned, his arms are low and relaxed, and his left foot is landing under his center of gravity.

But again, don't make too much out of comparing your form to others. As you become fitter, your form is going to get better because the muscles throughout your body that support you when you run are going to get more used to their new task. Also, in Chapter 11, I'll show you some basic strengthening exercises that can go a long way toward helping you run with better form.

The Least You Need to Know

- The best way to start a running program is by mixing walking and running and increasing the running portion as you become fitter.
- Prepare for the main part of your workout with a warm-up of gentle stretching and walking.
- After the main part of your run, ease the transition to a normal heart rate with walking and then more stretching.
- In the first few months of a running program, you should always go slow enough to be able to maintain a conversation.

- Side stitches are common for beginning runners and are usually caused by going too quickly.

- Instead of copying how others do it, run with the form that feels most comfortable for you.

Strutting Your Stuff: Where to Run

In This Chapter

- Safety rules for running
- Finding good places to run
- The best surfaces for running
- Running while traveling

When you decide to start golfing, it's pretty obvious where to go to practice your new sport. Same thing with tennis, swimming, and a lot of other activities—your venues are usually few and far between. But when you become a runner, the world is your oyster.

One of the great things about running, and one of the reasons that so many people can stick with it, is its convenience. You can run almost anywhere: streets, tracks, parks, trails, and so on. I even ran once on an airport runway in Venezuela, but that's something I'd rather not get into right now. My point is that with running, your options are almost infinite. Still, some surfaces are better than others. This chapter examines the advantages and disadvantages of the most common running surfaces and covers how to run safely on all of them.

Safety First

No matter where you run, you're going to run into trouble if you don't follow a few basic safety rules. Mind you, running isn't like rock climbing, where one false step can put an end to your career. As a runner, most of your safety concerns have to do with watching out for others. Unfortunately, distracted drivers and preying pouncers are part of our world.

Try to follow these basic personal safety guidelines for runners at all times:

- Always run facing traffic. When you're on roads, run defensively; assume that no driver sees you.

- Try to run with others. If you run alone, try to run where others are, such as parks, neighborhoods, or tracks.

- If you'll be running in the dark, wear reflective gear or a blinking light. The new generation of running lights are so light that you'll barely notice them, but drivers sure will.

- When you leave to run, tell someone where you'll be running and how long you plan to be out.

- Don't run the same route at the same time every day. Doing so makes it easier for someone to plan an attack.

- Know where phones, friendly homes, and open businesses are along your routes in case of an emergency.

- If you're especially concerned about your safety, consider running with your phone.

RULES OF THE ROAD

You'll see a lot of runners wearing iPods and other portable music devices. Don't be one of them. When you run wearing headphones, you're surrendering one of your main ways of staying alert. You won't be able to hear cars and potential bad guys. Save the music for getting psyched to run beforehand or for relaxing afterward.

- If you're verbally harassed, ignore it. Responding usually just spurs those people on.

- Be extra alert near thick bushes and other places where attackers can hide.

- If you're set upon by a dog, stop. If it persists, yell at it firmly. It will usually run away. Don't count on being able to outrun it.

- If you're set upon by an unarmed human, create as much of a commotion as possible, and try to escape. If the assailant is armed, don't resist, but try to get a good description to give to the police.

I know this sounds like a lot to keep in mind, but there are some strange people out there. Being on guard for them is better than letting them ruin your running by having their way.

Road Warriors

Now with the unpleasantries out of the way, let's look at where you should run. The most common place to run, and usually the most convenient, is the road. Most people can just step outside of their homes, hit the road, and be off on an infinite number of routes.

The three main types of routes that runners use are loops, out and backs, and point to points:

- Loops involve running a big circuit around your starting and finishing point.

- Out and backs are where you head out for a set time or distance, usually with just a few turns, turn around at halfway, and then retrace your steps home.

- With a point-to-point route, you start at one place and end at another. This type of route usually requires someone to drop you off or meet you at one end.

Roads are good places to run because you're usually familiar with the ones in your neighborhood. A lot of times, running in known territory makes a run go by more quickly mentally. The firm footing of most asphalt road surfaces means that you don't have to worry about turning an ankle, as you might if you're running on grass or rugged trails. Races are almost always going to be held on roads, so by training on them, you'll be used to that surface if you decide that you want to race. Roads are also a good choice because you can drive courses in your car before running on them so that you know what the footing, terrain, and distance will be like.

 TRAINING TIP

Devise your running loops with smaller loops in mind. That way, if you run into trouble or just don't feel up to your original plans for the day, you can cut your run short.

Of course, that firm footing comes with a price. Humans didn't evolve to run for hours at a time on asphalt. If you're new to running, you're probably going to be sore enough for the first couple of months. Pounding away on a hard surface will probably only make that soreness worse. That's why it's so important to have a good pair of running shoes if you're going to be taking it to the streets. (For more on running shoes, see Chapter 7.)

Another thing to be mindful of on the roads is the slant. Most roads tilt slightly from the center. If you're running against traffic, your left leg will be operating as if it's a bit longer than your right one. Also, your right foot will turn in a bit more when you land because you're on an uneven surface. Both of these stresses to your legs can lead to injury, so try to avoid roads that have a really obvious slant to them. Run toward the middle of the road if you can safely do so.

And let's not forget our good friend, the automobile. Regardless of what traffic laws say about sharing the roads, cars rule. Thanks to the millions of runners out there, things are definitely better than when I started running, when runners on the roads were looked upon as freaks. Today, at least, most drivers are used to seeing runners on a regular basis, but that doesn't mean that they're going to cut you much slack, especially if they're deep into a cellphone conversation.

The solution? Do your best to stay off of heavily traveled roads. Even in the busiest cities, you can usually find a mile or two of relatively open road. In addition to being safer, less traveled roads are just a lot more fun to run on because you can relax a bit more and feel a bit more like you're getting away from it all.

TRAINING TIP

Most runners have a few standard routes they do on a regular basis. Being on a course you're used to can make the miles go by faster because you'll have a better idea of how far you have to go and can dole out your effort accordingly. On days when you need variety, feel free to explore.

Although they're not really roads, I'll include bike paths in this section also because they're usually made of asphalt. Don't let the name fool you. Runners know that "bike path" is usually code for "nice place to run where you don't have to worry about cars." In Boston, for example, there's an asphalt path along both sides of the Charles River for about 9 miles in each direction. It's where most of Boston's runners congregate to get in some hassle-free miles away from busy streets. Most metropolitan areas have at least a few miles of bike paths. Seek them out.

Run Away from Sidewalks

There's not much to say about running on sidewalks other than that you should avoid it whenever possible. Sure, sidewalks are safer than roads with respect to cars, and maybe they don't feel all that much different from asphalt. But they're made from concrete and cement, which are some of the hardest surfaces around. When you figure that with every running step, you subject your body to a force equal to at least three times your body weight, it should be obvious that you want to do whatever you can to lower that impact shock.

RULES OF THE ROAD

When you're overtaking walkers or other runners, especially on a narrow path, alert them by announcing loudly, "On your left," when you're a few steps away from passing them. Otherwise, they might be startled if you suddenly breeze by them.

Another good reason to avoid running on sidewalks is that they seldom provide an uninterrupted surface for long. You're continually going up and down, up and down for driveways and curbs. This unevenness only adds to the pounding on your legs and is a good way to twist an ankle, too.

The only time it's worth clinging to sidewalks is when you're running in a busy section of a city. Even then, though, you'll probably be making your way to a park, bike path, or other better option for the bulk of your run. Otherwise, try to spend as little time running on sidewalks as possible.

Lap It Up: Tracks

Another of the most popular and obvious places to run is on a track. Its plusses are many:

- You can easily track (so to speak) your distance and/or pace, giving you a quantifiable means of monitoring your progress.

- You can stop immediately if something goes wrong.

- You're usually in a safe, secure area. Many tracks are lit for an hour or two in the evening in the winter.

- There are no cars to deal with.

- There are no hills to deal with.

- You often have easy access to water fountains and bathrooms.

- You don't have to worry about potholes, hidden roots, and other things that can trip you on roads or trails.

RULES OF THE ROAD

When you're running on the track, it's common runner's etiquette to cede the inside lanes to faster runners. If you hear someone from behind you yell, "Track!" that means to move to the outside to let them through.

Add to these advantages the fact that synthetic and rubberized tracks transmit about 20 percent less shock to your legs than asphalt does, and you can see why so many runners, especially beginners, find the track to be a safe haven. (Treadmills also provide a softer surface than roads and allow you to stop immediately if you run into trouble. Read about them in Chapter 9.) Another nice thing about outdoor tracks is that they're standardized. Almost all tracks at high schools in the United States are 400 meters around. If you didn't pay attention in school when the metric system was discussed, don't worry. One mile equals 1,609 meters. So 4 laps of a 400-meter track is 1,600 meters, just 9 meters (roughly 30 feet) short of a mile. It takes you only a few seconds to run 9 meters, so do what most runners do: ignore the difference, and count 4 laps of an outdoor track as a mile.

FOOTNOTES

Today, most outdoor tracks are 400 meters long because of what happened in the nineteenth century. Back then, the tracks in England—which is considered the pacesetter for modern track and field—were a quarter mile around, which is 440 yards. But when Frenchman Pierre du Corbertin began to push for the Olympics to be revived in the late 1890s, England wanted to be in sync with the rest of Europe, and the yard tracks were converted to metric distances to standardize measurement.

The biggest problem with running on a track is the tedium. I know I start feeling like a caged rat sometimes if I'm just running around and around on a track at an easy pace. Most runners find that running for more than half an hour on a track starts to get on their nerves. One way around this problem is to run with a friend in the outside lanes. The time will pass a lot more quickly if you're talking away with a buddy by your side. (And at the risk of contradicting myself, I'll count your iPod as a friend here, where there's no need to be on guard for cars and crazies.)

Another way to beat boredom on the track is to try to lose track of the number of laps you've run. Just like when you're running a new route on the roads, run for your usual amount of time, and figure that you'll cover roughly your usual distance.

Most longtime runners go to a track only when they want to do their one or two hard workouts of the week. During these workouts, they want to be on the track because they can precisely gauge their effort. They'll go to the track with a set workout in mind (such as doing *quarters*) and watch every second to make sure they're sticking to their plan as closely as possible. (For more on these types of workouts, see Chapter 19.) Why don't they run on the track most days? Because one of the greatest pleasures of running is exploring nature and enjoying a variety of scenery and terrain. Despite all of its other benefits, the track doesn't offer that variety.

DEFINITION

If you see someone running hard on the track for a lap at a time, he or she is doing **quarters.** They're called this because even though most tracks are measured metrically, runners usually ignore the small difference in distance and figure that 4 laps equals 1 mile. One lap, then, is a quarter of a mile.

Lack of variety is part of the reason that most longtime runners avoid indoor tracks. It can be pretty tough to get in runs of any real length on the indoor tracks that you'll find in the United States. Most of them require at least 10 laps just to cover 1 mile. I know this feeling all too well. When I started running again in the early 1970s, I ran mostly at an indoor track at the YMCA. Around and around and around I ran. Next thing I knew, I had covered half a mile. So once I felt a bit more confident about my running, I moved outside and rediscovered how much more fun it is to run in the great outdoors.

TRAINING TIP

If you're doing a distance run on the track, switch directions every mile. This switching will help you to keep track of your distance and will evenly distribute the stress of leaning into the curves to both of your hips. To further reduce that stress, run in the outside lanes, where the turns aren't as tight.

The other good reason to use indoor tracks only when you have to is that they're so small that the turns are very tight. Even more than standard outdoor tracks do, these indoor tracks place undue strain on the hip facing the inside of the track.

The Off-Road Option

Run on soft surfaces such as dirt, grass, or trails made of crushed stone, cinders, or wood chips as much as possible. These are the types of forgiving ground that, as a species, humans grew up running over. Think about how much more pleasant it feels on your feet to walk across your yard than it does to walk down the street. Multiply that difference not only by the much greater pounding of running, but also by the thousands of steps that you take in a run, and you reach the unavoidable conclusion that running on natural surfaces is one of the best ways to avoid injury.

When I was in college, I did a lot of my running on trails, and I loved it. There's something psychologically soothing about cruising through the woods. You're likely to feel more relaxed during and after your run than if you're always having to worry about whether a car is going to come tearing around the next bend. A lot of trails are shaded, too, so you stay cooler and aren't subject to the sun's rays.

FOOTNOTES

The Rails to Trails Conservancy converts old railroad lines into multiuse recreational paths. These are great places to run—they're free of auto traffic, they're usually scenic and have a soft surface, and they're always flat. The Conservancy currently administers more than 1,500 trails throughout the country, for more than 15,000 miles of running room. To find one near you, visit the organization's website (www.railtrails.org).

Finding convenient trails to run on can be tricky. Check with local hiking clubs and horse stables for sites in your area. And don't feel guilty about driving to a trail for a run. People drive to parks to sit around and eat hot dogs, so what's the harm in taking a short trip for a satisfying run in the woods?

Even if you can't run on trails on a regular basis, you can still reduce the pounding on your legs by seeking out soft surfaces wherever you are. I usually try to run on the small strip of dirt or grass by the side of a road rather than on the asphalt. Soon after I turned 40, I stopped doing this, figuring that with my ever-advancing age, I needed as sure a footing as I could get. Well, guess what happened? Soon after switching from the dirt and grass to the roads, I had my first real injury in years. Now I'm back to the side of the road whenever possible.

RULES OF THE ROAD

If you drive to a trail or park to run, bring dry clothes and fluids for after the run. That way, you can drive home comfortably and therefore more safely.

I originally made that switch away from dirt and grass because the footing on softer surfaces can be a bit tricky. Holes, roots, and uneven patches are a lot harder to see on grass than on a hard road or track. In my high school days, I once cut the bottom of my feet by running across broken glass that I couldn't see on the ground. And some trails, no matter how mentally soothing, are just too rugged for most runners to be able to maintain their normal stride.

Nonetheless, I remain convinced that all runners benefit from running on smooth, natural surfaces. Most of the best runners in the world, such as the Kenyans and Ethiopians, do the bulk of their mileage on dirt roads and trails. This training strengthens their leg muscles and tendons, and when they get on the roads, they can fly. The same will be true for you. Beginning runners, who might be heavier than veteran runners, will really benefit from the reduced pounding they get when running on soft surfaces.

Reach the Beach

I used to run a 10K (6.2 miles) race on the beach in Duxbury, Massachusetts. This beach was a firm, flat surface on which I could pretty much run with my normal stride. In other words, it was unlike most beaches. Despite what you might see in the movies, there's just not that much good running to be had on the sand. Most beaches are either too soft, so that your feet sink too far into the sand with every step to run normally, or, by the time you get to firm footing near the water, they're too slanted. In the latter case, you're asking for the same type of trouble as when you run on a slanted road.

There are exceptions, and some runners find a certain mystical element in running by the ocean when the footing is good. On the central California coast, there's a place called Pismo Beach. The sand at Pismo Beach is ideal for running. It's flat and firm for about 50 yards from the water's edge. I know a runner who has done two-hour runs there, finding great joy in watching and listening to the crashing of the surf just feet away. If you can find one of these rare runable beaches, they're a nice treat, although even the most Zen-like runner would find them boring on a daily basis.

Outer Destinations

Now that we've looked at where to run when you're in familiar surroundings, let's look at what happens when you're a stranger in a strange land. A lot of beginning runners, no matter how committed they are when at home, blow off their running when they're traveling for business or pleasure. That's a shame. You know how running is such a stress reliever in your day-to-day life. It's that much more of one when you're away from your usual routine. Plus, running in a new town or city allows you to experience it in a way that you can't if you confine yourself to meeting rooms, tour buses, and restaurants.

Finding good places to run when you're traveling can be difficult. Most inactive people don't have a good sense of distance. If you ask them where to run, they might mention a local park and not realize that it's not quite going to fit your running needs because it's only 100 yards across. Or they might know of a large enough place to run, but because it's a mile or two away, they'll think that it might as well be on Mars as far as being accessible.

As with other aspects of travel, a good solution is to do some investigation before you leave home. Get on the web and contact the local running clubs or running stores. If you can, do this before you make lodging reservations. When I'm in New York City, I always make sure that my hotel is no more than half a mile from Central Park, which is really the only place in Manhattan to get in some unimpeded miles.

 TRAINING TIP

When you arrive in an unfamiliar locale, always look for uncomplicated places to run. Keep an eye out for bike paths, parks, and other places that will have at least a mile or two of open space so that you won't have to risk getting lost or remembering routes that involve tons of turns.

These days, most cities have set aside some land for recreational purposes. It might not be great running, it might not be more than a mile or so of ground, and it probably won't be as beautiful as Central Park, but it can be the difference between being able to run and not. Besides parks, one common place to run is along waterfronts, such as along Lake Michigan in Chicago.

 FOOTNOTES

United States Track & Field maintains a database of more than 300,000 running routes around the country. You can search the database at www.usatf.org/ routes.

Don't forget that one of the keys to successful traveling is adaptability. This is as true with regard to running as it is to plane departures. If no good running options present themselves, make the most out of the hand you're dealt. When I was in postwar Vietnam in the early 1990s, the only place I could find to run without being overrun by traffic was a 600-yard loop through a zoo. This was hardly ideal, but circling that loop seemingly endlessly was a lot better than not running at all. In this country, if nothing else, you can usually find an outdoor track by looking for the nearest high school or college. Another easy option, especially for safe morning running, is to run around the perimeter of a mall's parking lot.

The Least You Need to Know

- No matter where you're running, the key to running safely is to be on constant guard for threats from cars, dogs, and suspicious humans.
- Streets and tracks are the most common and convenient places to run, but they have their drawbacks: streets are hard and can be dangerous, and tracks can be boring.
- The best place to run to avoid injury is on soft natural surfaces, especially dirt trails.
- Sidewalks and beaches are rarely good places to run.
- When you're traveling, you can find good places to run by contacting local running clubs or running stores, or checking online.

Morning, Noon, or Night: When to Run

In This Chapter

- How to find the time to run
- How running increases the amount of time in your day
- Deciding what time of day is best for you
- Making the most of your weekends

There's a guy in the Washington, D.C., area who is known to some as "Busy Running Man." That's because when he's spotted on the roads, he's running while wearing headphones and, incredibly, reading the morning newspaper. Is he an expert at maximizing the effectiveness of his time, having figured out how to do three things at once? Or is he among the world's worst at managing his time, always having to cram too many activities into too small an amount of time?

I tend toward the latter view. I say that because Busy Running Man seems to exemplify (admittedly in exaggerated form) what so many people think about running: so much is going on in their lives that it's a constant struggle to find the time for it. "I don't have the time" is the most frequent excuse that people give for not exercising regularly. That's almost never true. In this chapter, I'll show you how to find the time to fit running into your schedule, as well as detail the benefits of working out at various times of the day.

Fitting It in Your Schedule

As I said, a lack of time is the reason most often cited when people are asked why they don't exercise regularly. You're reading this book, so I'm not going to lump you into the always-looking-for-an-excuse category. What you want to know is where to find the time. But let's look at these people's claim nonetheless, if for no other reason than to keep you motivated if you hit a snag in your running program and start to think that your busy life means that your fitness must be sacrificed.

> **TRAINING TIP**
>
> People who think they don't have time to run because their day consists of running from one responsibility to another should consider this: in the average American home, the television is on for more than eight hours a day. Bypass one roundup of the latest local mayhem or an episode of *Mad Men,* and you've got more than enough time to get in a good workout.

Running Out of Time?

Usually, people who say that they don't have time for exercise have never made it a part of their life. They don't understand what it means to feel fit, so they don't place any importance on it. They've been taught that exercise is always drudgery, and they think that their life is hard enough as it is. Why would they take precious time to make it more so? Also, they think that they're already so tired all the time. Why run, and get more tired?

What Presidents and CEOs Know

Almost all of the 15 million regular runners in the United States are very busy. They hold demanding jobs; they're parents; they volunteer in their communities. But they know that the tiny amount of time that it takes each week to stick with a running program gives them a return that is monumental. The physical and psychological strength that they get from running increases the amount of "time" in their lives, if you take "time" to mean hours in which they feel vibrant, productive, and at ease with themselves.

Let's look at it another way and break things down mathematically: there are 168 hours in a week. You can maintain a good level of fitness by running for half an hour, four times a week. So there's two hours. Throw in another 15 minutes each workout for stretching, cooling down, and so on, and you're up to a grand total of 3 hours out of every week's 168.

Can't find three hours? Life too busy? Consider that people with seemingly over-whelming jobs—such as Allstate Insurance CEO Thomas Wilson, astronaut Leroy Chiao, and Columbia University president Lee Bollinger—are regular runners. They all know how running centers their day and increases the quality of the rest of their time.

When asked about people who throw out the I-don't-have-time excuse, former President George W. Bush, who ran six days a week during his first term, told *Runner's World* magazine, "I say they don't have their priorities straight. These are the same people who say they don't have enough time for their families. I don't take that as an acceptable answer. I believe anyone can make time. As a matter of fact, I don't believe it—I know it. If the President of the United States can make time, they can make time."

 TRAINING TIP

It takes a lot less work to maintain fitness than to acquire it. You can cut your training to just one third its usual level for a few weeks and not really lose any aerobic capacity. So if your schedule gets uncharacteristically hectic for brief periods, schedule just a few short runs a week, and you won't have to worry about starting from scratch when things return to normal.

None of this information is meant to belittle your busy life. It *is* a struggle to find the time to run regularly. I just wanted to make sure that you're convinced that it's a worthwhile struggle, and one that can almost always be won. Here are some ways to manage your running time so that it easily becomes a regular part of your day:

- Consider your run an integral part of your day, as you do going to work and spending time with your family.

- When planning your day, plan when you're going to run. Don't expect the time to magically present itself.

- If you struggle to run once you're home from work, treat running as an extension of your workday. Don't consider yourself "done for the day" until you've gotten your run in.

- Instead of viewing running as another responsibility, look upon your running time as a gift to yourself each day, when you get to spend quiet, quality time by yourself or with a close friend or two.

- Plan runs with friends one or two days a week. Give these meetings the same degree of commitment as you do other meetings during the week.

- Explain to your family and friends how special this time is to you. They'll be more likely to respect and support your running if you share with them why it's so important.

- If necessary, schedule your runs the same way that you do other parts of your life. Write them on a calendar, enter them in your personal organizer, or leave yourself a note.

Above all, keep a flexible approach rather than an all-or-nothing attitude. When things seem out of control at work, you don't just blow it off and head home for the day. You adapt to the situation and do the best you can. If work or other responsibilities has cut into the start of your usual running time, don't consider the day lost, and not run at all. If anything, you'll need running's stress relief more than usual. So get out the door for whatever amount of time is left to you. Then look at the time-consuming situation and see whether it's avoidable next time.

Morning Glory

The best time to run is the time of day when your normal schedule will most regularly allow you to run. For many busy people, that time is the morning. Studies of adult exercisers have shown the highest rate of regular compliance among those who work out is in the morning. It's no surprise why—other than the sandman, there usually aren't a whole lot of people placing demands on you at 6 A.M. But come the end of the workday, you might be pulled a million different ways, and it might be a lot easier to justify missing a run than to have to say no to people.

Most regular morning runners find that hitting the roads before work or school gives them energy for the whole day. It sure beats staggering out of bed at the last minute and starting your day in a stupor behind the wheel. Mentally, there are few greater feelings than starting your workday knowing that you've already achieved something personally significant.

Morning runners should take some extra precautions, however. Some studies have shown that regular morning runners get injured more often than evening runners. Your muscles are stiffer in the morning, and it's harder to feel as though you're making a smooth transition from rest to activity in the morning, especially when going right into a wake-up run. Additionally, most morning runners are trying to squeeze in a run without being late for work, so they might tend to skimp on a proper warm-up. The solution is to include time for some gentle stretching, and just some overall waking up, when you're setting your alarm clock for the next morning's run. Give yourself at least 20 minutes from when you get out of bed to when you get out the door.

TRAINING TIP

Carbohydrates ingested within 30 minutes of finishing a run are absorbed three times quicker than otherwise. This fuel replenishes your muscles and speeds your recovery from run to run, so don't let a tight prework schedule prevent you from getting something in your system between finishing a morning run and going to the office.

I know that this is precious time seemingly taken away from sleep. There are two things you can do to counter that feeling. First, if your entire wake-up/warm-up/run/cool-down routine is going to take an hour, then go to bed an hour earlier the night before. (Try not to do it the other way and get up an hour earlier than usual after going to bed at your normal time.) But what about all that stuff you need to do in the evening before you go to bed? My second bit of time-management advice is to save some of the little chores, such as paying a couple of bills or packing lunches, for that wake-up time I advise between getting out of bed and starting your run. If you've ever started the day by running as a beautiful sunrise unfolds, you know that the effort of getting out of bed is usually worth it.

The Lunch Bunch

Another of the main when-to-run options is the middle of the day. When I was training for the 1976 Olympics, I was employed as a teacher. Running before and after school every day was starting to get to me, so I asked for and received permission to run during my lunch hour. This was a huge help. It broke up my workday, gave me a boost for the afternoon, and allowed me to get in a better quality workout than when I was continually dragging myself out of bed to run. (I'm not much of a morning person.)

Running at lunchtime is also nice because, as with morning running, you have the postwork hours free to spend with family and friends. During the winter, running in the middle of the day often can be your only chance for any real sunlight until the weekends. This is also usually the warmest time of day in the winter.

TRAINING TIP

If you're going to run in the middle of a workday, start preparing for it about 15 minutes before your lunch hour. Stand up at your desk and do some gentle stretching of your back, neck, shoulders, and legs. This stretching will ease the transition from being an office stiff to a flowing runner.

The biggest problem you're going to face as a noontime runner is logistics. Your employers might not see the value in you dashing out the door every day for a vigorous run, especially if they're not exercisers and think that you're going to spend the afternoon asleep at your desk. That's why it's a good idea to do what I did and discuss your desire to run at lunch with your boss. As you should with your family, explain why this time is important to you. (You could also hit them with the statistics that show that the fittest employees take the fewest number of sick days.)

You might need more than the standard time allotted for lunch in your company to get in your run. It's not in your long-term best interest to sprint out the door at 12:01, return at 12:56 and be back, dressed, at your desk at 1:01. Account for the necessary pre- and postrun activities as you should when planning a run in the morning. Present your boss with a good plan, such as taking an extra 30 minutes in the middle of the day in exchange for arriving earlier or staying later.

After getting the thumbs-up from your boss, you're going to have to assess the surroundings. The number of businesses that have showers on site is growing, but they're still rare. Check for health clubs near your office at which you can stretch and shower afterward. If reasonable, this option is often a good one for helping to maintain your professional identity—you'll leave and return to work in your office attire, rather than your co-workers seeing you in shorts and a T-shirt.

When there's not an accessible shower, some runners towel off in the bathroom. This is a judgment call, based on your preferences, as well as the degree of formality of your office and the closeness of contact with your co-workers. Let's just say I wouldn't want to be around some runners a couple of hours after they've run if they had yet to shower.

Night Training

Hit the roads after a stressful day, and by the end of the run, you start to entertain the possibility that perhaps your boss only *seems* to be the devil incarnate. Even if you feel tired from a long workday, you usually feel better after you've warmed up when you run in the evening than at any other time of the day. Getting out for some miles after work is also a wonderful way to separate your professional life from your personal life.

 TRAINING TIP

One way to combine your running with your home responsibilities is to run with your dog. It can get its needed exercise and bathroom trips, and you can cross two things off your daily to-do list at once.

But consistently getting in your runs after work can be tough if you're not dedicated. You're seldom going to get a call early in the morning from your boss asking you to come in two hours early, but the same isn't true when it comes to staying late at the office. If you have a family, they might be in the reasonable, even endearing habit of wanting to spend time with you when you get home from work, rather than watch you dart out the door in your running shoes. There's also the matter of holding up others' mealtimes to consider.

Having someone to run with right after work can help mightily in sticking with it. Another solution is to start your run from your office. By the time you've finished your run, the traffic will be lighter, and you can go home and devote your entire attention to what's waiting for you there.

Weekend Warriors

As I said in Chapter 3, you want to progress intelligently with your running. That usually doesn't mean doing most of your running for the week on the consecutive days of the weekend. But that's what you'll see a lot of time-pressed runners do, figuring that they'll trash themselves on Saturday and Sunday and then have the workweek to recoup and do it all again the next weekend. That's not a good approach unless one of your main goals as a runner is to get injured.

Still, if it's always a major effort to find the time to run during the workweek, you can use the weekends to your advantage. Say you're running four days a week. Have Saturday and Sunday be two of those days. That means you only have to squeeze in two runs between Monday and Friday. Just be sure to plan intelligently. It's usually best to do your weekend running in the mornings. You can still sleep in some, go for a nice run, enjoy breakfast with your family, and then have hours free for whatever else you want to do.

The Least You Need to Know

- Almost everyone has enough time in their schedules for a regular running program.
- A good running program need only take 3 hours out of the 168 hours in a week.
- The best time to run is whatever time of day you'll consistently have the fewest demands on your time.

- Plan for and set aside your running time the same way that you plan other important parts of your life.
- Busy adults tend to have the highest compliance rates when they run in the morning.

Mo' Better Motivation

In This Chapter

- Developing good goals to stay motivated
- Setting the right types of goals
- Keeping written records of your running
- Running with others to stay motivated

Ask runners who have been running for six months or more if they hope to run for the rest of their lives, and almost all of them are going to say yes. That's the easy part—recognizing that your life is better because you run. What's not so easy is knowing how to stay motivated enough along the way to keep running.

Inertia is a mighty powerful force, and it can be tough to keep in mind how much better running makes you feel. So it can be difficult to resist that little voice that tells you that your life is hard enough as it is, so you just can't deal with running this week. Then one week becomes two, then three, and then you're way off track.

In this chapter, I'll show you some basic motivational strategies that I and other longtime runners use to keep ourselves on the road. If you get in the habit of using a few of the methods, not only will you want to run for the rest of your life, but you'll be psychologically able to.

Goal for It!

This book contains more than 100,000 words. That's a lot of writing! How do you go about tackling such a big project? You set intermediate goals and then set short-term goals to get you to those intermediate goals. You track your progress toward these short-term goals, all the while reminding yourself of the long-term goal, and when necessary and appropriate, you review what you've done to remind yourself how far you've come. That's the approach that I recommend for running as well. You need to set both short-term and long-term goals, you need a way to track those goals, and you need to monitor how you're progressing toward your goals, both to see whether they need to be revised and to remind yourself how far you've come.

For most runners, the ultimate long-term goal is to keep running for the rest of their lives. That's a pretty heady goal, and one that's hard to pin down. It's certainly my ultimate goal, but it's so vague that I can't use it as my main source of motivation. I set goals for a given year, and then within that year I set intermediate goals of what to focus on for a few months at a time. Within those few months, I set even shorter-term goals to guide me through a week or so of running at a time. Along the way, I'm constantly assessing things to determine what adjustments I need to make.

Keep It Real

To use goals to motivate you to run, start by setting short-term goals that you can achieve within three months. These goals should be specific and challenging, yet within your grasp. For example, your goal might be to be able to run 3 miles in less than 30 minutes at the end of 3 months.

 TRAINING TIP

Your goals should be attainable with a reasonable amount of work, but they should be challenging. If your goals are too easy to reach, you're more likely to get bored with your running.

To get to your short-term goal, you need to set shorter-term goals that follow a logical progression. After all, if you can now run 2 miles at a pace of 12 minutes per mile, and you keep doing that for the next 12 weeks, then you probably won't achieve your goal of 3 miles in 30 minutes. You need to map out intermediate steps along the way to get you from your starting point to your goal. Your intermediate goals should be two to three months away so that you can achieve several shorter-term goals. Two to three months is long enough for you to make some progress in your running and long enough to allow for the setbacks that all runners encounter occasionally. But it's also a short enough period of time that you can stay focused on the goal.

Being specific with your goals is the best way to make sure that you can track your progress. "I'd like to run faster" or "I'd like to lose weight" are amorphous goals. Three weeks into your running program, you're probably running faster, and if you've lost a pound, then you've lost weight. So why continue? But if you say, "I want to run 3 miles in less than 30 minutes by the end of June," or "I want to lose 10 pounds by the beginning of November," then you have something quantifiable to go after. You can chart a course toward meeting that goal, you can monitor your progress as you near it, and you can definitively say whether you achieved it.

The Means to Get to the Ends

The other big reason to be specific with your goals is because doing so will help you to know what to do to meet your goals. One of my big goals for my first year as a 50-year-old was to break the American record for 10 miles for a man of my age. That time is 52:53, which is just a bit slower than 5:15 per mile. So I knew that I needed to do some training at or faster than that pace to reach that goal. Contrast that goal with the vague statement that I wanted to run a fast time for 10 miles. What does that mean? How fast? How would I know what to shoot for in my training?

The same principles apply to your short-term goals. Do you want to be able to run 5 miles without stopping 2 months from now? Okay, then you know that to get to that goal, you need to work up to 3 miles, then 4 miles, and so on, at a pace that you can handle, rather than concentrating on how fast you're running.

RULES OF THE ROAD

You should write down your goals, but you shouldn't view them as being etched in stone. If you encounter an injury or other setback, but ignore it to keep working toward your goal, you'll only be setting yourself up for more setbacks. Only try to progress when you can do so healthfully; when you hit a physical setback, your goal should be to maintain, not improve, your fitness.

When you meet that short-term, three-month goal, give yourself a break! Promise yourself a meaningful reward while you're working toward the goal, then give yourself that reward when you meet it. The reward could be a nice dinner at your spouse's expense, or a new piece of running apparel, or a book or DVD that you've wanted for a long time.

TRAINING TIP

Just as you shouldn't be intimidated by your goals, don't be limited by them either. If you reach a goal ahead of schedule, reward yourself, and then set a new, slightly tougher goal.

Don't beat yourself up if you don't meet your goal. Instead, be honest about how much progress you made and evaluate why you didn't quite get to where you wanted. I tried and tried, but didn't break that age-50 record for 10 miles. The closest I got was 53:13, an agonizing mere 16 seconds off. Now I could have gotten down, told myself I stink, gone into a funk, and gotten apathetic. But what good would that do? Instead, I patted myself on the back for what I did achieve, and then looked at where and why I fell short. Did I set too tough of a goal? Was it unreasonable of me to expect to be able to achieve it based on my fitness when I started working toward the goal? Did I not work hard enough? Did I do the wrong types of things to get me to my goal?

Ask these kinds of questions, and remember: you've almost undoubtedly made some progress. Say your goal was to be 15 pounds lighter at the end of 3 months, but you've lost 10 pounds. That's still a tremendous achievement! Focus on congratulating yourself for what you have done, not beating yourself up over where you might have fallen short. The most important thing is that you've made the attempt. Learn from your experience and move on toward your next goal.

Logging On

The best way to track your progress toward your goals is to keep a *training log*. This log is a notebook, journal, spreadsheet, or even just random piles of paper in which you record key information about your running (see the following figure). A training log gives you an objective record of your progress as a runner. A lot of runners, including me, regularly consult their training logs to look at the work they've done in the past to provide motivation for the future.

The changes that running causes are subtle on a day-to-day basis, and memories are notoriously selective. Taken together, those two things can make it hard to get a sense of how your running is going. But if you mark key information a few times a week in your log, you have an undeniable record.

DEFINITION

A **training log** is the place where you record important information about your running. You should keep some sort of training log because it allows you to monitor your progress and learn from your mistakes.

When you're feeling down and thinking that you're not making any progress, you can look back and see that the run you just got back from that seemed to be a disaster would have been a major accomplishment just a few months ago. Many runners lack confidence in themselves and their abilities, and they downplay their accomplishments. By providing a visible manifestation of your running, training logs are great psychological comforters.

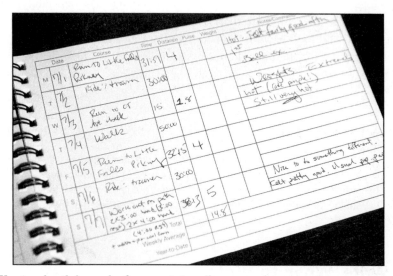

Keeping detailed records of your training allows you to better monitor your progress.

Your Very Own Guide Log

I like to use my training log to see how I'm chipping away at my goals. Consider that 10-mile race I talked about earlier. To get ready for that race, one of my key workouts was several repetitions of running hard for a mile, jogging very easily for a few minutes to recover, and then running hard again. As the race neared, I wanted to be sure that I was doing the hard miles at least a few seconds a mile faster than the pace I hoped to maintain in the race. After each workout, I wrote down my times for the hard miles. From week to week, I was able to see that my times were improving.

On the other hand, if I had seen that my times in key workouts and races weren't improving as I got nearer to that 10-mile race, then I would have known to revise my goal. My log would have helped me decide what was a reasonable goal in the 10-mile race.

Use your log the same way. If your goal is to lose 20 pounds in the next 4 months, track your weight in your log. That's a goal that you can mark your progress to, just as focusing on a race and trying to reach a certain level of fitness for it is for me. The same principle applies if you've been running a few miles a day and want to try to run more. Write down with pride when you run farther than you have in the past, so you have a record of the great strides that you're making.

Training logs also help you to learn from your mistakes. Say that lately you've been dragging. Every run feels harder than it should, and you just don't seem to be as eager to run as usual. You look back in your log, and notice that a few weeks ago, you had the flu, but ran farther than usual anyway (runners are stubborn!). Training logs can help to remove some of the mystery from your running. Over time, you'll be able to see what does and doesn't work for you.

RULES OF THE ROAD

Avoid the temptation to base your running around how impressive it will look in your log. If you're going to increase your mileage from week to week, do it because it will help you to meet a running goal, not just because it looks good in your log. Use your log as a tool to meet your goals rather than the source of your goals.

What to Write, When to Write

The more often you write in your training log, the more it can help you. Writing in your log within an hour of every run is ideal, because that's when the run is freshest in your mind. Another good time is soon before you go to bed, because you can put the run in perspective with the rest of the day. Try to write in your log at least twice a week so that you don't forget to include relevant information.

What information should you include in your training log? It depends on what factors are significant to you in determining your progress. Here are just some of the things that runners record in their logs:

- Distance run
- How long the run took
- How the run felt subjectively
- What the course was like
- What the weather was like
- Any ache or pain during the run
- Whether the run was a solo effort or with others

- Weight

- Morning heart rate

- Number of hours slept

- Any other exercise for the day

- Significant nonrunning events that might make running harder or easier that day, such as a late night at work

- Mileage for the week and month

- Goal for the coming week and month

- Assessment of progress toward goals

All of this information is more than most people want to write down a few times a week. At the minimum, I think you should include distance or time run, anything significant about the course or weather, anything significant about how you felt during the day or on the run, and, at least twice a month, how you're progressing toward your goals.

The Buddy System

The best way to stay motivated is to make your running interesting, easy, and enjoyable. The single best thing you can do to make your running easier and more enjoyable isn't getting the latest, greatest pair of shoes or eating just the right food, or putting on those cool running sunglasses. It's much simpler than that—run regularly with a friend. That person is your *training partner*.

DEFINITION

A **training partner** is a runner of similar ability whom you run with on a regular basis.

We've all heard about the loneliness of the long-distance runner. Yes, running can be an intensely solitary experience, and that's one of the main things that many people love about it. I certainly enjoy the opportunity to get away from the usual distractions with only my thoughts to accompany me. But if that's how you always run, you're missing out on one of the greatest and generally unknown aspects of running—the social side. Most people find that the miles pass a lot quicker when they've got a friend by their side.

Running with friends of similar ability is the best way to make your running more enjoyable.

As I said in the introduction to this chapter, inertia can be one of your toughest foes as a runner. Once you get out the door and start running, you've won the battle for the day. The best way to do that is to plan to meet a friend to run. Knowing that your friend is depending on you to be at such and such place at such and such time makes it very unlikely that you won't show. Once you show up, you'll start your run, and the workout will take care of itself.

Training partners can also help to motivate you during your run. If the two of you have planned to run 5 miles together, but you're feeling a little apathetic that day, you're a lot more likely to stick with your original goal for the day when you're with someone than if you're running on your own. That's why even the most solitary runners often try to hook up with others for their longest run of the week.

In the same way, training partners can help you to get more out of yourself on days when you've planned to run faster than usual. You're just a lot less likely to give up and take it easy if you and a friend are out there sharing the effort, helping each other reach your potential.

Not that running with someone else is all about mutual teeth gritting and pain withstanding. Running at an easy pace with others is one of my favorite social activities. Nonrunners often can't believe this, because they think that running always hurts and always leaves you breathless. The opposite is usually true when you run with a friend—you can't get yourselves to shut up! For a lot of people, running seems to loosen their tongues like a few drinks do. (Note that when you run with someone else, you'll regularly be seeing whether you can pass the talk test and are running at the right level of effort.)

RULES OF THE ROAD

It's okay to run occasionally with runners who are faster than you as a way to push yourself. But your regular training partners shouldn't be substantially faster than you, or you'll always be overdoing it. Conversely, if you regularly run with someone who is much slower than you, you'll be limiting your progress. A good rule of thumb is to try to find training partners who run within 30 seconds per mile of your normal pace.

How do you find training partners? The easiest way is to have a friend or spouse who runs at about the same pace as you, but don't worry if you don't. Most local running clubs hold group runs a few times a week. There, runners of similar pace levels will hook up, even if they don't know each other. You can also meet potential training partners through the people who finish near you in a race.

Avoid the Extremes

Consistency is the key to progressing as a runner. It's infinitely easier to stay motivated if you can see that you're able to steadily chip away at your goals. Try to avoid the extremes of overdoing it or not doing it.

Most of this chapter is about how to keep running. You want to know how to prevent those spells where you don't run for a week or two at a time and see your progress erode. Avoiding these spells is important because psychologically, periods of low motivation can feed on each other so that the less you run, the more frustrated you get, and the more you feel like giving up because your goals seem farther and farther away. Physically, it's important to keep at it because after as little as one week away from running, you start to lose the benefits. One study found that after only two to three weeks of inactivity, a group of runners lost almost half of their aerobic fitness. Talk about use it or lose it!

RULES OF THE ROAD

Common runner's etiquette is to let the slowest member of a group set the pace, rather than everyone straining to keep up with the fastest member of the group.

But consider the other extreme on the motivation scale. Runners are ambitious people; after all, no one is making you do this sometimes difficult thing. Just by starting a running program, you've shown that you are motivated. Problems can arise when that motivation runs amok. You can get so fired up that you start running more than you're ready for. In that case, you're *overtraining*. When that happens, you'll eventually either get injured or get so burned out that you won't want to run. In either case, you'll be as susceptible to seeing your fitness slip away as if you were undermotivated.

DEFINITION

Overtraining is running more than your body can handle for at least a few weeks. Overtraining can lead to injury and burnout. The amount of running that constitutes overtraining varies from runner to runner.

When you run more to get in a certain number of miles per week rather than to meet your goals, you're doing **junk miles.** This kind of running is just mindlessly accumulating miles, usually for the sake of having an impressive-looking training log.

The number of times that your heart beats in one minute when you're doing nothing is your **resting heart rate.** It's usually lowest in the morning when you're lying in bed, especially if you don't wake to an alarm clock.

Overtraining is most common in highly ambitious runners who think that more miles are always better than fewer miles. They base their training more on reaching a certain number of miles per week than on structuring their training to best meet their goals. As a result, they wind up running a lot of *junk miles.* Also, they usually don't meet their goals, and they get injured and feel flat pretty easily.

Because the amount of running people can handle varies so much from individual to individual, overtraining can happen at what might seem like a low level of mileage. If you go from being sedentary to running 15 miles a week within a month, you're putting far more stress on your body than if you were a longtime runner who increased his or her mileage from 40 to 55 miles per week. Unfortunately, overtraining isn't like a broken leg, where you definitely know what's bothering you. Its symptoms are many, and they can be caused by a lot of things besides just running too much.

Still, there are some ways to determine whether you're overtrained or to prevent overtraining in the first place. One of the best ways is to regularly measure your *resting heart rate,* or pulse. Over the course of several mornings, see how many times your heart beats in one minute when you first wake. If possible, try to take your pulse on mornings when you don't wake to an alarm clock. Your resting heart rate is usually going to be within a few beats of the same measure from day to day.

If your resting heart rate is more than five beats per minute higher than usual, something's up. You might be on the verge of getting sick, or you might be dehydrated, or you might be under a lot of stress. For whatever reason, your heart has to work harder than usual just to maintain your body's systems at rest. If that's the case, then think how much harder than usual it's going to have to work when you run.

If your morning pulse remains elevated for a few consecutive days, you need to take it easy. If you're not sick, or can't otherwise explain why your pulse might be higher than usual, then you're on the verge of overtraining. If you keep running at your usual level, you are risking injury and staleness.

Other signs of overtraining are the following:

- No desire to run on most days
- Lower energy during the day and when you run
- "Heavy" legs that don't feel better as you run
- An otherwise unaccountable drop in running performance
- Abnormal sleep (either too much or not enough)
- Unexplained, increased irritability
- Frequent minor colds and infections

The more of these symptoms you have had for at least a week straight, the more likely it is that you're overtrained. If so, cut your running by half and limit yourself to a very easy pace.

Two things are important to note here about overtraining. How much running it takes to make you overtrained depends on not only how much you've been running lately, but what else has been going on in your life. If there has recently been a lot of stress in your life, even if it's a lot of good stress, your usual running routine is going to take more out of you. Be more careful about not overdoing it when you're deep in the weeds of a major project at work, or you've just moved, or a loved one is ill in the hospital.

 TRAINING TIP

If your enthusiasm for running is lacking, it's usually not because you're overtrained. You probably just need to make more of an effort to add variety to your running. Try running in different locations, at different times of the day, faster or slower than usual, with a new training partner, and so on.

Also, variation in how you feel from day to day is unavoidable in running. So any of those signs of overtraining might hit you on a given day. Don't immediately assume that you're on the verge of falling apart. It's when a majority of them occur day after day that you're probably overtrained, not just when you're feeling a little sluggish. With more running experience, you'll be better able to know which warning signs are serious, and which ones are transitory and par for the course.

The Least You Need to Know

- Setting short-term goals to reach in the next few months keeps you motivated and focuses your running.
- Goals should be specific and challenging, but reachable.
- A detailed training log of important aspects of your running will help you progress toward your goals.
- Running with others of similar ability is one of the best ways to stay motivated.
- Avoid overtraining. It can lead to physical staleness, a lack of enthusiasm for running, and injury.

The Right Stuff

Running is a low-tech, low-hassle sport. You don't need special skis, the right type of wheel for your bike, or a different golf club for every shot. What you do need are good running shoes. They're the most important purchase you're going to make as a runner. You don't have to pay a ton for a good pair—about $75 to $90. But you will want to get a pair that fits your needs. In this part, you're going to uncover the right way to buy a good running shoe and find out what apparel and gadgets out there might make your running easier.

Sole Mates: Finding the Right Running Shoes

In This Chapter

- Why you need good running shoes
- The three types of road running shoes
- Finding the right shoe for you
- The best places to buy running shoes

Your most important purchase as a runner is the right shoe. Well, that and the left shoe. What I mean is that running is a simple sport. That's one of my favorite things about it. You don't need to buy a bunch of fancy equipment or fill out forms to become a member somewhere or coordinate court times with others. If you want, it can be as simple as just you and the roads.

But you do need good shoes—and not just any shoes, but good running shoes. When you run, your body absorbs a force of about three times your body weight every time you hit the ground. The right shoes will protect you from all the pounding. This protection will help to keep you from getting injured, and staying injury-free is key to enjoying your running. In this chapter, I'll show you what goes into a good running shoe, how to know which one is right for you, and where to buy them.

Why Running Shoes?

All sports have shoes made just for them, running included. But you'll often see beginning runners hitting the roads in any old shoe they have sitting around in the closet. Tennis shoes, boat shoes, basketball shoes—you name it, people think that they're okay to run in. That's too bad, because those people are probably going to hurt more than they should and not enjoy their running as much. Just as you wouldn't expect to shoot hoops well if you hit the basketball court in bowling shoes, you shouldn't expect to run well unless you're wearing running shoes.

FOOTNOTES

Not all runners think that shoes are essential. Ethiopia's Abebe Bikila set a world record when he won the 1960 Olympic Marathon. He did so running barefoot over the cobblestone streets of Rome. When he won the 1964 Olympic Marathon, however, he wore shoes.

What makes a shoe a running shoe? It's made for one thing, moving forward. After all, that's what you want to be doing as you make your way down the road. Unlike, say, a basketball shoe, a running shoe doesn't need to protect your ankles from side-to-side motion, nor does it need to help you jump. It just needs to help your body deal with the repetitive stress of putting one foot in front of the other, thousands of times per mile. So let me say this as clearly as possible: if you're going to run, get running shoes. Your body will thank you.

The Last Shall Be First: Shoe Construction

Running shoes vary greatly from one to another, but all good ones have these basics of construction in common (refer to the following figures):

- Outsole, the bottom of the shoe that hits the ground
- Midsole, the soft, cushioned part directly above the outsole
- Insole, the usually removable part on which your feet rest
- Upper, the top part of the shoe that holds the laces
- Heel counter, the sturdy back part of the shoe

FOOTNOTES

Those ubiquitous Nike waffle soles are aptly named. In the early 1970s, when the company was just starting, co-founder Bill Bowerman wanted a way to increase the shoes' traction. So he poured some raw shoe material into the family waffle iron and produced the studded sole that has become standard on most running shoes.

How these parts of a shoe are built and shaped is what makes one shoe good for you and another one not so good.

The outsole of a running shoe.

The midsole of a running shoe.

The insole of a running shoe.

The upper of a running shoe.

The heel counter of a running shoe.

In addition to the midsole, most modern shoes also provide cushioning through technologies that the various running-shoe companies have devised in their labs. The best known is Nike's Air cushioning. (It's so well known, in fact, that if you ask runners what shoe they wear, they'll often say, "Nike Air," rather than accurately name the model.) Other examples are Asics's Gel, Brooks's HydroFlow, and New Balance's Absorbz.

Although the running-shoe companies would vehemently deny it, most of these cushioning technologies are roughly equivalent for most runners. They all do a good job of increasing the amount of shock that the shoe absorbs, and therefore decreasing the amount of shock your legs absorb. Some shoes have these cushioning technologies only in the heel, some have them only in the forefoot, and some have them throughout the shoe.

The other major construction part of a shoe is its "last." Running geeks love to bandy about this term because it can be used in two ways, so it can confuse outsiders. For the purposes of this book, the last is how the shoe's upper is attached to its midsole. There are three basic types of last:

- Board lasting, in which the upper material is glued to a shoe-length board (usually made of paper fiber), and then attached to the midsole.

- Slip lasting, in which, as in a moccasin, the upper material is stitched directly to the midsole.

- Combination lasting, in which the upper material in the forefoot is attached directly to the midsole, as in slip lasting, while the upper material in the rear of the foot is attached to a board, as in board lasting.

You can tell which kind of last a shoe has by removing the insole. Once it's out, you'll see either a solid piece of material (a board-lasted shoe), a piece of material that runs to the arch area (a combination-lasted shoe), or stitches (a slip-lasted shoe). The best last for your shoe depends on how you run, as explained later in this chapter.

The term "last" can also refer to the shape of the shoe. To avoid confusion, this book uses the term "shape." There are three types of shoe shapes:

- Straight, in which the shoe is built straight along the arch.

- Semistraight, in which the shoe is built so that the forefoot points slightly toward the heel.

- Curved, in which the shoe is built so that the arch area appears partly carved out.

A shoe's shape is best determined by looking at it along the outsole. As with a shoe's last, which shape your shoe should have depends on how you run.

TRAINING TIP

Few things are more irritating during a run than having your shoe laces come undone. Double-knot your shoes before every run. Tie the knots snugly so that the shoe stays firmly in place during your run, but not so tight that you feel pressure across the top of your foot.

A final piece of construction lingo you may run across while shoe shopping is dual-density midsole. In many shoes, you'll see that the inside of the midsole will be darker than the rest. (It's usually gray.) If you push on this area, you'll notice that it's harder than the rest of the midsole. That darker, firmer area is a medial post, designed to add stability to the shoe. Shoes that have a medial post have a dual-density midsole, which means that part of the midsole is denser than the rest.

The Myth of the Perfect Running Shoe

Buying a running shoe is like buying a laptop computer: there's no accurate answer to the question, "Which one is best?" The right question is, "Which one is best for me?" Like laptop users, runners have different needs. I weigh 130 pounds and land with the greatest amount of force on my forefeet. That means I need a different kind of shoe than a heavier runner who lands with the most force in the heel, just like someone who does graphic design has different computer needs than an accountant.

All Feet Aren't Created Equal

The best running shoe is the one that best suits how your body, especially your feet, adapts to the stress of running. You want a shoe that best complements how you move through the gait cycle (what running geeks call biomechanics—how your body parts move together).

DEFINITION

Overpronation is when your feet roll in too far after they've hit the ground. If you overpronate but don't run in shoes that control the excessive motion, you'll likely be injured. **Supination** is when your feet roll to the outside after they've hit the ground. Less than 10 percent of runners supinate. Those who do need shoes with more-than-average cushioning.

Running shoes are constructed to address what happens when your feet hit the ground. Ideally, your foot lands on the outside heel, rolls in until your heel is aligned under your lower leg, then becomes rigid as it propels you forward. About half of all runners are blessed with something close to this kind of biomechanics. But many runners' feet roll in too far or continue to roll in as the foot prepares to push off; this type of footstrike is called *overpronation*. And a small minority of runners' feet don't roll in enough; this type of footstrike is called *supination*. The following figures illustrate these three types of running biomechanics.

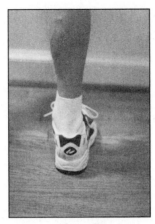

Overpronation (feet rolling in too much).

Neutral stance (feet rolling in about the right amount).

Supination (feet not rolling in enough).

The Three Types of Road Running Shoes

To address the different biomechanical needs of different runners, shoe companies play with the basics of construction. The shoes that they produce as a result create a continuum of models from heavy, ultrarigid ones to light, flexible ones. There are three main types of road running shoes:

- Motion-control shoes, which are designed to combat overpronation

- Neutral shoes, which are for runners without significant biomechanical problems

- Flexibility shoes, which are designed to provide maximum cushioning for supinators

Although this list is simplifying things a bit, these broad categories are helpful to keep in mind when you start your search for the right running shoe.

I'm assuming here that your first pair of real running shoes will be a standard pair of road running shoes. Those really popular trail running shoes aren't what you should start your running career in, because as a new runner you're going to want to experiment with what types of surfaces you like running on the most. Trail running shoes are made specifically for the conditions you'll find on rugged trails. I'll say more about trail running shoes in Chapter 23, which is devoted to trail running.

Back to the three types of road running shoes. Motion-control shoes usually contain these features:

- Combination or board lasting

- A straight shape

- A medial post that extends to the arch

- A thick midsole

- Heel and forefoot cushioning technologies

Because of these construction features, motion-control shoes are usually the heaviest ones on the market.

Neutral shoes usually contain these features:

- Combination or slip lasting

- A semistraight shape

- A small medial post

- A medium-thickness midsole

- Heel cushioning technologies

As you can see, these middle-of-the-road models are designed to suit the majority of runners.

Flexibility shoes usually contain these features:

- Slip lasting

- A curved shape

- No medial post

- A thin midsole

- Forefoot cushioning technologies

Flexibility shoes are usually among the lightest on the market.

Which Type Should You Wear?

There are many ways to make an educated guess at which type of running shoe is best for you. If you're already running, look at the forefoot of your old shoes. (Don't bother looking at the heel, because almost all runners land on the outside heel. It's what happens after landing that determines your needs.) Neutral runners usually see wear in the center of the forefoot; overpronators often find wear near the big toe; supinators may find wear toward the little toe. Also, examine your old shoes from the back when they're on a level surface. Do the heel counters tilt in significantly? If so, you're probably an overpronator.

Also, if you've had any running injuries, these can give clues as to your biomechanics. Overpronators tend to get injuries caused by soft-tissue fatigue, such as tendinitis and knee problems, because of the extra motion required of their muscles, tendons, and ligaments. In contrast, supinators subject their bodies to great amounts of shock because their feet move through too small a range of motion. As a result, they're susceptible to such injuries as ankle sprains, stress fractures, and shin splints.

If you're new to running, have a friend watch you from behind or videotape while you walk and run. Have your friend note what happens to your feet after your heel has landed. If it looks as though the inner part of your heel is still in contact with the ground when you're pushing off to the next stride, then you're probably an overpronator. If your heel appears relatively flat when you push off, you're probably a neutral runner. And if it seems that your foot is moving toward the outside as you push off, you're part of that rare breed of supinators. A good sales clerk at a running shoe store should be able to make the same assessment for you.

Shoe Wear, Tear, and Care

Like everything else in this world, running shoes eventually break down. They just seem to do so much more quickly than other shoes. Remember, with every running step, you create a force of about three times your body weight. Even for the lightest of us, that's a lot to ask our shoes to put up with. So with more miles, your shoes begin to deteriorate. The outsoles get worn out. The midsoles compress. The uppers start to tear. Next thing you know, that shoe that used to feel so good is making your knees ache with every step.

RULES OF THE ROAD

Your shoes will last longer if you have more than one pair because they won't get broken down as quickly from run to run. Buy two similar, but slightly different, models. Running in different shoes on different days more evenly distributes the pounding on your feet and legs.

Most runners can comfortably wear their shoes for 500 to 600 miles. In fact, none of the cushioning technologies used in today's shoes are designed to last more than 800 miles. Trying to squeeze more miles than this out of your shoes is the runner's version of being penny wise and pound foolish, because it can lead to injury. In the early 1970s, I once wore clean through the outsole of a pair of running shoes; no wonder my calves were killing me at the time! So watch the wear and tear on your shoes. It's a good idea to keep track of how many miles you have on a pair of shoes so that you can better estimate when you need new ones.

Even if you don't meticulously record the mileage on your shoes, always keep an eye on them. If you've worn through a spot in the outsole, ditch 'em. The shoe is so worn down that it's going to throw off your normal stride, and that's a good way to get injured. You should also check the heel counters. If you set your shoes on a level surface and look at them from the back and see that the heel counters point in significantly, they're no longer doing their job of providing support.

After a few hundred miles, you'll probably also start to see wrinkles in the midsole. These wrinkles mean that the midsole is getting compressed and can no longer absorb as much shock as when the shoes were new. When your shoes get in this condition, press a fingernail in the midsole. If doing so leaves a mark that doesn't quickly disappear, it's time for new shoes. Lastly, if you start to notice little aches and pains that you can't attribute to other causes, your worn-down shoes are probably the reason.

You can also extend the life of a shoe by doctoring the inside. I think most of the arch supports and inserts that come with running shoes are weak. As your shoes get a bit worn, you can take out the standard-issue inserts and replace them with a couple of the many commercial inserts available at running shoe stores. Many of these inserts supply extra cushioning, which I find to be helpful as the midsoles of my running shoes compress.

TRAINING TIP

When your running shoes get wet, stuff them with newspaper or place them in front of a fan. Keep them away from heat, because heat can ruin the midsoles.

Shopping for Shoes

These days, there are shoes on the market that cost more than the per capita income of some developing nations. Do you really need to spend $150 for a pair of shoes? No doubt, shoes that cost that much are well made, but that doesn't mean they're necessary. Many running shoes have more to do with marketing hype than with helping you to run better. Let's face it: like other people, some runners are driven by status. They just have to have the newest shoe with all the fancy colors and the cool logos. If that's you, and if it helps you feel better about yourself as a runner, then by all means, purchase the high-ticket items.

RULES OF THE ROAD

Like car manufacturers, shoe companies like to introduce new models all the time. If you find a shoe that you really like, consider buying more than one pair. If you don't, it might be off the market by the time you're ready for a replacement pair.

Dollars and Sense

Almost all runners can find shoes that suit their needs for $100 or less. If you're a beginner, I don't think you should spend more than that because you're probably still learning what type of shoe you need. You'll be less likely to be honest about abandoning a model that doesn't work for you if you've just plunked down several days' pay for it.

 TRAINING TIP

Shoes that have too high a heel can shorten and weaken your calf muscles and Achilles tendons. Using your index finger, measure the back of a shoe from the sole to the top of the midsole. The heel shouldn't be much higher than from the tip of your finger to your first knuckle.

At the other end of the scale, unless you can find discontinued models on sale, try not to spend less than $60. I know that the dollars can add up fast if you're only getting 400 miles out of a pair of shoes. But shoes that retail for less than $60 are often cheaply made, without enough support and cushioning. They're made in mass quantities out of inferior materials and are dumped on unsuspecting shoppers in megastores. They can lead to injury, and, well, they just don't feel as good as "real" running shoes. Isn't staying injury-free and enjoying your running worth that extra $10 a few times a year?

The Best Lace Places

The best place to buy running shoes is in a specialty running shop. This is especially the case if you're not sure which shoes to buy. Sure, you'll find a decent selection of shoes in sporting goods stores and even department stores, but those stores lack the knowledgeable salespeople who can help you find the model that's best for you. The same lack of knowledgeable help is a drawback to buying your running shoes online. The workers in a running store are going to be runners like you, who know how important it is to find just the right shoe and who spend their time fitting only runners, not runners along with basketball, football, soccer, and baseball players.

Also, a running specialty store is likely to stock a wider variety of models. The second-tier running companies, who pretty much concentrate on running shoes and don't have big national promotions budgets, make some of the best shoes out there. But these shoes are often hard to find unless you go to a running store.

At a running store, you'll be encouraged to pick up, examine, and try on several models until you find the right match. If the staff won't let you take a short test run in a shoe you're interested in, or if all their recommendations are for the higher-priced models, take your business elsewhere. Keep the following tips in mind when trying on running shoes:

- Try on both shoes—one of your feet is probably bigger than the other.

- Try on shoes in the afternoon, evening, or after a workout. Your feet are their largest at these times.

- Try on shoes while wearing your running socks and any inserts you plan on wearing.

- The shoes should flex where your foot does—in the forefoot, not in the middle of the arch area.

- When you stand up, there should be a thumb's width from the end of your longest toe to the front of the shoes.

- The shoes should feel comfortable immediately, rather than needing a break-in period.

Once you find a model that works for you, then it's okay to buy it wherever you can find it the cheapest. Several online distributors and mail-order businesses sometimes offer significant savings over what you'd pay in a store, but I don't recommend buying shoes through the web or catalogs unless you've previously used the model you're buying.

For More Information ...

Other runners are your best source of information on specific models. Runners can get pretty darned opinionated about their shoes, so sometimes you have to take their shoe advice with the proverbial grain of salt. But don't be afraid to ask other runners about which shoes have worked best for them (bearing in mind that they might have different needs than you). If a lot of runners tell you that they don't like a certain shoe, avoid it. Not heeding that advice is like ignoring a group of car owners who all tell you how their transmission went after only 15,000 miles on a certain model.

The two national running magazines, *Runner's World* and *Running Times,* do shoe reviews throughout the year, and soon after post the reviews on their websites. The reviews do a good job of telling you which of the new models might be right for you.

One note of caution: although the shoes in these reviews have been tested by the people writing the reviews, the authors usually don't have enough time before their deadlines to run more than 100 miles in any model. As with a car, it's often how a shoe holds up in the long run that determines how happy you are with it. So if you hear rumblings about a shoe from other runners that disagree with what the reviews say, listen to the runners. They'll likely be speaking from past the 100-mile mark.

The Least You Need to Know

- Running shoes are the most important purchase a runner makes because good shoes help to prevent injuries.
- There's no such thing as the perfect running shoe, only the perfect running shoe for you.
- What happens when your feet hit the ground determines which running shoes are best for you.
- Expect to pay between $60 and $85 for a good pair of running shoes.
- Most runners can get 500 to 600 miles out of a pair of shoes before having to buy new ones.
- Running specialty shops are the best places to buy running shoes.

From Top to Bottom: The Right Running Apparel

In This Chapter

- How much running apparel you need
- The best types of fabrics for running
- Staying comfortable while running in the cold
- The features of a good sports bra
- The best socks for running

My standard outfit for schlepping around the house is an old T-shirt from a race and a pair of jeans. That's true for a lot of runners. You paid for the shirt anyway when you signed up for the race, and wearing it is like donning a scrapbook.

Look around the next time you're in an area with a lot of runners, and you'll notice those shirts being worn for running, too. But more and more these days, you'll see people running in stuff that looks more like what skiers and mountain climbers wear. Sometimes you'll see even the most staid, middle-aged guys running down the street in tights.

What's going on here? Do you really need all these different types of clothes to be a runner? In this chapter, I'll describe what basic clothes I think all runners should have and how to know what to wear for increased comfort.

What Do You Really Need?

As you may have picked up by now, I'm a pretty simple guy when it comes to running. Despite what the apparel makers would have you think, you don't need all that much gear to run comfortably year round. In addition, bear in mind that you probably already have some clothes that will fit the bill. Also, you don't have to get all of your gear at once; you can buy it as you need it. Good running apparel will last for several years, so consider your purchases an investment in your health and comfort.

RULES OF THE ROAD

T-shirts from old races are the runner's unofficial uniform, but be careful what you wear when: it's an unstated but universal rule that a real runner never wears the shirt from a race in that year's event. You'll look a lot cooler if you have on the shirt from the same race of a few years ago, or better yet, some obscure race from years ago.

If you're going to run comfortably in most parts of the United States throughout the year, you should have the following in your running wardrobe:

- A couple of pairs of running shorts

- A couple of short-sleeve and a couple of long-sleeve T-shirts

- A *singlet*

- Either a pair of *tights* and a heavy top made of similar material or a *running suit*

- Gloves and a hat that fit snugly

- For women, a couple of *sports bras*

- A few pairs of running socks

Obviously, the more you have of each item, the less often you have to do laundry. (Or, if you're not the frequent laundering type, the less your home will smell.) More importantly, as you accumulate a nice amount of running apparel, you don't have to worry about whether your gear has dried from your previous run.

The running apparel industry is even more style driven than the running shoe industry. Unlike shoes, running apparel doesn't change that much from year to year in terms of construction. Pretty much the same types of materials are used every year, and what varies is how they look. You can often find top-quality gear for discounted prices at specialty running stores because they want to make way for the next season's lines.

DEFINITION

A **singlet** is a tank top designed for running. Because singlets are more ventilated, they are better choices than T-shirts. Most serious racers wear singlets in competition even in weather as cold as 40 degrees.

Tights are snug leggings for running in cold weather that don't restrict your freedom of movement.

A **running suit** is a pair of pants and a matching jacket that are warm enough for cold weather running but not so heavy that they restrict your form. Some runners prefer them to tights because they are looser and leave more to the imagination than tights do. Running suits are also known as track suits or warm-up suits.

A **sports bra** is a snug-fitting bra made of the same materials as other exercise gear. You might also hear them called jog bras, because Jogbra was the name of the first company to widely produce sports bras, much like people tend to call all copy machines Xerox machines.

Fashion and Function

A lot of runners think that what I'm saying here only applies to the hard-core, high-mileage runners. "But I only run a few miles a day," they say. "Why do I need special clothes for running?" You'll see them hit the roads in the winter wearing their old cotton sweats and a parka.

Sure, you can run in that stuff. I certainly put in my share of miles in baggy cotton sweats, heavy coats, and long johns 35 years ago. But even though back then there wasn't a whole lot of other options, I had the sense that there had to be a better way. I've tripped and fallen because of getting caught on my droopy drawers. And this stuff accumulates water and ice like nobody's business. Back then, my gear always seemed heavy and cold.

TRAINING TIP

Get whatever length and type of running shorts you feel most comfortable with. Most runners prefer some kind of split on the side of the shorts to provide greater freedom of movement. Look for shorts that have a decent key pocket on the inside.

So now, when there are better options, I don't understand not taking advantage of them. You want to do whatever you can to make your running easier. Why wouldn't you want to be as comfortable as possible when you run? I have a friend who I run with once in a while. In the winter, this guy likes to run without a hat, no matter how cold and wet it is. And remember, I live in New England, where it can get plenty cold and plenty wet. I've been on runs with him where his hair has had icicles forming on it because he was so cold and wet. I guess it's a macho thing for him, but to me it just seems silly. Running can be difficult enough on its own. Do what you can to make it easier.

At the other end of the weather spectrum, when it's really hot, you might wonder why you should wear a singlet. Nobody says you have to, but more men who used to go shirtless anytime it got above 70 degrees now wear singlets, even when the temperature is in the 90s.

Why? First, nearly all singlets are light in color. This color reflects the sun's rays. Speaking of the sun, singlets provide burn protection. Runners can be as vain as anyone else, and a lot of men used to take pride in their bronzed torsos. But now we know so much more about how exposure to the sun can lead to skin cancer. I think that's why more men are taking a little bit of cover under singlets. And let's face it—some people are too self-conscious about their bodies to parade around town in only a pair of shorts.

Cotton Isn't King: The Best Fabrics for Running

I'm a pretty low-tech guy. I'm also a creature of habit and convenience. So when I reach into my drawer for something to run in on a moderately warm day, I'm going to pull out a cotton T-shirt from a race. Some of my running partners can't believe how much of my running I do in those shirts. They pay for high-tech gear instead of running in the shirts they get for free from signing up for races.

What do they have against the classic cotton T-shirt? Same thing that I have against running in cotton sweats. Cotton feels great against your skin—when your skin is dry. But work up a sweat, and cotton absorbs all of that moisture, and your shirt clings to you. If it's cold outside, you start to feel cold. If it's hot, you get hotter, because your sweat just continues to gather on your shirt rather than evaporating and therefore cooling you like it's supposed to.

What's the alternative? Apparel made from fabrics that provide *wicking*, or, as the apparel designers like to say, moisture transport. When it's hot, the apparel moves sweat from your skin to the surface of the garment. There, it evaporates, so you get cooled. You also feel more comfortable because your running clothes aren't clinging to you as much. When it's cold, and you sweat (it does happen), you stay warmer in wicking fabrics because the moisture isn't held against your skin, so your skin doesn't start to feel clammy.

Most high-tech warm weather gear is made of *CoolMax*. Some companies have their own version of a similar fiber, but the principles behind the construction are the same. Shopping for running shorts and singlets is therefore pretty much a no-brainer, given that nearly all of the companies use the same materials. Go with what you like and what fits you best.

DEFINITION

Wicking is a term used to describe the process of apparel moving moisture from your skin to the surface of the garment. This process keeps you drier and more comfortable during the course of a run. Because cotton absorbs water so easily, it does a horrible job of wicking.

CoolMax is the running apparel industry standard for a moisture transport fiber. Its four-channel construction creates 20 percent more surface area than regular fibers do, so it quickly wicks moisture away from your skin to keep you dry. CoolMax retains 8 times less moisture than nylon and 14 times less moisture than cotton.

Microfiber is a broad classification of fiber that's used in a variety of running gear. It's usually nylon or polyester fibers, tightly woven so that sweat vapor can escape from the inside while the fiber remains quick drying and wind and water resistant from the outside. Microfiber apparel usually has a soft, silky feel.

Most running shorts these days have a CoolMax liner and some sort of *microfiber* shell or outer part. At first glance, the shell might look like the 100 percent nylon shorts that were standard for running shorts 30 years ago. But feel them, and you'll notice how much more comfortable they are. They do a heck of a lot better job with the elements than the old nylons did.

Winter Wear

I've run through enough Boston winters to know that you're only defeating yourself if you skimp on your cold weather apparel. But getting some basic high-tech gear doesn't have to bankrupt you.

The key to dressing comfortably for winter running is *layering*. You've probably heard about layering from outdoorsy types. What they mean when they talk about it is the same as what I mean—wearing a few light layers rather than one bulky one as a way to stay warmer and more mobile.

> **DEFINITION**
>
> **Layering** is dressing to run in the cold with a few light layers. Dressing this way keeps you warmer than wearing one layer of heavy clothes because heat is trapped between the layers. Layering also keeps you more comfortable because a few light layers allow greater range of motion, and as you warm up, it's easy to remove a layer.

You could pile on three cotton shirts and technically meet the several-light-layers definition, but once you get going on your run, you sure wouldn't be comfortable, for all the reasons I talked about in the previous section. For running, each layer has a purpose, and there are different types of fabrics to meet the different purposes of different layers.

The Base Layer

The layer closest to your skin, the base layer, should wick moisture away from your skin to the next layer. So what you want for this layer is a material that is like CoolMax, but a bit heavier. A well-known example is polypropylene. Most of the apparel companies have special names for their versions of these slightly heavier fabrics. All of them have the same basic construction. The thin fabric consists of two layers. The one closest to the skin is what the apparel people call hydrophobic, or water hating. It moves sweat to the top layer of the material, which is what is called hydrophilic, or water loving.

Merino wool base layers are increasingly available. They have the benefit over synthetic fibers of staying soft and odor-free even after several runs before you wash them. And their production is a lot more eco-friendly. But they're also about twice as expensive.

In dry, windless conditions down to the low 40s, many runners feel comfortable with just this base layer on. (It's got to be pretty cold before you need more than one layer on your legs when you're running.) So if that temperature sounds like close to the coldest you'll be running in, you're pretty much set with a pair of tights and a snug top made from one of these microfibers.

Running Suits

Sometimes you want a layer on top of your base layer. This is where running suits often come into play. These suits act as an outer shell to keep out wind, snow, and rain while allowing sweat vapor to move from your base layer to the surface. The most famous example of an outer layer fabric is Gore-Tex. Gore-Tex is pretty bulky for running, however. You can still find running suits made from Gore-Tex, but they're not the most comfortable suits on the market anymore. Newer materials, such as ThinTech and Activent, do as good a job of keeping wind and water out, but they're lighter and more breathable.

I'm a running suit guy much more than a tights wearer, but that's a matter of personal preference and, like wearing those cotton T-shirts, probably just a habit. If you live where running in the winter is going to mean pretty frequent run-ins with cold precipitation, then I'd go with a suit over the tighter stuff. Under your suit you can wear a pair of shorts and whatever thickness of shirt you need to feel comfortable.

In the nastiest winter weather (I'm thinking of my co-author up in Maine), you probably want a third layer between the base and shell layers. This layer is called an insulating layer. You want a top for this layer that's going to be pretty much a duplicate of your base layer so that it will help to keep moisture off of your skin.

RULES OF THE ROAD

If it's cold enough to run in tights, then you should probably have gloves on. That's because when you run in cool weather, more of your blood circulates in the core of your body, so your extremities get colder. Many runners wear gloves even if they're out in only shorts and a long-sleeve T-shirt.

Should You Top It Off?

When to wear a hat, like so many apparel choices, varies from runner to runner. We've all heard that a lot of body heat is lost through your head. To some runners, this fact means that they always want something on their head. But other runners, especially those who produce a lot of heat, know that this fact means that if they wear a hat, then their hair will get wet with sweat. When this happens, your hair can freeze, and you'll be a lot colder than if you didn't have a hat on. For about $25, you can find hats made of materials with wicking qualities to solve this dilemma.

Another good compromise is to wear a band that just covers your ears. This band protects your ears, which can be especially susceptible to frostbite, but it also allows you to blow off a little steam.

The Gloves Controversy

The gloves versus mittens question is also up to you. Mittens trap heat better, but running in them doesn't feel as natural as running in gloves does. But gloves can make your hands feel colder because your fingers are more spread out. Again, it depends how you react to cold. You can find gloves and mittens with wicking qualities for about $15. When the weather is not especially frigid, cotton gardening gloves, which cost only a few dollars, work fine.

Chest Protectors: The Importance of Sports Bras

There's no evidence that running damages breasts. Still, almost all women runners, regardless of breast size, prefer to run in a sports bra. It is a must-have piece of apparel for women runners.

> **FOOTNOTES**
>
> Two women created the first running bra in the late 1970s by sewing two jock-straps together. This bra was their attempt to come up with a better alternative to what women runners commonly did then—wrapping themselves in ace bandages or wearing a size-too-small bra. The creators of this prototype went on to found the company Jogbra.

What you wear over your sports bra depends on the weather and your modesty. During the hottest parts of the year, some women have no qualms about heading out for a run with nothing on top but their sports bra. Sports bras aren't revealing like other bras, and you're going to stay more comfortable in the heat the less that you have on. After all, those men you see running without shirts are doing so to stay cooler, not to improve their social lives. Understandably, some women aren't going to feel comfortable being seen like that in public. If that's you, go with a lightweight singlet over your sports bra. A few companies even make combination tops, with the bra built into the singlet.

Because your sports bra is going to fit snugly against your skin, you want it to have some wicking properties. Try a cotton/polyester blend. The polyester will move sweat to the surface and will provide more durability than cotton alone. If you need extra support, look for a bra that has Lycra in it as well.

Keep these fitting tips, offered by the American Running Association, in mind when choosing a sports bra:

- A sports bra shouldn't have exposed seams inside, because these can chafe you.
- The shoulder straps should be about ½ to ¾ of an inch wide. Straps that are narrower than that might dig into your shoulders.
- Don't buy a sports bra with clasps; these can dig into your skin. Get a sports bra that slips over your head.
- The bra should have a wide elastic chest band to keep it from riding up.
- Get a bra as close as possible to your usual size. If you can't fit your thumb under the shoulder straps and elastic chest band, it's too small. If a bra slips off your shoulders, it's too large.

Unlike what you might do with regular lingerie, don't buy a sports bra off the rack because it's your size. Always try it on before you buy it. In the dressing room, run in place, swing your arms around, and so forth, to make sure that it will move with you.

Sifting Through Sock Selections

Given that a few running nuts out there hit the streets without wearing shoes, it shouldn't be too much a surprise to learn that some runners choose to run without socks. But most runners have learned that they're probably going to be more comfortable if they run in socks. The inside materials of shoes can chafe unsocked feet during a run. And your running shoes probably smell nasty enough without sweat pouring right into them from otherwise uncovered feet!

There's certainly no lack of socks to choose from. That broad selection is good, because you're going to go through running socks like no other item of running equipment, shoes included. The good news is that you can find high-quality socks for running for just a few dollars a pair, although, as with everything else in running apparel, you can pay three or four times that much if you want top-of-the-line stuff.

I run in pretty basic, low-cut, white socks. As with shoes, the most important features are fit and comfort, not high-tech claims. Socks are usually available in two to four sizes. Make sure you wear the size that fits your foot. Wearing a sock that's too loose or too tight is as bad as wearing a shoe that's the wrong size.

How thick a sock you run in depends on what's most comfortable to you. Some runners like extremely thin socks because they like to feel the road when they run. On race day, especially, many runners want as little sock as possible. But sometimes, socks that are too thin will slip around inside a shoe. This can lead to blisters and can detract from a shoe's stability.

Other runners are from the more-is-better school and like a thicker sock because it provides more cushioning. But if your socks are too thick, they can make your shoes too tight and inhibit your normal biomechanics. Runners who have more than one pair of shoes will sometimes wear different thicknesses of socks with different shoes. This strategy makes sense, given the importance of a sock fitting just right within a shoe.

You might see socks specially marketed as running socks. What this usually means is that the socks have extra padding across the ball of the foot, toes, and especially in the heel area. This extra padding cuts down on shock and protects important areas that can blister. There's also usually padding or a tighter area through the arch to allow the shoe to fit more closely and add better arch support. Some runners don't like this feature because they think it feels too constraining. Again, you should go with what feels best to you.

As with other pieces of running apparel, socks come in many other fabrics beyond the old standby cotton. Cotton is a fine choice for colder weather running—it's very comfortable, and you probably won't be sweating so much that the sock will absorb much moisture. But when it's warmer, cotton can cause problems. Once the cotton fibers become saturated with moisture, the socks might bunch up inside your shoes and cause blisters. It's just not a whole lot of fun to be running down the road on a hot day and feel your wet feet squishing around in your shoes.

Socks made of synthetic fibers are usually better about wicking moisture away from your skin. The most commonly used synthetic fibers in running socks are acrylic, polypropylene, and CoolMax. Sometimes these fibers are blended with cotton, and sometimes they'll make up the whole sock. Polypropylene and CoolMax socks work well year-round. In the heat, they keep your feet drier, and when it's cold, they keep your feet warmer by keeping moisture away from the skin. The same is true of Merino wool socks.

The Least You Need to Know

- You can buy enough apparel to run in comfortably year-round (shorts, shirts, and cold-weather gear) for less than $300 total.
- In moderate weather, cotton clothes are fine to run in, but in hotter or colder weather, they can be uncomfortable once they get wet.
- For the greatest comfort in hot and cold weather, run in clothes that have wicking qualities, which is the capability to move moisture from your skin to the garment's surface.
- The key to staying comfortable during winter running is to dress in layers.
- A good sports bra should fit snugly and have wicking qualities.
- The most important features of running socks are fit and comfort, not the type of fabric they're made of.

Gadgets on the Go

In This Chapter

- What running watches and digital chronometers can do for you
- How to use a heart rate monitor
- The lowdown on GPS units
- The joys of running strollers
- What to know before you buy a treadmill

One of the things I like most about running is that it's so low tech, and I'm not just saying this because I still have trouble uploading photos to Facebook. I like how elemental running is—usually, it's just you, a decent pair of shoes, and Mother Nature. That part of running is never going to change—running down a dirt road on a lovely spring day is pretty much the same today for me as it was 40 years ago.

In those 40 years, however, a lot of new gadgets have been introduced that are supposed to make running better. I don't like most of them. They just get in the way of the basic act of getting out the door and moving under your own power. In fact, I suspect that one of the reasons for running's growing popularity is that it acts as an escape from the overly digitized world.

That said, there are a few gizmos that I think can be helpful to many runners. In various ways, running watches, heart rate monitors, odometers, running strollers, and treadmills are gadgets that can add to the enjoyment of your running by making it more convenient and productive.

Watch It

If I had to pick just one gadget for runners soon to be banished to a desert island, it would be one of the most basic. Out of all the techno devices crafted for runners over the last 40 years, there's still none better than the digital running watch.

Marking Time

The best thing about running watches is that they give you freedom. This statement might sound counterintuitive—isn't timing your run going to make you feel more pressured? Not when you do it correctly.

Yes, many runners use their watches to meticulously record all of their *splits*, that is, their intermediate times en route to a longer distance. That kind of timing can be good, especially when you're doing specific workouts to improve your performance at an upcoming race. When you're doing these kind of workouts, it's sometimes hard not to feel like your entire worth as a runner for the time being is decreed by your watch.

DEFINITION

Splits are times en route to a longer distance. For example, most 10K races have markers at every mile along the way so that you can check your mile splits. Knowing your splits is the best way in a race to know if you're running at the right pace to meet your goal.

But one of the main ways that I use my watch is on a regular, easy run when I feel like exploring. I love the feeling of freedom that running can give you—you head out your door, and it's completely up to you where to go. If 10 minutes into your run, you feel like taking a detour off of your usual route, well, who's stopping you? When you have a running watch on, you can make that detour and not wonder if you ran farther or shorter than usual. That's because the main feature on these watches is a stopwatch, or chronometer. All you have to do is start the chronometer at the start of your run, go wherever you want, and stop the watch when you stop running.

Say you normally run for half an hour. If you feel like you're running at about the same pace that you usually do, then you most likely are. There's no use in quibbling with yourself about a potential extra tenth of a mile here or there. It'll all even out eventually. This frees you to start your watch, head off in an unfamiliar direction for 15 minutes, turn around and run home.

TRAINING TIP

Don't time every one of your runs. When you know that you're going to run one of your regular routes, and you're just planning on running easy, you don't need to time yourself. It's very easy to become a slave to your stopwatch. This can lead to overtraining and detract from the fun of running.

The chronometer feature is especially useful when you're traveling and have to run in completely alien territory. When I'm in a new place, I start my watch, run at my normal training pace for however long I want, and rest assured that I've gone about as far as I would at home. Using your watch this way is also a good way to make new courses at home. Say you have a loop through your neighborhood that you're calling a 3-miler. See roughly what your average time is for that loop over the course of several runs, and then chart out other courses that you can run in that time. These new courses will be about the same length as the neighborhood loop.

FOOTNOTES

What did runners who didn't like holding stopwatches during a race do before digital chronometers were invented? Many would wear a regular watch and hold the hands at noon until the race started so that they could easily calculate their time en route.

Things That Go Beep in the Night

A key feature on a running watch is the countdown timer. You program the watch to count down a certain time, at the end of which it beeps for a few seconds, and then it starts counting down again until it beeps, and so on, until you make it stop. Runners will use this feature if they want to alternate bouts of hard and easy running. For example, you may start your countdown timer and run hard. After two minutes, the timer beeps, which is your signal to run very slowly. Two minutes later, it beeps again, and you start running hard, repeating the process as often as you want.

Yes, it's easy to feel like a Pavlovian dog when you use this feature, but it is very helpful when you're doing faster running of the sort that is detailed in Chapter 19. That's especially the case when you don't have access to a measured surface such as a track, or when it's dark out and you might have a hard time reading your watch. Many runners rely on this "countdown training" to guide them through their hard running in the winter.

You can find a good running watch with a chronometer, lap counter, and countdown timer for about $50 (see the following figure). Get one that's water-resistant so that you can wear it in the rain. If you run in the dark often, look for one with an illuminating backlight that you can easily switch on and that stays lit for a few seconds.

A running watch helps you monitor your progress as a runner.

Heart Rate Monitors

Running, like all aerobic exercise, is all about getting your heart rate up. All of those benefits of running that I told you about in Chapter 2 come when you raise your heart rate above a certain level and then keep it there for at least 20 minutes. In Chapter 3, I showed you good ways to know whether you've reached that range, including the talk test and the perceived effort scale. For most people, those vague guidelines are enough to be able to tell whether they're working hard enough to get the physical benefits of running.

But some people figure that if fitness all stems from what your heart rate is, then why not go right to the source? Why not measure your heart rate (pulse) while you run to make sure that you're at the right intensity? Enter the heart rate monitor. It enables you to check your heart rate throughout your run without having to stop and do any sort of counting. You just look down at your watch as you would to check the time—but even that isn't necessary with some models. With these models, you program the range of heart rate that you want to run at, and the monitor beeps if you get above or below that range.

The ABCs of Effort

Before looking at heart rate monitors specifically, let's delve a bit further into heart rate in general. There are many good reasons to use your heart rate as the guiding force in your running, but doing so has drawbacks as well.

Training by heart rate is good because if you know what numbers to use, there's no more accurate way to gauge your running. When you head out for a run around your neighborhood, how do you know what your pace is? Even if you compare your splits along the way to what you usually run, who's to say that you know what the earlier times mean? If the terrain is hilly, or the weather is warm, or you've been fighting a cold, or you got a bad night's sleep, your pace from day to day will be affected. Heart rate training proponents like to point out that heart rate monitors take all of those factors into account, and they do so in a way that helps you to progress in your training with less risk of injury and burnout.

The theory is that your heart rate can reach two extremes: your resting heart rate and your *maximal heart rate*. Remember resting heart rate from Chapter 6? It's the lowest number of times that your heart beats in a minute. Generally, your resting heart rate decreases as you become fitter because as your heart becomes stronger, it doesn't have to work as hard to pump the blood that your body needs when you're sitting around or sleeping. The average American has a resting heart rate of 72. Aerobically fit people usually have resting heart rates of around 60, and some hard-core distance runners have resting heart rates of 40 or lower.

DEFINITION

The greatest number of times that your heart can beat in a minute before it plateaus is your **maximal heart rate.** This figure doesn't change as you become more fit; what changes is how hard you have to run to reach it.

Your maximal heart rate is the highest rate that your heart can reach. Unlike your resting heart rate, it doesn't change as you become fitter. Your maximal heart rate is set at birth. Past the age of 30, it decreases by about one beat each year, although it doesn't decline as rapidly in very fit people. Most beginners should run at about 60 to 70 percent of their maximal heart rate. In that range, you're going fast enough to get the benefits, but not so fast that you're continually out of breath and running so hard that you're more likely to get frustrated or injured. In that range, exercise should feel good.

Your resting heart rate and how hard you have to work to run in the 60 to 70 percent range vary from day to day. Heat, hills, stress from work, lingering fatigue from a few bad nights of sleep, dehydration, caffeine—all of these factors can elevate your heart rate. What this means is that if you monitor your training by your running pace, then maintaining that pace is going to be harder from one day to the next. If it's 50 degrees outside and you've spent a restful day with the Sunday paper and you run on a flat course, your nine-minute miles are going to feel a lot easier than if it's a hot Wednesday, the office was miserable, you started your day with three cups of coffee, and you're running a hilly course.

Heart rate monitors allow for these differences. In a sense, your heart doesn't care about all that stuff that happened today at the office. It just wants to be worked at a level of effort that's between 60 and 70 percent of its maximum. That's going to mean running slower after that stressful day at the office than on that blissful Sunday. No big deal—you've achieved the same aerobic benefits from both runs.

Getting to the Heart of the Matter

Okay, so this heart rate training might be for you. But how do you know if and when you're in that magical 60 to 70 percent of maximal heart rate that gives aerobic benefits without increased risk of burnout and injury?

If you're going to train between 60 and 70 percent of your maximal heart rate, then you need to know what that top figure is. Unfortunately, any formula that you use to calculate your maximal heart rate is going to be inaccurate. The formulas are based on the average maximal heart rates for a person of a given age. Trouble is, your maximal heart rate may be as much as 20 beats above or below this average. Remember that maximal heart rate is something you're born with; it isn't a reflection of your fitness.

 TRAINING TIP

> Heart rate monitors are also helpful when you do a form of aerobic exercise other than running. If, say, you're cycling or working out on an elliptical trainer and aren't sure if you're getting a good workout, wear a heart rate monitor. Work out at the same intensity level you would running, and you'll be getting in a solid effort.

If you have a base level of fitness and want to find your maximal heart rate, here's how. If you run a 5K race and can honestly say that by the end you were working as hard as you can, then your heart rate at the finish is probably within a few beats of your maximal heart rate. Or try this test: warm up with some very easy running for 10 minutes or so. Do a few accelerations of 15 to 20 seconds at a pretty fast pace. Catch your breath, and then run as hard as you can for two minutes. Pace yourself so that you maintain about the same speed throughout. If you run as hard as you can, you'll most likely be within two to three beats of your maximal heart rate by the end of the run. If you aren't sure whether you gave an all-out effort, jog for 10 minutes and repeat the test. Some runners find that they get a slightly higher heart rate if they perform this test uphill.

Im-Pulse Purchases

Almost all heart rate monitors work the same way. You wear a thin plastic chest belt around your torso, at about sternum level (refer to the following figure). At the same time, you wear a wristwatch receiver. (These receivers can double as a chronometer.) The belt picks up your heart rate and sends that signal to the receiver. There, your current heart rate is displayed.

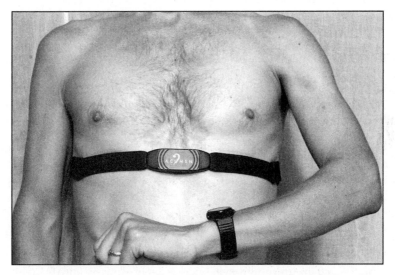

A heart rate monitor can tell you if you're running at the right intensity.

Most monitors have a feature that enables you to program in a floor and ceiling rate. If you go above or below these rates, the monitor will beep, and you'll know that you're out of the heart rate zone that you want to be in.

For example, if 60 percent of your maximal heart rate is 108, and 70 percent of it is 126, then you could program the monitor to beep when you go below or above this range. Then you would know either to pick up the pace or to slow down. If you're going to buy a heart rate monitor, I think you should get one with this feature; it makes you more likely to do your normal run without checking the receiver all the time, and it helps to build that ability to listen to your body instead of always relying on signals from the monitor.

Measuring Milestones

When most people say "I run 25 miles a week," they know they're not literally speaking the truth—it's quite unlikely that they covered exactly 25.00000000 miles last week. Rather, they've estimated the distance, and accept that over time, it doesn't really matter if they really ran 24.7 or 25.6 miles the previous week. Most runners guesstimate their mileage in this way, figuring they have a rough idea of how far their favorite courses are; while some might be shorter or longer than they're said to be, things average out over time. But if you're the type of person who doesn't like these sorts of loose ends, a runner's portable odometer might be for you.

Going, and Knowing, the Distance

Portable odometers have been available for years, but not since, fittingly enough, the start of the twenty-first century has technology advanced enough to allow for the devices to be accurate enough to bother with.

Many runners—including lots of new runners still finding their footing in the sport—have trouble feeling confident that how far they *think* they ran is anywhere close to the truth. That's especially the case when you're traveling and have to make do on unfamiliar courses. In those circumstances, if you're not comfortable estimating the distance you've covered based on time, it's nice to have some sort of quantification of your efforts. Portable odometers can also be liberating in the same way that watches can. That is, they can encourage you to explore new loops or trails near your usual running courses, secure in the knowledge that your effort is faithfully being recorded.

Running by Satellite

The most accurate of these new devices rely on global positioning system (GPS) technology. The most popular version consists of a GPS receiver that you wear on your arm and a watch/monitor that are wirelessly connected by a radio signal (see the following figure). The receiver scans the skies for satellite signals, and then transmits precise speed, distance, and pace readings to the watch in real time. In other words, you get constant updates on how far you've run, what your average pace has been during your run, how fast your last mile was, and so on. Pretty cool, huh?

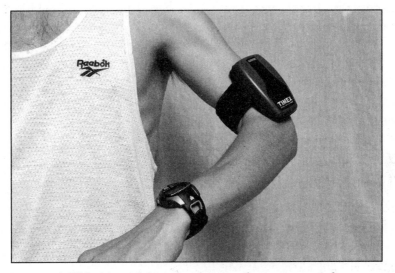

A GPS unit can help you track your mileage more precisely.

Now before you run out and spend the $150 or so on one of these, I should point out a few things. First and most important, as with pretty much any running gadget, you need to determine if a GPS system is really going to improve your running. If you're comfortable doing like most runners do and roughly figuring the distance of most of your runs, then (like me) you're probably not the sort to buy one of these things.

Also, the GPS technology is hardly foolproof. The greater the cloud cover, and the more winding the path you're running on, the greater the likelihood that you'll lose the GPS signal. (When this happens, the unit estimates distance for the time the signal is lost based on a complex set of mathematical equations.) In other words, if you wear one while running through a forest on an overcast day, you're just as well going low tech.

And Baby Makes Two

As I said in Chapter 5, one of the most common excuses for not running is "I don't have the time." As I hope I've convinced you, that's almost never the case. But I tend to be a little more understanding when I hear new parents cite a lack of time. As the father of two girls, I know that, especially in the early years, it's tough to justify doing anything that isn't directly related to the care and feeding of the household's newest resident. Yet I also know how important during that stage it is to do things that are for *you*, not seemingly everyone else in the world. One way to tend to the tykes while not missing your miles is by using a *running stroller*.

Mobile Baby Sitting

Their appeal is obvious. Often, runners who are new parents see their mileage slip for want of a simple half hour here or 45 minutes there. Running strollers allow you to stick with your running program without having to endlessly shuffle schedules or find a babysitter who's willing to work for an hour at a time.

The first running strollers in the United States were introduced in 1984 by the Baby Jogger Company. They were so successful that, like Rollerblade or Q-Tip, the company's name has become nearly synonymous with all similar products, regardless of manufacturer. Running strollers have become lighter and kinder to their occupants in the last 25 years, but the basics have remained unchanged—aluminum alloy spoke wheels, a synthetic fabric seat in a lightweight frame, a retractable canopy to protect from the elements, a sturdy harness to keep your baby strapped in securely, storage pouches, and foldable frames for easy storage (see the following figure).

DEFINITION

A **running stroller** is a sturdy baby transporter designed to be pushed while you're running without importing significant shock to its occupant.

Most strollers are designed to accommodate babies as young as six weeks old up to five-year-olds. Weight limits vary among models, but 70 pounds is pretty standard.

It's important to remember that while you're working up a sweat pushing a running stroller, little Junior is reclining into the face of a slight head wind. So keep the kids bundled up! Also, little babies need help with neck support; you can use a rolled-up cloth diaper or a neck roll (available at baby-supply stores).

A running stroller can help you get in a run without worrying about child care.

The Cost of Child Care

Expect to pay around $300 for a good running stroller. Considering how one allows you to keep with your running at one of the most stressful times in your life, this sounds like a pretty good bargain to me. If your budget is especially tight—and which new parent's isn't?—you can often buy a used model from a runner whose children have outgrown the stroller.

RULES OF THE ROAD

Most races discourage people from covering the course while pushing a running stroller because you're likely to hinder other runners.

Other than which one allows you the most normal running motion, one of the biggest matters to consider when comparison shopping is what your normal running courses are like. Basically, the bumpier the road, the larger the wheel you'll want to keep the ride smooth for your newest training partner.

Terrific Treadmills

A runner I know went to bed one Friday night planning to meet a couple of friends for a long run the next morning. When he woke up, he could barely leave his basement apartment, much less meet his friends—more than 2 feet of snow had fallen overnight! Being the compulsive sort, this dedicated runner hit the roads anyway and somehow slopped his way around in the blizzard for his daily run. The next day, he did the same. The next day, he had Achilles tendinitis so badly that he was incapacitated for more than a month.

"If only I had a treadmill," he thought. An increasing number of runners have obviously had similar experiences and thoughts, because in the last 15 years, more treadmills have been sold than any other piece of home exercise equipment. The big reason? Convenience.

> **RULES OF THE ROAD**
>
> You get the same aerobic benefits from doing the same workout outside or on a treadmill. Mechanically, though, the two runs are different. Outside, you push off against an unmoving surface; on a treadmill, you keep up with a moving belt. So do some outdoor running to prepare for races if you do most of your mileage on a treadmill.

The Fast Lane on the Beltway

It doesn't take a blizzard to spur some runners to hop on a treadmill. Many owners just aren't big fans of heading out in the dark and cold nearly every day for more than a quarter of the year. Treadmills are a great way to stick with your running through the toughest parts of the year (see the following figure). And that can mean summer, too—some runners retreat to treadmills when it's scorching outside, but air-conditioned inside. How bad can it be to always have a nice, cool bottle of water within reach? Busy parents also appreciate treadmills because they solve the child-care question. These runners keep Junior occupied nearby while they hop on the treadmill for their 30 or 40 minutes of running.

Treadmills have long been a favorite of runners returning from or nursing an injury. The belt on most of them is padded, so you're assured a softer, more level surface with surer footing than you would probably find outside. There's also the matter of control. You can have pretty much any kind of workout you want on a good treadmill, all at the touch of a button. You can play with the incline setting to simulate a hilly run, adjust the pace setting to get in some fast running, or just keep the pace constant and see how long you can comfortably keep up.

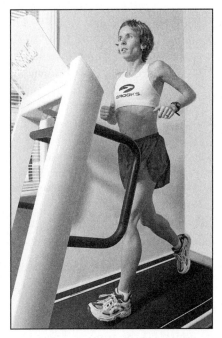

A treadmill allows you to get in a safe run regardless of the conditions.

Notice that I said "pretty much any kind of workout." One of the few types of workouts that you can't have on a treadmill is a visually interesting one. That's the main drawback of treadmills—it can be very difficult not to feel like a gerbil in a cage. (This is why some runners refer to them as "dreadmills.") No matter how bad the weather, I would prefer to run outside most days. I like looking at my surroundings, encountering Mother Nature, and all that. But that's me. If treadmills help to make your running easier, then I'm all in favor of your using one.

 TRAINING TIP

To account for the fact that you're not overcoming wind resistance when you run on a treadmill, set the treadmill's grade at 1 percent to better equate running at a given pace indoors and outdoors.

Milling About

How do you know if a treadmill is for you? I strongly recommend that you use one frequently before going out and buying one. Who among us doesn't have a piece of home exercise equipment that accumulates dust more than it does usage? If you think regularly using a treadmill might be for you, join a health club for a month. See what it's like to run on a treadmill a few times a week. Be honest with yourself about whether you'll continue to do so after you've put down some pretty serious bucks to have one in your home.

 TRAINING TIP

Don't take the readouts on a treadmill's console too literally. The speed is usually displayed accurately, although it's not uncommon for them to be off a bit. The calories burned display almost always overstates things. Stick with the rough figure of 100 calories per mile.

Here are some ways to beat boredom on treadmills:

- Watch the TV news or your favorite sitcom. Next thing you know (you hope), half an hour is up.

- Listen to motivational music.

- Don't stare at the console—the time will pass more slowly if you do.

- Break your run into segments of various lengths and paces rather than one long haul at the same pace on the same grade.

- Have a friend run "with" you on an adjacent treadmill. Runners of vastly different ability can run side by side on treadmills.

- Run in front of a mirror to monitor your form.

- Visualize yourself out on your favorite running route. Imagine where you would be on that route 10 minutes into your run, 20 minutes into your run, and so on.

- Adjust the incline and pace settings frequently to better simulate an outdoors run and to break up the run mentally.

If you have a treadmill in your home, don't stick it in that musty corner of your basement. You're just not going to be motivated to get on it a lot that way. Create as pleasant a setting as you can.

Putting the treadmill near a window gives you the chance to breathe some fresh air during your run, so at least you're not foregoing all the benefits of running outdoors. If you can't be near a window, try to have a fan nearby to keep the air circulating. You're probably going to sweat more on a treadmill because there's not the wind resistance that you encounter outside. So keep a towel handy.

Making the Grade

You've determined that having a treadmill in your home will improve your running by making it more convenient. What do you need to know before you buy one?

First off, you better have a nice bit of disposable income if you want to buy one that's worth the trouble. Although treadmills are available for as little as $400, they're not suitable for regular running. Their belts often stop running smoothly once you put in some miles on them, they're much more likely to break down with regular use, and some of them barely go fast enough to allow you to run with normal form.

 RULES OF THE ROAD

Before running on a treadmill, stand at the edge of the belt and get the machine going at a slow walking pace. Then step on the belt and gradually increase the speed to your desired pace.

Most treadmill devotees say that a good benchmark price is $1,500. Spend that much, and you can be pretty sure that the combination of features and construction will allow you to run smoothly on the treadmill for several years. Of course, there are manufacturers who will be happy to sell you a treadmill for more than twice that much. These high-end models are a little better, but as with buying a car, once you get to a certain level of quality, you start getting diminishing returns for your extra money.

Because of the expense involved, you should be sure that you're going to use your treadmill regularly before investing in one. If you do decide to go shopping for one, keep these buying tips in mind:

- Shop at a store that offers several models, that will deliver and assemble your treadmill, and that provides a maintenance contract.

- Take your running gear to the store and run on the model you're interested in for at least 10 minutes. (If the store won't let you, take your business elsewhere.)

- Be sure that the treadmill doesn't shake at the top speed that you plan to run on it.

- The machine's top speed should be faster than the fastest that you plan to run on it. Same thing for elevation. It's not good to frequently run a treadmill at full power.

- You should be able to change the controls easily while you're running without having to alter your form drastically.

- The control panel shouldn't shake while you're running.

- To keep you from tripping, the belt should start and stop gradually, and the handlebars should be reachable, but not intrusive.

You also should consider how loud the treadmill is when you're running on it. How much noise is acceptable for you depends on where you'll be using your treadmill and whether others will be near while you're using it.

The Least You Need to Know

- The best gadget ever invented for runners is the digital sports watch. You can find high-quality watches with all of the features you need for about $50.

- Training with a heart rate monitor to determine whether you're running at the right level of effort is the most accurate way to keep from running too hard or too easy.

- Running strollers allow busy parents to get in their miles without having to hire a babysitter or otherwise disrupt their routine.

- Running on a treadmill can help you stick with your running by giving you an alternative to uncooperative weather.

- Don't buy a treadmill for your home until you've run enough on one elsewhere to be sure that you'll use it regularly.

Body Shop

Keep running, and you'll be on more intimate terms with your body than you have ever been. This muscle feels this way, that muscle feels that way. Runners are nothing if not focused on their bodies.

This part is all about making your body the best it can be for your running. You'll learn ways to stretch and strengthen some parts of your body in order to make your running easier and prevent injury. You'll also find out about treating injuries, establishing a good runner's diet, starting activities that can aid your running, doing special things that can help women runners, and finding ways to run in any kind of weather. I guarantee that by the end of this part of the book, you'll know how to keep your body in top working order for running.

Stretching: The Truth

In This Chapter

- Why all runners should stretch
- The right way to stretch
- The best times to stretch
- Essential stretches for runners

This has happened to almost everyone who has run for a while: you're pushing against a wall or car or other big, immovable object, with one leg bending toward the object, the other behind it and straight. Invariably, someone comes along and says, "Need help holding it up?"

Ha, ha. What these people often don't know is that you're doing one of the classic runner stretches, the wall push-up. It might look funny, but it sure does a great job of stretching your Achilles tendons and calves, which can get sore and tight with running.

As you probably know, those aren't the only parts of your body that can get sore and tight from running. In this chapter, I'll show you how to stretch to increase your *flexibility* throughout your body so that you can run with more efficiency and fewer injuries. I'll also let you in on a related secret that has helped to keep me on the road for so many years.

Flexible Flyers: Why Not to Be a Tightwad

Before showing you how to stretch, I want to tell why you should stretch. Some runners never stretch and try to cover up the real reason they don't (laziness) with silly theories. The main reason offered for not stretching is summarized by the supposedly rhetorical question, "You never see a racehorse stretch, do you?" What they're trying to say is thoroughbreds seem to be able to run pretty well just by running. To suggest that humans need to do more to run is to argue with nature.

DEFINITION

Flexibility is your ability to move through a full range of motion. Along with aerobic capacity, muscular strength, and muscular endurance, it's one of the key components of fitness. When you're more flexible, running is easier because muscles, ligaments, and tendons don't have to work as hard to maintain a given pace. Maintaining decent flexibility is an important aspect of remaining injury-free.

Yes, it's true that you don't see racehorses stretch. You also don't see racehorses sit behind a desk 8 hours a day, or run on asphalt, or start running after being sedentary for the previous 40 years. So maybe when we're all bred solely to run fast and spend our days trotting around on dirt tracks, we can forego stretching. In the meantime, all runners, at least of the human variety, should stretch.

As running strengthens your muscles, it also shortens and tightens them. This is especially true of the prime movers on your back side: your Achilles tendons, calves, hamstrings, butt, and back muscles. You will feel better running, as well as most of the rest of the time, if these muscles are limber and can move through a wider range of motion.

By way of analogy, think about in which instance you'd rather launch into a sprint: immediately after having been driving for the past two hours or after having walked around the block? Intuitively, you know that you feel better running when you're looser, no matter what the racehorse fans would have you believe. And just as you're more limber at a specific time if you've been moving around, you're more limber in general if you regularly incorporate stretching into your running program.

Another important reason that all runners should stretch is because properly doing so will lower the risk of injury. Note that I said "properly." I'll get to what that means in a bit. What I want to say here is that the anti-stretchers will often give you anecdotal evidence about runners they know who stretch and still get injured. To that I say, "Yeah, and ...?" No one has ever claimed that if you stretch you'll never get injured. And when it's done wrong, it most definitely can cause injury.

But when stretching is done right, it can help keep you injury-free. That's true for the same reason that a short, taut rope is more likely to break under a given amount of force than a longer one of the same strength. In both cases, the shorter, tighter fiber is being asked to do a relatively greater amount of work, and eventually, it will tear from the task. When your muscles and connective tissues are more supple, they can more easily absorb and distribute the repetitive shock that running subjects them to.

How much time should you allow for stretching? The program I outline in this chapter should take only about 15 minutes to do. If you can do that 4 times a week, that's only 1 hour out of the 168 hours in a week. I don't think that's too much time to spend to contribute significantly to making your running easier, more enjoyable, and less interrupted by injury.

Don't Go Ballistic: The Right Way to Stretch

What is the right way to stretch? A good way to understand the right way is to know more about the wrong ways. The bouncy, jerky stretching you might remember from gym class is called *ballistic stretching*. It's bad because when you make a movement that lengthens a muscle, its initial reaction is to contract. Think about what happens when you briefly extend a coil, and then suddenly let it go. The same quick return to a shorter state happens when you stretch ballistically. This type of stretching increases, rather than lessens, the amount of tension in your muscles. In some cases, it can cause the muscles to tear. That's not a great way to lower your risk of injury.

DEFINITION

Stretching your muscles with quick, jerky movements is known as **ballistic stretching.** Avoid this method. If you stretch too suddenly and for too short a time, your muscles are likely to become strained, not more limber.

Gradually stretching a muscle to the point where you feel a slight pulling sensation is known as **static stretching.** This is the right way to stretch. Static stretching helps muscles to stay limber.

The right way to stretch is to do so comfortably, gently, and consistently. Improving, or at least maintaining, your flexibility is similar to improving your endurance. As explained in Chapter 3, the key to progress in your running is to find a comfortable level of effort and to work out regularly at that level. As you stick with that approach, your endurance will increase, and you can gradually run more, or faster, without any more effort.

The same is true with stretching. Regardless of the specific exercise you're doing, you want to find a point where the muscles you're working on are stretched just enough so that you can feel it, but not so much that it's obvious you're overdoing it. This type of stretching is known as *static stretching*. As with the first part of your running program, when in doubt, ease up. It's better to stretch a muscle a bit less than to overdo it.

RULES OF THE ROAD

Do your stretching on a firm, but comfortable, surface. If the surface is too hard, such as a wooden floor, you're not going to be able to relax. If it's too soft, such as a bed, you won't be able to do the stretches properly. A plush carpet is good. You can also find padded stretching mats for about $10.

As with boosting your endurance, when it comes to flexibility, slow and long are better than fast and short. You should hold all stretches for at least 15 seconds. Thirty seconds is even better. This amount of time encourages increased blood flow to the muscles you're concentrating on, which will gradually elongate them. When you comfortably hold a stretch for 15 to 30 seconds, the muscles will relax. This reduction in muscular tension is what makes you feel looser, both right after the stretch and from day to day when you're consistent with your flexibility program.

After the stretch, relax the muscles you're working on for the same amount of time. Then do the stretch once more, again holding it for 15 to 30 seconds. By the end of the second time you've done a certain stretch, you'll probably notice that your flexibility in that area is greater than when you began, just like your normal training pace is easier 10 minutes into a run than at the beginning.

TRAINING TIP

Do your stretching in a pleasant environment. Many runners like to find a quiet spot where they can relax and focus on their stretching without any distractions. Many runners also like to listen to music while stretching. Listening to a few of your favorite songs is a good way to help pass the 15 or so minutes that you should spend stretching.

Scheduling Stretching

In an ideal world, all of my runs would go something like this: a gentle warm-up of slow walking and running, lasting about 10 minutes; then 10 to 15 minutes of stretching; my planned run for the day; then 10 to 15 minutes more of stretching. Following this format would mean that when I start the first bout of stretching, the warm-up would have increased blood flow to my muscles, thereby increasing their ability to stretch without injury. That prerun stretching would also mean I'd start my run less creaky and could more readily feel comfortable at my regular training pace.

The postrun stretching would help my muscles and connective tissues maintain their length until it was time to start the whole thing over the next day.

Like I said, that's how things would go in an ideal world, but in reality things are different. I'm not saying that I shouldn't do the routine I've just outlined, just that I don't. I don't want to be hypocritical here and describe some perfect stretching routine if it's one I know I almost never do. I'm a big believer in keeping running simple. The easier it fits into your busy life, the more that you're likely to stick with it. In terms of stretching, that means hitting upon a routine that you'll do consistently, even if it's not the ideal one.

You can get pretty much everything that you need out of your flexibility program by doing it either before *or* after, rather than before *and* after, your run. So which is better: before or after? If it's going to be one or the other, go with after.

If you limit your stretching to before your run, you won't get as much out of it. First, your muscles are colder and tighter then, so you won't be able to stretch as far comfortably. It's also easier to overstretch then and potentially hurt yourself. There's also a good chance that you'll rush through your routine if you still have your run in front of you; time may be short, and you want to get out the door! All of this is especially true for the many runners who train in the morning before work.

Contrast that with stretching after your run. Your muscles are warm and more receptive to being gently elongated. For this reason, stretching after a run just feels so much better. You're also likely to be more relaxed after your run.

RULES OF THE ROAD

To get the most out of your stretching, do your flexibility routine in clothes that won't inhibit your range of motion. Running shorts and a T-shirt are ideal. You want clothes that are loose enough so that you can move through a full range of motion, but not so baggy that they're going to get in the way.

Sometimes, you might not have time right after your run to stretch. In those cases, you can still get most of the benefits of stretching by finding a short chunk of time elsewhere in the day. I think you'll make a lot more progress in all areas of your running if you have a flexible (ha!) approach rather than an all-or-nothing outlook.

TRAINING TIP

If you stretch after you run, change into warm, dry clothes first. Get something to drink and bring it with you to where you'll be stretching. Both of these things will encourage you to spend the time stretching rather than rushing off to the shower or refrigerator.

Essential Stretching Exercises for Runners

Given that the human body has more than 500 muscles, you could spend all day stretching if you really wanted to work on your flexibility. But you have better things to do than that, right?

What you want to know is which of those more than 500 muscles tend to make your running better. Certainly, you can get more involved than what I'm going to recommend here, but all runners should have a stretch that they do regularly for these areas of the body:

- Feet and ankles
- Calves and Achilles tendons (the backs of your ankles)
- Hamstrings (along the backs of your legs)
- *Iliotibial band*
- Hips and butt
- Groin
- Back

DEFINITION

The **iliotibial band** is a thick, fibrous band of tissue that runs along the outer leg from the hip to the knee. It often becomes tight in runners, especially those who run on slanted surfaces.

You'll notice that these areas are almost all on your back side. Although it feels great and is beneficial to stretch body parts along your front, such as your quadriceps muscles in your thighs, it's the ones along your back side that you have to give the greatest amount of attention.

Everyone has his or her favorite stretches for these various parts. I like to tweak traditional stretches if I can find a way to isolate a body part that I'm having trouble with. So don't think that the exercises I describe are the only ways to stretch these key body parts. Start with what I explain here, and if you find a way to alter these stretches that works better for your sorest, tightest spots, feel free to experiment.

No matter how closely you follow the routine I outline here, keep these basic guidelines in mind:

- Stretch at least four times a week to maintain and improve your flexibility.

- Stretch on a flat, firm, comfortable surface.

- Stretch in warm, dry clothes that won't restrict your range of motion.

- Hold each stretch for 15 to 30 seconds, release it and relax for the same amount of time, and then repeat these two steps.

- Breathe normally while stretching.

- Stretch only to the point of mild sensation.

With those caveats in mind, let's look at the basic stretches on the following pages that all runners should do some version of.

Feet/Ankle Stretch

As illustrated in the following figure, start the feet/ankle stretch by sitting with one leg flat and straight on the floor; the other leg should be at roughly a 90-degree angle, with your heel on the floor so that the toes of that foot point toward the ceiling. Grab the toes of your bent leg and pull them toward your chest. After 15 seconds, point them as far as you can in the other direction. You should feel the stretch along the top of your foot, where it joins your ankle. Relax your foot, then repeat the stretch in both directions. Switch the position of your legs, and do the stretch twice for the other leg.

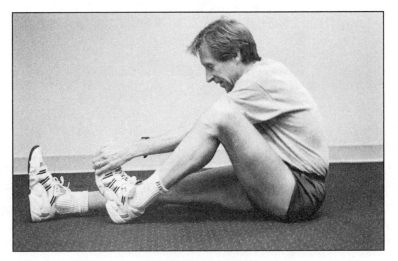

The feet/ankle stretch.

Calves/Achilles Tendon Stretch

To stretch your calves and Achilles tendons, stand facing a wall with the palms of your hands flat against the wall and your toes pointing toward the wall, as shown in the following figure. You should be at arm's length from the wall. Place one foot about 10 inches in front of the other. Lean into the wall, bending your forward leg. You should feel the stretch in the calf muscle and Achilles tendon of your back leg. Relax, then repeat the stretch for the same leg. Switch the position of your legs, and do the stretch twice for your other leg.

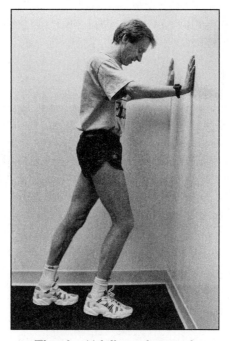

The calves/Achilles tendon stretch.

Hamstring Stretch

Begin the hamstring stretch by lying on your back, as shown in the following figure. Wrap a towel or rope under the ball of one foot. If your hamstrings are very tight, keep the other foot on the floor with the knee of that leg bent. If you're more flexible, straighten both legs flat on the floor. Slowly raise the foot with the towel around it toward the ceiling. Don't use the towel or rope to pull your leg down; instead, push your foot up. Straighten the leg being stretched only as far as feels comfortable. You should feel the stretch along the back of your raised leg. Relax, and then repeat the stretch for the same leg. Switch the position of your legs, and do the stretch twice for your other leg.

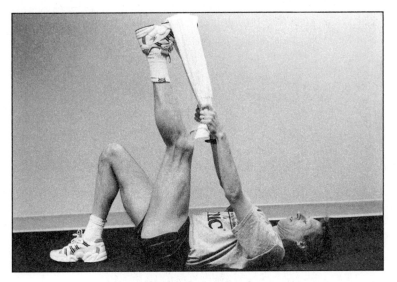

The hamstring stretch.

Iliotibial Band Stretch

To begin the iliotibial band stretch, sit with one leg bent at roughly a 90-degree angle, as shown in the following figure. Keep the other leg straight and flat on the floor. Place the foot of the bent leg just over the outside knee of your straight leg. Place the elbow of your opposing arm on the outside knee of your bent leg. Push the knee of your bent leg toward your opposing shoulder. You should feel the stretch along the outside of your bent leg, anywhere from the hip to the knee. Relax, then repeat the stretch for the same leg. Switch the position of your legs, and do the stretch twice for your other leg.

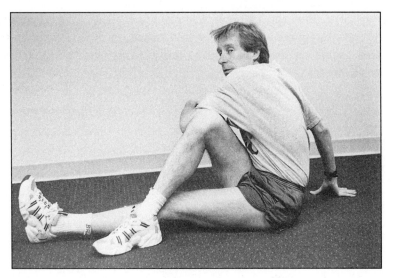

The iliotibial band stretch.

Hips/Butt Stretch

Lie flat on your back to begin the hips/butt stretch. Draw one leg toward the other at a 90-degree angle with your opposing arm. Gradually pull your bent leg across your straight leg, as shown in the following figure. You should feel the stretch in your hips and deep in your butt. Relax, then repeat the stretch for the same leg. Switch the position of your legs, and do the stretch twice for your other leg.

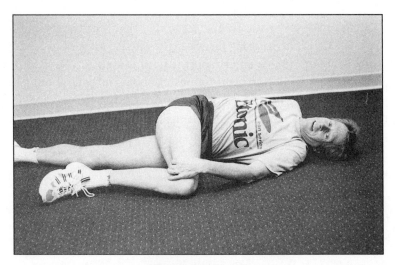

The hips/butt stretch.

Groin Stretch

To stretch the groin area, sit with the soles of your feet against each other. Place your elbows against the insides of your knees. Gradually push your legs down so that the outsides of your knees approach the floor. You should feel the stretch on the upper insides of your thighs. Relax, then repeat the stretch.

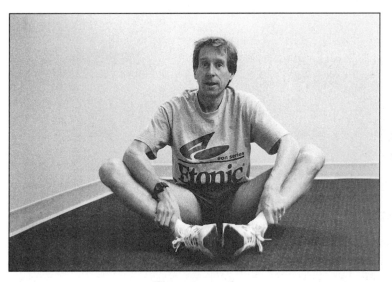

The groin stretch.

Back Stretch

Kneel on the floor with your knees at a 90-degree angle to begin the back stretch. Your back should be flat and your arms locked, with your palms flat on the floor. Simultaneously tighten your abdominal muscles and tilt your pelvis toward your head so that your back arches like that of a stretching cat, as illustrated in the figure. You should feel the stretch from the top of your butt through your lower back. Relax, then repeat the stretch.

The back stretch.

It's no stretch to say that if you spend a few minutes a day a few times a week doing these exercises, you're going to enjoy your running more. As with running itself, moderation and consistency will get you farther than extremes of overdoing and underdoing a stretching routine.

The Least You Need to Know

- A good flexibility program will increase your enjoyment of running and lower your risk of injury.
- You can contribute significantly to your flexibility with just 4 15-minute stretching sessions per week.
- The best way to stretch is slowly and gently, holding each stretch for 15 to 30 seconds.
- The best time to stretch is right after you run.
- The most important areas for you to stretch are on your back side, especially your calves, hamstrings, butt, and back.
- Getting a good sports massage a couple of times per month will greatly improve your flexibility.

Pumped Up: Strength Training for Runners

Chapter 11

In This Chapter

- Why all runners should do some form of strengthening work
- Why strength training doesn't mean gaining unwanted weight
- Essential strengthening exercises for runners
- How to detect and correct muscle imbalances

I'm 5'9" and weigh about 130 pounds. Based on that, you might be as ready to take advice from me on how to get stronger as you would from Rush Limbaugh on how to take vows of silence. I don't pretend to know everything there is to know about lifting weights, but I don't need to. What I know, and what you should care about, is what few simple exercises to do a few times a week to run easier and more smoothly. That's a lot different than what Arnold Schwarzenegger would probably have you doing, but when was the last time he won the Boston Marathon? In this chapter, I'll show you why and how all runners should do some form of strengthening work, as well as some special leg-strengthening exercises that some runners should do.

Ever Notice That Runners Are Skinny?

Before getting down to business, I want to set a few things straight. And no, I'm not just doing this because I'm tired of having sand kicked in my face. Look at pictures of top runners at any distance from the mile on up, and you'll notice one common trait—they're all really skinny! Especially in the arms and torso, these are bodies that make people think more about prison camps than peak health. This impression is particularly prevalent with male runners, in part because our society still equates masculinity with brute strength.

But appearances can be deceiving. Yes, it's true that in comparative studies, distance runners usually score below average in tests of *muscular strength*, as measured by a one-repetition maximum. But that's largely because of the fact that their weight is also below average. When the figures are adjusted to take into account strength for body size, runners have average strength.

For most people, looking like the people who win the New York City Marathon is just never going to happen, especially given that almost nobody is going to put in the number of miles that top runners do day after day, week after week. So don't let the looks of a few genetic freaks—I'm including myself here—discourage you from running. You're probably going to lose some weight as a result of your running, and I assume that most of you see that result as good. What you're not going to lose is relative strength.

Hurry Up and Weight

So if running isn't going to make you so weak that you need help bringing in the Sunday paper, then why am I saying that all runners should do some strengthening work? For starters, because everyone should, in the same way that everyone should do some sort of regular aerobic exercise. The American College of Sports Medicine recommends that all adults do two or three *resistance training* sessions per week to maintain and build muscular strength. This recommendation makes sense to me. Being cardiovascularly fit, as you will become through running, is certainly the most important aspect of being fit, but it's not the only one.

More specifically for runners, you'll be able to progress more in your running if you include some basic strengthening exercises in your program. Remember what I said about running form in Chapter 3: you run best when your whole body moves in sync. This type of movement means, among other things, that your upper body flows right along with your legs, rather than being somewhat awkwardly perched atop your legs, contradicting their every move. When you have a basic level of strength in your upper body, you can hold yourself better and more upright as you run. This ability will make a given pace feel easier.

The Core of the Matter

Everyone talks about *core strength* these days, but runners have been hip to the importance of strong hips and abs since at least the 1960s. Ron Clarke, who set several world records in the 1960s, used to say that a distance runner couldn't be too strong in the middle. What he meant was that when you run, the shock that comes every time that your feet hit the ground is transmitted throughout your body if your midsection is strong. Strong stomach and back muscles absorb some of that shock, rather than confining it to your legs. The result is that your legs have to put up with less impact force and won't get as overloaded with potential wear and tear.

Clarke knew how important it was for the midsection of your body to remain stable and supportive when you're in motion. When you run, your midsection acts as a fixed base while your legs work as levers relative to that base to propel you forward. If the torso and pelvic muscles that form your fixed base are weak or fatigue quickly, then you can't maintain good running form. By improving the strength and muscular endurance of your midsection, you provide a more stable base of support for your legs to work from. This improvement will allow you to maintain your stride length as you tire.

DEFINITION

Core strength refers to how your abdominals, hips, lower back, and butt muscles work together to maintain an efficient body posture when you're in motion. Runners with good core strength can maintain their form better as they tire and are less susceptible to injury.

In addition, many people have weak abdominal muscles, which allow your pelvis to rotate forward and put more strain on your hamstrings. (Sitting in a car and at a desk for hours a day is a big culprit here.) This creates a less efficient body position for your running and also increases your risk of lower back problems. The abdominal and lower back exercises I'll describe in a bit will improve your core strength, and thereby help you avoid these common running form problems.

TRAINING TIP

Don't neglect your strength training program when you're away from your usual routine. When I'm traveling and don't have access to weights or machines, I do exercises such as push-ups and pull-ups.

Essential Strengthening Exercises for Runners

As with the stretching routine I laid out in the preceding chapter, the purpose of this section is to show you the minimum of what I think you should do in strength training, not present a one-size-fits-all strength training program. You might have noticed that everything I've said so far about strengthening exercises refers to upper body work. That's what I'm going to focus on here. I'm not saying that runners can't benefit from doing resistance training for their legs, just that I don't think that doing so is as necessary for all runners as the upper body work.

Later on in this chapter, I'll show you a few leg exercises that you might have reason to do, but for now, I'm going to stick to my keep-it-simple mantra. All runners should do some form of strengthening exercises for these areas:

- Abdominal muscles

- Back

- Shoulders

- Chest

- Triceps

These key upper body parts contribute to running more smoothly. When these areas are stronger, you'll be better able to maintain good running form when you get tired.

In some of the exercises that follow, I use small dumbbells. For years, I've used 12-pounders. Again, this is the kind of weight that Arnold Schwarzenegger probably picks his teeth with. That's fine. I'm just working at maintaining a decent level of upper body strength that will help in my running. Those 12-pound dumbbells are what work for me. Find a weight that you can use comfortably throughout the exercises.

TRAINING TIP

If you do your strength training at a time other than right after your run, do something to limber up a bit before delving into the exercises. One good way is to work through the exercises you'll be doing with little or no weight for resistance.

Regardless of whatever weight you use, follow these guidelines in your strength training program:

- Use a weight that you can comfortably lift 12 times.

- After you do all the exercises, relax for a few minutes, and then repeat the set.

- Do this workout two or three times a week.

- Don't lift weights on consecutive days.

- Schedule your strength training sessions for your easier running days or for days when you don't run.

- If you have the time, do these workouts after you do your stretching routine.

- Do these exercises in the same comfortable clothes that you do your stretching in.

- Do the floor exercises on the same firm, comfortable surface that you stretch on.

RULES OF THE ROAD

Never sacrifice strength gains for safety. You should always be able to maintain good form while doing your strengthening work. If your form deteriorates during a set of exercises, use a lighter weight.

Keep these guidelines in mind as you review the basic exercises on the following pages.

Crunches

Lie on the floor with your back and head flat against the floor to begin the crunches. Bend your knees so that your heels rest on the floor. Cross your arms across your stomach. While keeping your back straight and your butt on the floor, slowly raise your upper body until your shoulders are level with your knees, as shown in the following figure. Try not to curl your upper body toward your knees; instead, imagine that it's being pulled by a string toward the ceiling. Slowly lower your upper body until your back is flat on the floor. Repeat this exercise 25 times.

Crunches work your abdominal muscles.

Back Strengthening

To begin the back strengthening exercise, lie down with your stomach and thighs against the floor. Prop yourself up on one elbow with your upper arm at a 90-degree angle to the floor, keeping the opposing leg straight and flat. Raise the other arm and the opposing leg to shoulder level at the same time, as illustrated in the figure. Hold for a few seconds, then relax and repeat the exercise with the other arm and leg. Do this exercise 10 times with each set of opposing arms and legs.

Back strengthening.

Shoulder Press

To begin the shoulder press, stand straight with a small dumbbell in one hand. The arm with the weight should be bent so that the palm of your hand is facing away from you and the weight is roughly at shoulder height. Straighten your arm and slowly push the weight toward the ceiling, as shown in the following figure. Slowly return to the starting position. Repeat the exercise 12 times for each arm.

Shoulder press.

Chest Strengthening

Lie down with your back flat, your knees bent, and your feet on the floor to get in position for the chest strengthening exercise. Keep one arm against your side. In the other, hold a small dumbbell while extending the arm perpendicular to your torso, as shown in the following figure. Slowly raise the weight until it's over your chest, and then slowly lower it to the starting position. Repeat this exercise 12 times for each arm.

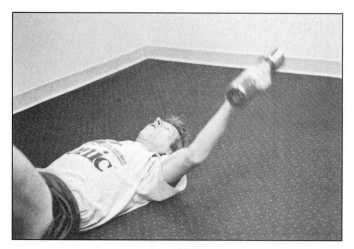

Chest strengthening.

Triceps Strengthening

To begin the triceps strengthening exercise, lie on the floor with your back flat, your knees bent, and your feet on the ground. Grip a small dumbbell with both hands. Rest your arms on your torso so that the weight is lying near your waist. While keeping your arms straight, slowly pull the weight behind you until it touches the floor behind your head, as shown in the figure. Slowly return to the starting position. Do this exercise 12 times.

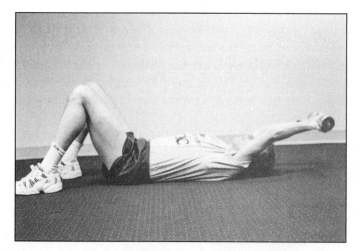

Triceps strengthening.

Get the Imbalance Right

Some runners should also do simple leg strengthening exercises. These runners are people who are susceptible to one of three common *muscle imbalances* that can occur between *opposing muscle groups* in the legs: the hamstrings and quadriceps; the calves and shins; and the adductors and abductors. Read on to see whether you have one of these imbalances.

> **DEFINITION**
>
> **Muscle imbalances** result when opposing muscles don't have the right ratio of strength between them. In runners, the muscle along the back, such as the hamstrings, may become overdeveloped and too tight in relation to the muscles along the front, such as the quadriceps. This imbalance can harm your form and make you more susceptible to injury.
>
> **Opposing muscle groups** are muscles in the same part of the body that work in opposite directions. For example, the biceps muscle in the arm flexes the elbow, and the triceps in the back of the arm extends the elbow.

Upper Leg Equilibrium

Ideally, your quadriceps (your thigh muscles) should be about 25 percent stronger than your hamstrings. In other words, if you were to go to a gym, you should be able to lift 25 percent more when doing leg extensions (which work the quadriceps) than when doing leg curls (which work the hamstrings). But running can overdevelop your hamstrings while doing relatively nothing for your quads. An imbalance in the strength ratio between the two muscles might show up as chronic knee pain because the tendons around the knee can become strained by having to work extra hard to compensate for tight, too-strong hamstrings and relatively weak quads. When your quads are stronger, they can absorb more of running's impact shock that is otherwise distributed to the knees.

> **TRAINING TIP**
>
> If you belong to a gym, ask a fitness instructor about exercises on machines that work the same muscles I'm recommending you focus on. For example, using a leg extension machine is a good way to strengthen your quadriceps.

If you have an imbalance in this area, try this at-home remedy. Fill a gym bag with shoes. While sitting on a chair, dangle the straps of the bag across the top of one foot. Lift the bag by straightening that leg. Do this exercise 12 times for each leg.

Below-the-Knee Balance

As with your hamstrings and quadriceps, your calves may get too strong and tight while your shins get relatively weaker when you run regularly. You might have this imbalance if you have chronic Achilles tendon problems. To strengthen your shin muscles, write the alphabet in the air with your big toe. It sounds strange, but try it. You'll feel right away how effective this exercise can be.

Thigh Therapy

Thigh muscle imbalances happen to the best of us. Long-time runners are more susceptible to this imbalance than are beginners because with a lot of running, the abductor muscles (on the outside of your upper thigh) get stronger while the adductors (on your inner thighs) aren't worked all that much. The problem is that these muscles are supposed to rotate your hips through a full range of motion, so when the adductors become too weak, and the abductors have to do too much work, you get hip pain. If you have this problem, strengthen your adductors by sitting on a chair with a soccer ball between your thighs and squeezing the ball several times.

The Least You Need to Know

- You'll run more smoothly and with less effort if you regularly do some basic upper body strengthening.
- You only need to do strengthening exercises two or three times a week.
- The types of strengthening exercises that runners should do aren't the kind that will make you add unwanted bulk.
- Runners should concentrate on exercises that strengthen the abdominals, back, arms, and shoulders.
- Some runners should do leg strengthening exercises to correct muscle imbalances that can lead to injury.

The Aches and the Pains

In This Chapter

- Why runners get injured
- Preventing running injuries
- Treating running injuries
- The best doctors to see for running injuries

Being injured is the pits. Many times, you can't run at all. Even if you can run with your injury, you usually have to cut back on your usual distance and slow down. Your running just isn't as much fun. Suddenly, your running, which is supposed to help with the stress in your life, adds to it.

Unfortunately, injuries are a part of the sport, and a common one at that. By some estimates, more than half of all runners are injured enough every year to have their training interrupted for more than a week. Now that I've completely depressed you, here's the good news—injuries are common, but they're usually predictable and preventable.

Most running injuries come from trying to do too much too soon at too quick a pace and ignoring the body's signals that it's on overload. So before looking at how to treat common running injuries, I'm going to show you how to avoid them. I hope that after reading the first part of this chapter, you never have reason to read the second.

Are Injuries Inevitable?

Most running injuries are *overuse injuries*—they stem from repeatedly stressing an overworked body part and ignoring the early warning signs that something is wrong. They're different from the sudden, acute injuries you might associate with playing football or going skiing.

DEFINITION

Most running injuries are **overuse injuries.** These injuries occur gradually as a muscle, tendon, ligament, or, more rarely, bone repeatedly has to absorb more shock or work through a greater range of motion than it's prepared to.

Why do runners get injured? Remember, when you run, your bones, muscles, tendons, and ligaments deal with forces of at least three times your body weight with each step. In order to continue running, your tissues must be able to withstand these loads, even when they're repeated thousands of times per day. An injury is a failure in your body to handle these repetitive forces.

What causes muscle strains, tendinitis, ligament damage, and stress fractures? Either the forces to which body parts are subjected are too high, or they're repeated too many times. In other words, injuries occur because of too much impact shock with each step, the cumulative effect of too many steps, or a combination of the two.

Most running injuries occur because of the repetitive nature of the running stride. When repeated thousands of times per run, even a slight imperfection in how your feet roll through the gait cycle, for example, can lead to problems nearly anywhere in your legs. That's why you need to take a global view of a running injury—you want to look at not only the area that's bothering you, but what about your running is causing that area to hurt.

Conquering your injury, then, means two things: treating the immediate symptoms, and figuring out what went wrong to cause them. Take care of the symptoms, and you get to start running normally again. Figure out and eliminate the root causes, and you're more likely not to be sidelined by that injury again.

Even if you're not injured, you should always be thinking about how to prevent injuries. Good running habits are so important, because the majority of running injuries can be prevented by eliminating the root causes. To eliminate these root causes, you need to increase the ability of your tissues to tolerate a force repeatedly and/or decrease the cumulative amount of force.

You can increase the ability of your tissues to tolerate repeated forces by doing the following:

- Regularly stretching the major muscles, tendons, and ligaments that are worked when you run.

- Correcting muscle imbalances that require a given body part to work harder when you run than it's designed to (see Chapter 11 for how to correct muscle imbalances).

- Increasing your mileage and intensity gradually so that your body has a chance to adapt to an increased workload.

Be sure to read Chapter 10 carefully if you're regularly bothered by soft-tissue (muscle and tendon) injuries.

The second main way to prevent running injuries is to regularly reduce the cumulative amount of shock that you subject your body to. Among the ways to do that are the following:

- Running on soft surfaces, such as dirt and grass, whenever possible.

- Running in shoes that have adequate cushioning and that have extra cushioning in the appropriate place if you land hard on a certain part of your foot.

- Running the appropriate number of miles to meet your goals, not just mindlessly amassing miles. Even the best-constructed body will eventually break down with too many miles.

 TRAINING TIP

A good mental outlook is crucial to conquering an injury. When I have a little injury that's interrupting my training, I tell myself that overcoming it is the most important aspect of my running for the time being. Make getting better your next short-term goal and track your progress toward meeting it as you would any other goal.

You'll also reduce the amount of shock to your body if you run at an appropriate weight. Beginning runners who might be overweight should therefore be especially careful about running on soft surfaces in well-cushioned shoes.

Should You Run on It?

Judgment calls are a big part of being a runner. You're always weighing a seemingly endless number of issues in trying to answer some basic questions, such as how far, how fast, and when and where to run. If you're injured, there's an even more basic question to consider: should you run? Here's where injuries can get the most tricky. If you don't run on your injury, it's not going to bother you. Push this logic to its extreme, and it'll never bother you—never run, and I can guarantee you that you'll never have a running injury.

The standard medical advice for all injuries used to be don't run for two weeks. If it bothers you when you start again, take another two weeks off, and keep doing so until you're better. That's not very helpful advice for most running injuries. If all runners stopped running every time they got a little ache or pain, some of them would almost never run!

What you want to know is how to finesse your ache or pain so that you can keep running without doing more damage. After all, a little knot in your calf that loosens up after 10 minutes of easy running is a lot different from an aching hip that makes you limp around the office, and then only gets worse when you try to run on it. How much and whether you should run with your injury depends on how it feels not only when you run, but also the rest of the day.

RULES OF THE ROAD

It's okay to run with aches, especially those that lessen as you run. But never run with pain, especially if it worsens as you run.

Although there aren't hard and fast rules for running while injured, here are some general guidelines:

- If you don't notice any pain during your run, but have pain after a run or when you get up in the morning, it's okay to run your usual run at your usual pace.

- If you notice pain during your run, but it doesn't interfere with your normal running form, it's okay to keep running, but stay close to home so that you can get back quickly if things deteriorate.

- If the pain becomes worse the longer you run, limit your running to however long you can run before this deterioration starts.

- If the pain causes you to alter your usual running form, don't run with this injury until you can run normally at a relaxed pace. Running differently because of an injury will make other body parts more susceptible to injury, because they're being asked to work harder than usual to compensate for the injured part that you're favoring.

- If your pain interferes with your normal, day-to-day nonrunning activities, the only running you should even think about doing is to the nearest sports medicine doctor's office.

If you're injured and can run, or even if you just feel the beginnings of an injury, try to run primarily on flat surfaces. Running downhill increases the pounding on your legs, and running uphill forces your tendons and muscles to work extra hard. When you're already flirting with disaster, you don't need either. In all of these cases, consider taking anti-inflammatories and applying ice to the painful area a few times a day.

Running Hot and Cold

Ice should always be your first line of defense against injury. If I notice the slightest little ache, I like to ice it after my run and a couple of other times during the day, too, if possible. A few minutes of preventative care can work wonders in keeping a little nagging pain from developing into a disruptive injury.

Why ice instead of heat? The reason is that most running injuries are a result of soft body tissues (muscles, tendons, ligaments) that have become inflamed. Blood vessels get damaged and swell; the greater the swelling, the worse the injury, and the longer recovery is going to take. Icing the inflamed area causes the blood vessels to constrict. This reduces the swelling because less blood flows to the injured area and the damaged tissue relaxes. This not only reduces the pain you feel, but also speeds healing, because as the tissue's metabolism is slowed, there's less tissue breakdown. Heating an inflamed area worsens, rather than improves things. Heat has the opposite effect of ice, so the blood vessels of the injured area become that much more swollen.

Always ice an injury for at least 5 but no more than 20 minutes. The area should become red and numb, not white and numb. After running is the best time to ice, because the tissues will be the most swollen, but you'll speed recovery if you can find a few other times during the day to ice. Rub the ice in circular motions on the injured body part.

> **TRAINING TIP**
>
> If you have a large area to ice, consider creating an ice wrap. A bag of small, frozen vegetables, such as peas and corn, is good for this. Another solution is to keep a mixture of three parts water to one part alcohol in a bag in the freezer. Because the alcohol won't freeze, the bag will have some give to it.

The Agony of Da Feet

Most people would say that runners have nice bodies, or at least they would until they got a look at runners' feet. Your feet can take a lot of abuse, and all that pounding and sliding around and sweating can cause quite a stink if left unattended. More important than looks, some runner's feet develop problems that can sideline them from more than the "World's Prettiest Toes" contest.

Tending to Toes

Most toe problems you're going to get as a runner are cosmetic rather than serious. The most frequent visitors will be black toenails, which are so linked with the sport that the condition is also known as runner's toe. Runner's toe happens when the nail is either pressed down too much on the bed that underlies it or the nail separates from the bed. In either case, blood pools between the nail and the bed. Eventually, the nail turns black.

When this condition is caused by the nail being pressed into the bed, it's almost never painful. The nail gets very hard, and it looks like hell, but it won't bother you. Sometimes, the nail loosens rather than hardens, and this is usually uncomfortable. New runners whose toenails aren't used to much wear and tear will get these more than longtime runners. If your black toenail is wobbly, sterilize a needle, and then use it to drain the blood from under the nail, as you would drain a blister.

Runner's toe is usually caused by ill-fitting shoes. If your shoes aren't long enough, your longest toe (which in some people is the second toe) will slam against the front of the shoe. You might also irritate your nails by running on a course that has a lot more downhills than you're used to, because your toes are going to rise up a bit more than usual on the downhills to help you brake. Wet shoes, either from sweat or rain, are also a leading cause of runner's toe.

Poorly fitting shoes may also cause blisters, "hot spots," and other irritations on the tops of your toes. When a pair of shoes causes blisters during your first few runs, then you've probably bought shoes that are too small. Cover these irritated spots with one of the many second-skin products on the market, which provide a soft layer between your skin and feet, and you'll usually be fine.

Healing Your Heels

The most common running injury to the heel area is called plantar fasciitis. (See the drawing of the human body to determine if you have this or any of the other injuries discussed in the rest of this chapter.) This condition is an inflammation of the plantar fascia, a fibrous band of tissue that runs from the heel to the toes. You'll feel pain along the inside bottom of your foot anywhere from the heel through the arch. Many times, the pain is the worst when you step out of bed in the morning or when you've been sitting for a long time, and then it improves during the day as the plantar fascia has a chance to loosen up.

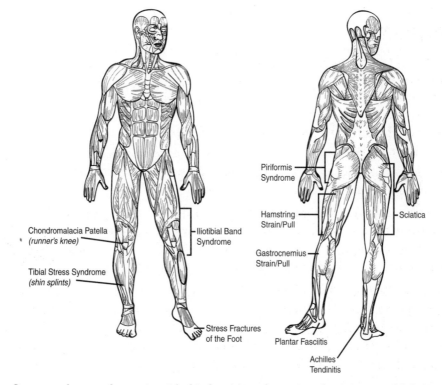

Chondromalacia Patella
(runner's knee)

Tibial Stress Syndrome
(shin splints)

Iliotibial Band
Syndrome

Stress Fractures
of the Foot

Piriformis
Syndrome

Hamstring
Strain/Pull

Gastrocnemius
Strain/Pull

Sciatica

Plantar Fasciitis

Achilles
Tendinitis

Compare where you have pain with this drawing to determine what injury you likely have.

The plantar fascia most often becomes inflamed because it has to work through more of a range of motion than it's designed to. When your heel strikes the ground, the pressure on the heel pulls on the plantar fascia. If your calf muscles are too tight, or if you overpronate but don't wear shoes with enough motion control, then you're most likely to develop plantar fasciitis. Also, high-arched, rigid feet can predispose you to this injury because when your heel lands, your foot doesn't move enough, so the plantar fascia has to absorb more shock.

The best treatment for plantar fasciitis is icing. Ice the bottom of your foot from heel to ball. Most people with plantar fasciitis can run on the injury. Cut back if the pain gets worse, not better, as you run. Preventative steps include increasing the flexibility of your calves and Achilles tendons, and making sure that your shoes have the proper combination of motion control and cushioning.

Leggings

Continuing our tour up the trail of woe, let's look at running injuries that you feel above the feet. Bear in mind that although these injuries occur above the foot, they are usually caused by something that goes wrong at footstrike.

Achilles' Last Stand

The Achilles' heel for some runners is the Achilles tendon. That's because the Achilles tendon—a cordlike structure that connects the heel to the calf muscles—has a fairly limited range of motion.

If you have Achilles tendinitis, you'll know it because nothing else causes sharp pain in that area. The pain, which can also be a burning sensation, will be anywhere from an inch above your heel to the bottom of your calf. In bad cases, you'll be able to see how inflamed the tendon is, because it will be visibly swollen compared to your healthy Achilles tendon.

Achilles tendinitis is often caused by many of the same things that lead to plantar fasciitis, including tight calf muscles and overpronation. Sometimes it can be caused when the back of your shoe sits too high against your heel. (This is why you'll see many running shoes with notches at the top of the heel counter.)

In addition to the standards of icing, anti-inflammatories, and cutting back on your running if your normal form is altered, here's another trick for beating Achilles tendinitis: wear heel lifts in your street and running shoes until the problem goes away. The lifts will take some of the pressure off your inflamed tendon by elevating it.

A simple, at-home method is to cut a half-circle that fits your heel from corrugated cardboard. Be sure to put a new one in at least once a day as the cardboard gets compressed. In the long term, be extra careful about stretching, and get out of the habit of wearing high-heeled shoes, which can shorten and tighten your calves and Achilles tendons.

Stopping Shin Splints

Shin splints—or what the running doctors call tibial stress syndrome—are one of the most common injuries for new runners. That's because they're usually caused by muscle and tendon weakness in the front or inside of the lower leg. With more running, these areas become strong enough to handle the increased stress they're being subjected to. Weak arches can also lead to shin splints by making the shin muscles work extra hard to raise your arches when you run. Shin splints can lead to stress fractures, so you want to beat them before they beat you. (See the following section "Stressed Out" for more on that lovely injury.)

Shin splints are tiny tears of the front lower leg muscles away from the shin bone (or tibia). At first, you might notice a pulling or vague aching sensation in the area after you run. The pain can become sharp, usually after you've run for a certain amount of time. The area around the shin may become inflamed, or lumps may form where the muscle tries to reattach itself.

I don't mean to sound like a broken record here, but the best immediate treatment for shin splints is the standard: ice, anti-inflammatories, and cutting back on your mileage. And another thing I keep harping on: run on soft surfaces whenever possible. Shin splints are one of those injuries that people sensitive to running's pounding get; that's why beginners, who haven't built up as much resistance to pounding, get them much more frequently than longtimers. So reduce that pounding by running on more forgiving ground.

Stressed Out

Stress fractures are tiny, incomplete breaks or cracks in a bone. They can occur many places in the body, but runners most often get them in the shin bones. They're caused by too much repetitive stress to bones that are overworked. That's why stress fractures occur gradually—over time, the bones are asked to do just a little bit more than they're ready for, and the shock is great enough to cause a slight crack.

Stress fractures are different from a standard broken bone because with a stress fracture, there's not a sudden, obvious incident when the bone breaks. Rather, the pain begins gradually, usually as a slight twinge, and only intensifies as you continue to run on it. Trust me, though—if you get a full-blown stress fracture, there will be no mistaking that you're hurt. With every step, sharp pain will shoot from your foot up your leg, and it will get worse the longer you run on it.

 TRAINING TIP

When you're coming back from an injury, err on the side of caution. The last thing you want to do is come back too quickly and retrigger your injury. If you had to take some time off, allow twice as much time as you were off to build back to your regular mileage.

The general rule for distinguishing a stress fracture from a shin splint is this: if the pain in your shins is dull and diffuse, it's more likely to be shin splints. If the pain is sharper and concentrated over a smaller area—usually no bigger than a dime—it's more likely to be a stress fracture.

Stress fractures are almost always caused by some of the errors that I outlined earlier in this chapter—increasing mileage and intensity too quickly, wearing shoes without enough cushioning, and doing too much of your running on hard surfaces. Runners who don't include enough calcium in their diets are also susceptible.

Unfortunately, when you have a stress fracture, you need to stop running. Otherwise, you're just asking for it. The bone will continue to rupture, and you could develop a complete break, which will add considerably to your downtime. So if you feel the beginnings of a stress fracture, take a few days off and ice the area (which will probably be a little tender and swollen, and maybe even a bit warm to the touch at first). If you definitely have a stress fracture, you're best off not running for at least four weeks, as well as avoiding other weight-bearing activity during this time. If it's still bad when you restart, stop again, and see a doctor.

The Knee Bone's Connected to the …

The fear that most people have of runners' knees—crippling arthritis—is largely unfounded. That doesn't mean that runners don't get knee injuries, though. In fact, in one survey of runners, injuries to the knee were more common than injuries to any other body part.

Let's face it: the knee is one of the most poorly "designed" parts of our body. This tiny little shifting piece of bone acts as the brace between our feet crashing into the ground and almost the entire rest of our body. Add to that the stress of running on asphalt, overpronation, and, for some, being overweight, and it's a wonder that there aren't more knee injuries!

The two most common knee injuries for runners are iliotibial band syndrome and, appropriately enough, runner's knee (what the professionals call chondromalacia patella). As explained in Chapter 10, the iliotibial band is a thick cord that runs from the pelvis to the outside of the thigh and connects just below the knee. It helps to stabilize your thigh muscles and knee when you run. Usually, you'll feel pain on the outside of your knee, but you might also feel it along the outside of your hip. The pain can be sporadic from day to day, but it usually comes on after you've run a set distance.

Bowlegged runners are susceptible to this injury. They should concentrate on regularly stretching the iliotibial band to make sure that it can work through a wide enough range of motion when running. And anyone can get it if they regularly run on uneven surfaces, especially the same side of an overly slanted road.

In the short term, you're best to limit your mileage to just below the level at which you usually start to feel pain. In the long term, be smart—work on increasing the band's flexibility, and run on level surfaces. If you have no option but to run on slanted roads, regularly switch directions so that one leg isn't always made to run as if it were longer.

In runner's knee, repeated stress on the knee causes inflammation and softening of the cartilage under the kneecap. This prevents the kneecap from tracking normally over the end of the thigh bone. You'll usually feel pain around or behind the kneecap; it might get worse when you climb stairs.

Overpronators are especially susceptible to runner's knee because the knee has to compensate for the extra inward rotation of the lower leg. Among relatively new runners, weak thigh muscles are often a leading cause of this injury. Your thigh muscles help to align your knee and keep it straight. If they're not as strong as they should be, they may not be able to help the knee guide itself along its proper course.

In addition to icing the entire area around your knee, you can get some relief from runner's knee by avoiding steep downhills, uneven surfaces, and other factors that are going to require your knee to do extra work to stabilize itself. (You also might want to avoid the tight turns of indoor tracks.) If you're repeatedly bothered by pain around your kneecap, get running shoes with better motion control.

Don't Get Hamstrung

Longtime runners suffer from injuries in the hamstring, hip, and buttock area more than beginners. Our hamstring problems are low-grade, chronic microtears that accumulate over time and usually because of neglect. Most of these injuries are the result of poor flexibility in these areas, and veteran runners who don't have good stretching habits are notoriously tight from knee to butt.

But beware of hamstring problems if your job involves long periods of sitting. Sitting for long periods can shorten your hamstrings and the surrounding muscles and tendons. Try not to sit for more than an hour at a time. In your runs, ease into your normal pace to give the large muscles along the back of your legs a chance to warm up.

Which Doctors to Run To

When should you see a doctor for a running injury? Most injuries, especially the soft-tissue overuse injuries, don't need medical attention, especially if you treat them right from the start. When an injury drags on, or when you keep running on it and you get injured elsewhere, you start entering the gray area of when to get help. Certainly, any runner whose injury interferes with normal, daily activity for more than a week without improvement should seek medical help.

If your injury is a problem only when you run, then when and how soon to see a doctor is up to you. If your self-care routine doesn't seem to be working, then you should probably see a doctor who might be able to diagnose and treat the underlying cause. You should also see a doctor if you repeatedly get injured in the same small part of your body. This type of injury means that you have an underlying weakness or structural deformity. A good sports medicine doctor will be able to get to the root of the problem so that the area won't plague you throughout your running career.

RULES OF THE ROAD

If you have a slight muscle tear, don't vigorously stretch the area; doing so might increase the inflammation. It's better to exercise it gently to increase the flow of blood and healing nutrients to the area.

What types of specialists should runners see? That depends on your injury. Foot and lower leg injuries can be treated by orthopedists or osteopaths (I'll say more about them in a minute), but they're most often treated by podiatrists. Podiatrists have the initials D.P.M. (doctor of podiatric medicine) following their name. Podiatrists complete four years of training at a college of podiatric medicine and a residency. They are licensed to perform surgery and prescribe medicine.

Podiatrists focus not only on feet, but also on problems elsewhere that are caused by feet. This focus makes them among the runner's best medical friends, because so many running injuries are caused by faulty feet. A podiatrist can determine whether factors such as overpronation or weak arches are contributing to problems in your biomechanics and setting you up for injury. These types of structural problems in the feet are often treated with *orthotics*. Podiatrists are the best professionals to see to determine if you need orthotics, and they're trained to cast the devices for you.

DEFINITION

Orthotics are devices worn in shoes to combat an underlying structural problem in the feet. They're usually prescribed by a podiatrist. Hard orthotics help to limit your foot's motion, so they are made for overpronators. Soft orthotics are made for people with rigid feet to help absorb and distribute some of the pounding of running.

Knee injuries are most often treated by orthopedists, although some knee problems are caused by problems in your feet and can therefore be addressed by podiatrists. Orthopedists are medical doctors (M.D.s) who treat injuries to bones, muscles, tendons, and ligaments. Orthopedists have a reputation for performing surgery, and although a good sports medicine orthopedist will always favor more conservative treatment first, many runners are leery of seeing orthopedists for this reason.

Running injuries above the knee are also often treated by orthopedists. Another good type of doctor to see for these ailments is an osteopath. Like M.D.s, osteopaths (D.O.s) are licensed to practice all branches of medicine, prescribe medication, and perform surgery. In general, they're trained to view the body more systematically, so they're likely to look at a runner's injury from the standpoint of unearthing the root cause rather than just treating the symptoms.

The Least You Need to Know

- Most running injuries are caused by overuse and can be prevented.
- Increasing mileage gradually, running on soft surfaces, and having good stretching and strengthening habits are some of the best ways to prevent injuries.
- Most running injuries will go away with a combination of rest and conservative treatment.
- Apply ice, not heat, to new running injuries.
- A trip to the doctor isn't necessary for most running injuries.
- If you have to see a doctor, which one is best depends on what type of injury you have. Seek out a sports medicine doctor for the best diagnosis and treatment.

Eating on the Run: Deciding on Your Diet

In This Chapter

- What runners eat
- The best diet for runners
- Sports bars and gels
- Timing your meals with your runs

Food is fuel. Even if your main motivation for starting a running program is to lose weight, you're not going to make it very far down the road if your muscles don't have the fuel they need. That fuel comes almost entirely from one source—what you eat.

Unfortunately, that pretty simple concept is misunderstood by scores of runners. Remember what I said in Chapter 10 about how carried away some runners get arguing about stretching? Well that's nothing compared to what you'll hear said about the runner's diet. My goal in this chapter is to cut through all the chatter and state a few dietary facts. By the end of this chapter, you'll know the basics of a good diet for runners and what *isn't* necessary nutritionally.

Do Running Nuts Live on Berries?

As I've said, one of the questions that I'm asked most frequently has to do with whether my knees bother me because of all those miles. Probably the second-most popular question I hear is, "You eat *that?*" This question comes about when I'm doing something as innocent as having a cup of coffee. It also happens if I'm enjoying a muffin, putting cream cheese on a bagel, or having a glass of wine with dinner.

Somewhere along the way, most people got the notion that being a runner means living off of the twigs and nuts that you gather out of your backyard. When running first achieved mass popularity in the 1970s, the sport was seen as part of a new movement for Americans who had decided that it was time to take charge of their health. So in the public mind, running became associated with health food stores, megavitamin doses, and drinking nothing but carrot juice and purified water.

I think that's too bad. Not because running can't be an incredibly big step toward taking control of your health. No, the problem is that people who are new to running have been led to believe that starting an exercise program also means a simultaneous radical change in your diet. That's not true, and it saddens me that some people might view running as off-putting because of this image.

That doesn't mean that being a runner means eating whatever you want. Yes, I'm as well known in some circles for my legendary consumption of junk food as I am for my marathon victories. And as I've hinted, I still like to indulge myself occasionally. Eating is one of the major pleasures of life, and who doesn't like to live a little now and then?

But as you become fitter through your running, you're probably going to be motivated to make changes in other parts of your life that will improve your health, such as getting more sleep and eating better. Running can help you to acquire an appreciation for simpler, heartier foods, which usually fuel you better and don't bother you as much when you run. The upshot is this: most runners find that they feel better if they make a few simple, healthful changes in their diets. But that doesn't have to entail shopping only at the local organic produce shop. As most longtime runners will tell you, one of the great things about running is that all those miles often mean eating more and not gaining weight.

The Real Runner's Diet

If runners' diets seem strange to most folks, that's because most people don't eat as most nutritionists advise. That's another way of saying that the best diet for runners is the one that everyone should eat. This diet should be low in fat and include a moderate amount of lean, high-quality protein; the majority of calories should come from carbohydrates, especially in the form of fresh fruits and vegetables and whole grains.

More than sedentary people, runners gravitate toward this type of diet because it makes them feel better. As you become fitter, you become more in touch with your body and with how it feels when you put certain things in it. I mean this both in the short term—those slices of bacon just don't seem to taste as good right after a morning run—and long term, as you learn how some foods fuel your running better than others.

Although your diet is important to your overall health, it's not the key to your running; your training is. No amount of dietary manipulation is going to make up for miles logged. A good diet is important because it will allow you to get the most out of your running, not because it's going to make you a better runner.

> **RULES OF THE ROAD**
>
> Runners should have healthful diets for the simple reason that everyone should. Running doesn't mean that the nutritional rules don't apply to you. There's a history of high cholesterol in my family. About 20 years ago, I was shocked to discover that my cholesterol level was in the 230s, even after so many years of so many miles. Once I made some simple changes to lower my fat intake, my cholesterol level went down into the healthful range.

Carbs: A Runner's Best Friend

Carbohydrates, or just "carbs" to most runners, are your body's main source of energy for aerobic exercise. One gram of carbohydrate contains 4 calories. Your body converts the carbohydrates you eat into glucose, a simple sugar. Glucose is then either used immediately by your body for energy or converted to glycogen, which, as Chapter 2 explained, is the fuel stored in the muscles that power your running. When runners "bonk" or "hit The Wall" and have to slow dramatically, they've run out of carbohydrates. (Chapter 22 discusses this situation.)

> **DEFINITION**
>
> **Carbohydrates** are sugars that fuel your muscles during exercise. You eat them in both complex form (such as pasta) and simple form (such as honey). You should get 60 to 65 percent of your calories from carbohydrates.

Carbohydrates are classified as either complex or simple. This classification has to do not with how philosophical they are, but with how they're constructed chemically. Complex carbohydrates are starches, such as grains, and simple carbohydrates are sugars, such as the fructose found in fruits. Common food sources of carbohydrates include fruits, vegetables, pasta, rice, bread products, cereals, and jellies.

You should aim for 60 to 65 percent of your calories to come from carbohydrates. This amount will keep your muscles well fueled so that you'll be able to meet your training goals. A high-carb diet chosen from the right sources also means that you're more likely to be getting all of the nutrients that you need because fruits, vegetables, and grains are packed with vitamins and minerals.

Most of the carbohydrates that you eat should be either fruits and vegetables or complex carbs such as pasta. Aim for this level of carbohydrate intake each day:

- 10 to 12 servings of grains (one serving equals a slice of bread, ½ cup of cooked pasta, half a bagel, or 1 ounce of cereal)

- 5 to 7 servings of fruit (one serving equals a medium-size piece of fruit, half a grapefruit, or 4 ounces of juice)

- 4 to 5 servings of vegetables (one serving equals 1 cup raw vegetables or ½ cup cooked)

But aren't starches going to make you fat? No. Starches are complex carbohydrates. They contain 4 calories per gram, just like the carbohydrates found in fruits and vegetables. If you gain weight from eating a lot of starches, that's from eating more calories than you burn, not because of anything inherently fattening about starches. The reason that people think that starches are fattening is that they're often eaten with high-fat foods that contain a lot of extra calories. You butter your bread, fry your potatoes, or have pizza with sausage and extra cheese.

Where's the Beef?

Protein is in every part of your body, from muscles to hair. Protein from your diet helps to build and repair muscles and regulate hormones. If you don't get enough protein, you'll recover from injuries and infections more slowly. One gram of protein contains 4 calories.

 TRAINING TIP

Many runners exclude dairy products from their diets. This is a mistake because low-fat and nonfat dairy products are excellent sources of protein and they provide calcium, which is essential to keeping your bones strong enough to withstand running's pounding. Aim for two to three servings of dairy products a day.

About 15 percent of your calories should come from protein. That's less than most people eat. The recommended amount of protein means 2 to 3 servings each day, with a serving size being as small as 2 ounces of chicken or 2 teaspoons of peanut butter. Chow down on a half-pounder at your favorite burger place and right there you've exceeded your protein needs for the day. A good guideline to follow is that your servings of protein should be no bigger than a deck of cards.

So for most people, getting 15 percent of their calories from protein is going to mean eating less protein than they're used to. The exceptions are people who restrict their protein intake because they think that it's good nutrition to exist on nothing but bagels, salads, and rice cakes. That's taking things too far the other way.

What's wrong with eating too much protein? It means that you're probably falling short in your carb intake. This shortfall could hurt your running because protein supplies a very small percentage of the energy for your running. Also, unless you choose carefully, the protein that you eat might come in a high-fat package, such as a marbled T-bone steak. Eating extra protein doesn't build bigger muscles any more than eating pig's feet helps you to grow extra toes. Extra protein that you eat mainly gives you very expensive urine.

The Skinny on Fat

Many of us are all too familiar with fat, but fat isn't all bad. With 9 calories in a gram, or more than twice the amount of a gram of carbohydrate or protein, it's a concentrated energy source. It's what your body burns at low levels of activity, such as when you're sitting at a desk or walking easily. Fat supplies and transports some vitamins, helps to maintain nerve fibers and cell membranes, insulates you from the cold, and cushions internal organs.

RULES OF THE ROAD

Don't go overboard on eating low-fat foods. You need some fat in your diet, not only for essential body functions such as digestion and providing cushioning for organs, but also because fat adds taste and texture to your meals. Also, many manufactured nonfat foods, such as pastries, have as many or more calories per serving than the foods they're meant to replace.

In a good diet, 20 to 25 percent of your calories come from fat. This amount is less than most Americans eat—the average is almost 40 percent of calories from fat. Eating too much fat means that you're not getting the carbs you need to restock your muscles from run to run. It's also bad for your health because a high fat intake has been linked to heart disease and some cancers. And extra fat from your diet is easily stored as extra fat on you.

If you emphasize getting 60 to 65 percent of your calories from carbohydrates, with plenty of fruits and vegetables in the mix, it will be easier to get your fat intake into the 20 to 25 percent range. Choosing lean cuts of protein, such as white chicken meat instead of a greasy cheese steak sub, also helps.

Putting It All Together

Worrying about this percentage of carbohydrates and that percentage of fats sounds like a lot of work. How can you reasonably eat this way without taking a calculator with you on every trip to the kitchen? And what about when you eat out? Relax. The key to a good runner's diet isn't math, but making the right food choices. After all, a meal of butter, beef jerky, and cola can supply you with the right amounts of carbohydrates, protein, and fat, but it's a disaster nutritionally.

Concentrate on getting the number of servings for each food type that I've emphasized. The percentages will take care of themselves if you focus on a variety of wholesome carbohydrates, fruits and vegetables, low-fat dairy products, lean cuts of meat, and legumes. Here's a tip: carbohydrates, such as whole grains, vegetables, and beans, should cover most of the space on your dinner plate. Protein should be the accompaniment, not the centerpiece that many people make it. This guideline is true both at home and when you eat out.

 TRAINING TIP

Don't forget the most important thing to consume on a regular basis—water. Drink at least 10 8-ounce glasses of water a day, plus however much you lose sweating on your runs.

Sports Bars and Other Goop

Sports bars or energy bars didn't exist in their current incarnation until 1986. Now you can't stop at a convenience store without having approximately 80 gazillion to choose from.

Energy bars and gels aren't necessary for most runners.

Why have they become so popular? Several reasons, many having to do with great marketing. The main useful reason is that they provide a couple of hundred of easily digestible calories that your body can use almost immediately for energy.

RULES OF THE ROAD

Energy bars are usually fortified with vitamins and minerals, but this isn't a reason to eat them. You shouldn't use energy bars or any other fortified product to try to make up for a poor diet. Get your vitamins and minerals from naturally occurring sources. If you choose to eat energy bars, do so for the real reasons they're made.

An increasing number of runners find a use for these products in their busy lives. Runners usually eat these bars within 90 minutes of a run when they're dragging and want something to eat that won't bother them during the run. These bars certainly fit that bill. Runners also eat them soon after a hard or long workout, when they want to get something in their system to speed recovery but can't yet stomach "real" food. And for people on the go, they're easy to carry and eat at any time.

No runner *needs* an energy bar, however. After all, Frank Shorter had already won his second Olympic Marathon medal 10 years before the first energy bar was sold. As an example, a Malt-Nut PowerBar contains 225 calories, with 83 percent of them from carbohydrates, 10 percent of calories from protein, and 7 percent from fat. It can sell for as much as $2. Eaten together, a bagel and a banana contain 275 calories, with 84 percent of them from carbs and 8 percent each from protein and fat. They taste better than energy bars to most people, are just as convenient, and cost about half as much.

What about energy gels? These puddinglike gooey glops are increasingly favored by marathoners, both as something to take for a little extra energy during long training runs and as a performance booster on the run during the race. Costing about $1 each, gels come in plastic containers about the size of a takeout ketchup packet, so they're easy to carry. They're also a lot easier to take on the run than energy bars.

Most gels contain about 100 calories of simple carbohydrates, about the amount that you'll burn in a mile of running. Research has shown that when you're exercising and consume simple carbohydrates such as these, the carbs are absorbed directly into your bloodstream for instant energy. (That's why sport drinks work well, too.) You need to drink several ounces of water soon after consuming a gel to help its absorption. If you're not carrying fluids with you, time it so that you finish downing your gel soon before you'll have access to liquids, such as a water fountain or aid station in a race.

Who needs energy gels? Technically, nobody—as I said, people did long training runs and marathons before these products were invented. Nonetheless, I've certainly come to appreciate the little midrun boost I get from a gel during a run. However, I use gels only when I'm going to be running for more than 90 minutes. If you don't run this kind of distance, then save your money.

FOOTNOTES

Sport bars and gels are a big improvement over what runners used to consume in long races. In the early part of this century, it was common to give runners whiskey and brandy late in a marathon!

If you are going to be working up to running for that long, then gels can help you. Plan to eat one when you're about two thirds of the way through your run, such as 10 miles into a 15-miler. Some runners consume two or more on really long runs.

Popping Pills: Vitamins and Other Supplements

Burdock root, ginseng, beta-carotene, chromium, brewer's yeast—the list of wonder substances that are supposedly going to dramatically improve your health and performance is endless. We Americans are always looking for that magic pill that's going to help us lose weight, feel great, have more energy, and, what the hey, why not have it prevent baldness and improve our sex lives at the same time? But the truth is that you can't eat your way to being fit any more than you can eat your way to a college degree or a successful career. These achievements all take a lot of steady, hard, and sometimes not terribly exciting work. Yet the nutritional supplement industry, to the tune of nearly $5 billion a year, has somehow convinced people that health and fitness can be achieved differently.

Vitamins and other supplements are often marketed as energy boosters or some such vague claim. Problem is, vitamins and minerals don't provide energy. Food does. More specifically, the calories in food do. Only foods and drinks that contain calories provide energy.

What do vitamins and minerals do, then? Vitamins are like your body's spark plugs—they are catalysts to reactions within your body. Minerals are elements that form and regulate the body. If your car wasn't firing properly, you might get the spark plugs fixed. But once you got your spark plugs up to normal operating level, you wouldn't throw four more under the hood and expect your car to run better. You would just be wasting your money with your misunderstanding of what keeps your car moving down the road day after day.

Same thing goes for taking vitamins beyond the base level needed for good health. No studies have found increased performance in runners who take megadoses compared to runners who have a normal intake. In fact, no studies have shown increased performance caused by any of these kinds of supplements, be they vitamins, minerals, or substances not even recognized as necessary for normal human functioning, such as bee pollen. The right nutrition for good performance is pretty much the same as it is for good health, regardless of your level of activity.

Most nutritionists would say that it's okay to take a daily multivitamin as a sort of health insurance, but even that shouldn't be necessary if you regularly eat a wide variety of healthful foods. Vitamins and minerals from food are always better than the same substances from pills. When you get vitamins and minerals from food, you're more likely to regularly be eating properly. For example, getting enough vitamin C from your diet means that you're eating a decent amount of fresh fruits and vegetables. Having to meet your vitamin C needs with a pill means that you're going to be hurting in other areas nutritionally, such as fiber and other disease-protective substances best found in food.

Just Veggin' Out

As I said at the beginning of this chapter, expect to get questions about your diet once people find out you're a runner. A common one—often said with a slight tilt of the head and a bit of concern about your sanity—is, "Do you eat meat?"

People become vegetarians for a variety of reasons, and it's not my place here to pontificate one way or the other on the moral, economic, health, or other reasons for doing so. What matters here is the more basic matter of whether it's possible to be a successful runner while eating a meatless diet.

The short answer: of course it is. I've already told you how, for most Americans, excess protein is a much greater risk than lack of protein. And for runners, it's running low on carbs that will get you into trouble late in a long run. Vegetarians, of course, need to be a little more mindful than meat eaters on this matter, and to make sure that their meals over the course of a day supply all of the necessary amino acids. (The old advice that this matching of protein types has to occur at every meal has been discarded.)

I'm assuming that if you decide to become a vegetarian, you'll be doing your nutritional homework and will educate yourself on how to obtain the nutrients that most people get from eating meat. After all, someone who lives off of donuts, chips, fried cheese, and beer could call himself a vegetarian, but if that's your diet, then in both health and running terms, you have more immediate concerns than how to account for passing up burgers at the Memorial Day cookout.

Timing Mealtime

Balancing when to eat and when to run can be tough. And that's not just because if you work during normal business hours, then you're probably running when most people are eating breakfast, lunch, or dinner. No, what I'm talking about here is learning how to schedule your runs so that your most recent meal doesn't come back for a second tasting 15 minutes into your run.

This is one of those areas where you're going to have to experiment to find what works best for you. I know some runners who can polish off a lumberjack's breakfast seconds before heading out the door for a morning run and others who swear that they'll have troubled stomachs their entire run if they eat the slightest morsel within several hours of training. There's not much you can do about where you fall on the rockgut scale. When in doubt, err on the side of caution.

Most runners find that they feel much better if they wait at least three hours after their last meal before they run. Running too soon after eating is a big reason that beginners often get side stitches—when you run, your body diverts blood to the exercising parts of your body. You don't want a big meal in your belly demanding to be digested when your heart and legs need all the attention from your circulatory system that they can get.

On the flip side, there's also great variation among runners concerning how soon they eat after a run. Some runners step in the door and start munching; others don't feel hungry for hours. This amount of time is going to be different even for individual runners from run to run—when it's hot and you finish your run dehydrated and overheated, you're probably not going to be as immediately hungry as on a 50-degree day. The harder you run, the more time you'll probably want to allow before your next meal.

FOOTNOTES

At a race in Japan once, I startled all the runners near me by popping a potato in my mouth just minutes before the start. I had a few stomach problems during that race, but knew that my opponents were completely psyched out. I won.

Again, experiment to see what works for you. But here's an important finding from the exercise science labs: if you consume some carbohydrates (it can be in solid or liquid form) within the first 30 minutes of the end of your run, your muscles will absorb those carbohydrates 3 times as fast as before your run. Although the rate at which they refuel slows some after those first 30 minutes, your muscles remain extra receptive for the first 90 minutes after a run.

Why does this absorption matter? Because the gains that you make in your running that allow you to progress occur during the recovery phase following a run. By getting some carbs into your system soon after finishing your run, you therefore speed up the recovery process. You'll feel better on your next run, and you'll be better able to nail each of your workouts and progress closer to your goal rate.

Carb refueling is especially important after longer-than-usual runs. Many times, when runners are dragging several hours or even the day after a long run, it's because they waited too long to restock their muscles. As I said, some runners just don't feel like eating any time near after finishing a run. That's okay, but even they would feel better from run to run if they got in the habit of getting a minimal amount of carbs in.

Keep in mind that I'm talking about only 100 to 200 calories in the first hour or so. That's a bagel or a couple of pieces of fruit. If you have a supersensitive system, liquid carbs are fine (and they'll also help you to get in the important habit of drinking soon after your run). That can mean a sport drink or some diluted fruit juice. Diet sodas don't count because they contain no calories, and therefore no carbs.

The Least You Need to Know

- A good diet will help you to stay healthy enough to run to your ability.
- You can't eat your way to becoming a better runner.
- The best diet for runners is the same diet that all people should eat.
- You should get 60 to 65 percent of your calories from carbohydrates, 15 percent of your calories from protein, and 20 to 25 percent of your calories from fat.

Crossing the Divide: Cross-Training for Runners

In This Chapter

- What is cross-training for runners?
- Why runners should cross-train
- How to blend running with other sports
- How to equate cross-training time with running mileage
- The best cross-training activities for runners

Tom Fleming, an old marathon rival of mine who is now a coach, asks, "Have you ever seen a Kenyan on a StairMaster? The top runners aren't in the water or biking or using some fancy piece of machinery. They're running." Of course, he's talking about runners who want to compete with the best in the world. But what about you? Should you supplement your running with other aerobic activities? If so, which ones? In this chapter, I'll show you why I think most runners should do some form of cross-training, how to account for your cross-training time, and which cross-training activities are best for runners.

What Is Cross-Training?

Like cooking, *cross-training* is one of those formerly precise terms that has been used in so many ways that it has come to mean pretty much whatever the user wants it to. Just like people call popping a frozen dinner in the microwave cooking, you'll hear people say that they're cross-training when they're mowing their lawn, shoveling snow, or heading out for a night of dancing.

I want to use a narrower definition. For the purposes of this chapter, cross-training means aerobic exercises that you plan as part of your regular running program. With this tighter definition, I think that most runners, especially beginners, can benefit from cross-training.

> **DEFINITION**
>
> For runners, **cross-training** is using aerobic exercises besides running to supplement your running mileage. It implies planning these activities as an integral part of your program to develop parts of your body that running neglects, as well as to fight injury, burn calories, and boost your aerobic capacity.

Cross-training doesn't mean anything that you do physically in addition to your running. Household chores, walks around town, and so on, should be seen as part of your everyday activities, not as cross-training. Doing yoga or lifting weights doesn't count as cross-training either. Although these stretching and strengthening exercises are important for runners to do (as explained in Chapters 10 and 11), they don't provide the aerobic benefits that cross-training activities do.

> **TRAINING TIP**
>
> When planning activities to supplement your running, don't forget to occasionally include the option of inactivity. Sometimes, especially on the day after a difficult or long run, your best bet for consolidating the gains from your work is rest rather than more exercise.

Should You Cross-Train?

So what about my old buddy Tom Fleming's point, that if you want to be a good runner, then you should run? After all, you don't become a better cook by washing dishes. First of all, remember that he's talking about runners who are trying to be among the best in the world. These people live by their running mileage, much as a factory lives by the number of widgets it produces per day. (I should know. Having averaged 130 miles per week for most of the 1970s and 1980s, I was one of these people.)

I'm not suggesting that you replace running with other aerobic activities, but that you supplement your mileage with them. Among the benefits of doing so are the following:

- **Fewer muscle imbalances, which are a leading source of injury.** For example, running strengthens and shortens your hamstrings while pretty much neglecting your quadriceps (thigh muscles). But cycling does just the opposite, so combining running with riding helps your legs to keep the proper ratio of strength between front and back muscles.

- **Greater aerobic capacity.** A lot of runners can take only so much pounding from running each week before their bodies start to break down. If you find what that level is for you, stay just below it, and add other activities, you can continue to develop your aerobic base beyond what you could just through running. To a large degree, your heart doesn't distinguish what exercise is making it pump more vigorously.

- **Greater weight loss.** You'll be able to work out more often without getting injured.

- **A more interesting exercise routine.** Some people love running so much that they don't need other activities to stay motivated. But a lot of runners find that they look forward to working out more if they alternate among a few sports.

- **The chance to work out with nonrunning friends.** You probably have friends who aren't going to join you for a 5-mile run, but they might go for an hour's bike ride with you.

Finally, even the most hard-core runners become cross-trainers when they're injured and are desperate to maintain their fitness. If you can run as much as you like without getting injured, can meet your weight goals through running only, are endlessly fascinated by doing just one activity, and regularly do stretching and strengthening exercises that develop whole-body fitness, maybe you don't have to worry about cross-training. If not, read on.

Cross-Training Time

You wouldn't expect to feel comfortable running if you did it only once a week, but that's the approach that many runners take to their alternative exercises. This approach isn't a good idea, because you'll never become adept enough at the activity for it to contribute significantly toward your fitness. So when you find a second sport that works for you, try to practice it at least twice a week.

Unless you're injured and are cross-training as a substitute for running, don't let your
aerobic alternatives take precedence over your running. For example, you don't want
to put in such a long, hard effort on a bike that your running is compromised for the
next few days. Once you get used to your activity, treat it the same as an easy running
day. You shouldn't be sore or overly fatigued from your cross-training.

One of the best times to schedule cross-training into your routine is on the day after
a hard or long run. The exercise will help to remove waste products that might have
built up from the previous day's effort and will help work out any stiffness, but you
won't be subjecting tired legs to as much pounding as if you ran.

Comparing Apples and Oranges

One of the reasons that hard-core runners don't do more cross-training is because
they don't know how to compare it to their running. The major way that they track
their progress is to recite their weekly running mileage to anyone who will listen.
A 5-mile run is a 5-mile run is a 5-mile run, so if you only run, keeping records is
pretty easy. But what about a 2-hour bike ride, a half hour in the pool, or 45 minutes
on a stair machine? How do these compare to running miles?

My advice is different than what most people are going to tell you. I say, don't worry
about it. That's because I'm recommending that you cross-train to *add* to your running, not *replace* it. In that case, there's not much point in obsessing about whether
3 cycling miles equals 1 running mile and how many minutes on a rowing machine
equal 1 mile of running. To paraphrase Sigmund Freud, sometimes a two-hour bike
ride is just a two-hour bike ride.

Measuring Progress by Effort

If you're cross-training because you're too injured to run, then you want to have some general idea of whether you're doing enough in other sports to compensate for your lack of running. Even when you're cross-training to supplement your running, it's nice to have some general idea of how much work you're doing in a language you're used to. So at the risk of contradicting what I said in the preceding section, try this: figure that you're getting roughly the same cardiovascular benefits as running for every minute that you cross-train at a similar intensity to the level of effort that you normally sustain while running.

If 4 miles in 40 minutes is an average, medium-effort run for you, then sustaining that level of effort for 40 minutes on a stair machine will provide roughly the same aerobic benefits. Your heart doesn't care what's getting it going, so long as it's an activity that uses major muscle groups for an extended period. Admittedly, this system is imprecise, but I would rather add cross-training to horseshoes and hand grenades and consider "close enough" as being worthwhile than worry too much about exact trade-offs.

After all, those same runners who so precisely say, "I ran 43 miles last week" are deluding themselves unless all of their running is on precisely calibrated courses. Most days, they're making rough estimations about how far they ran based on the amount of time they were out for. I don't see much harm in taking the same approach to cross-training.

However, notice that I said, "every minute that you cross-train at a similar intensity to the level of effort that you normally sustain while running." That's different than just counting the number of minutes that you cross-train. On a stair machine, for example, you'll often spend the first 10 minutes or so getting going; if so, those 10 minutes aren't really at the same intensity as the first 10 minutes of most runs. During a two-hour bike ride, you're likely to spend a nice chunk of that time going downhill, *drafting*, *coasting*, and so on.

DEFINITION

When you run or ride behind someone else doing the same activity, you're **drafting** off of that person. This can save you considerable energy because some of the work you do while exercising on land is pushing your way through the air. In a 5K race on a windy day, drafting can make a given pace as much as 10 percent easier.

When you're on a bike and moving, but not pedaling, you're **coasting.** Because of the ease of coasting, it can be tough to sustain a good workout while cycling. Therefore, you should avoid coasting too much.

If you're new to a sport, it can be difficult to gauge accurately how hard you're working. It might seem as though you're really putting in a good effort, but that could be because your legs are easily tired by the unaccustomed motion, rather than because you're working at a high heart rate. Many runners experience this kind of fatigue on their first few bike rides.

If you have a heart rate monitor, use it when you cross-train to gauge whether your pulse stays in the neighborhood that it usually does when you run. (To learn how to use heart rate monitors, see Chapter 9.) Otherwise, expect to spend at least the first few workouts in a new sport learning how to assess your effort.

Choose Your Supplement!

Now that you're convinced cross-training is a good idea, which sport should you pick? The following sections examine the best cross-training options for runners. Keep in mind that in choosing these activities, I'm interested more in what sports best complement running than in which ones provide the best isolated workout.

The Pool Is Cool

If I had to pick one supplementary activity that would help you the most as a runner, it would be swimming. Once you get your stroke down, swimming has many benefits: you can work hard enough to sustain a solid effort; it's a great upper-body strengthener; it's a *nonimpact* activity; and the kicking is terrific for loosening tight tendons and muscles in your feet, ankles, and legs.

DEFINITION

Nonimpact activities, such as swimming and water running, involve no pounding.

The other great use of a pool for runners is water running. This activity is pretty straightforward: you head to the deep end of the pool, usually with a flotation device on, and start running in place. After a few times, it will feel pretty much like running on land. Water running is especially good for injured runners who don't want to lose their land legs during a layoff, as well as for cross-training runners who get injured beyond a certain level of mileage, but don't like other activities. As with swimming, you have to work a little harder than you would on land to maintain the same heart rate. Many pools now offer water running classes.

TRAINING TIP

Make convenience the most important factor in deciding which cross-training activities to do. In theory, swimming may be an excellent complement to your running, but not if getting to a pool on a regular basis is a major logistical battle for you.

The two main drawbacks to swimming are convenience and gauging effort. Finding a suitable pool (one that's big enough to legitimately swim laps in) that isn't too crowded and that has decent hours can be a real challenge. If you don't have good technique, you'll spend your swim flailing around rather than giving your heart a good workout.

Even when you do become adept, comparing swimming to running takes a little extra math. Because you're supported by the water, and because you stay so much cooler than when working out on land, your heart will beat about 15 fewer times per minute for the same effort. So you really have to keep at it to keep your pulse near what it is when you run. Kicking vigorously with your legs is a good way to do this.

For the same reason, runners who do water running often spend much of their time simulating the sorts of hard workouts I'll describe in Chapters 19 and 20. That is, after a few minutes of warming up, they'll alternate high-intensity bouts with short recovery periods for most of the time they plan to spend in the pool. This helps to keep their heart rate elevated throughout the workout, and it makes the time pass more quickly.

Spinning Your Wheels

Cycling has long been a favorite of cross-training runners. Besides the fact that the two exercises complement each other in developing your legs, both give you that great feeling of exercising outside. Cycling can be almost as convenient as running if you don't live in a high-traffic area, and because you cover so much more distance, it's a great way for runners to discover other places to enjoy their favorite sport.

 RULES OF THE ROAD

Just like running, all sports have safety rules unique to them. If you're going to spend a lot of time doing a supplementary activity to your running, learn the safety guidelines for that sport.

The main drawbacks to cycling are weather and money constraints. As Chapter 16 explains, you can safely run in just about any conditions. But even the most committed cyclists have to reconsider things during and after heavy rains and snows when they're likely to take a spill. (If you've ever fallen while riding 20 miles per hour, you know that it does a bit more damage than tripping over a root on a run.) Also, once it gets below 30 degrees, cycling outside remains uncomfortable no matter how hard you're working because of the windchill that you generate. It's also not the safest practice to ride in the dark.

Financially, a good bike and the necessary equipment (helmet, gloves, shoes, and so on) can easily cost you at least $1,000.

Indoor cycling can involve less hassle and cost, but a lot more boredom. It can be tough to stay on these machines for long enough to get a real workout in. Spinning classes are a good option if you have a tough time motivating yourself to stick with stationary cycling.

 TRAINING TIP

If there's a piece of exercise equipment that you regularly travel to a gym to use, buying one for your home will help you to work out on it more often if you can afford it.

Assuming you're of the right mindset, probably the most reliable cycling-as-cross-training option is to put your outdoor bike on a training stand or rollers. That way, when the weather is nice, you can enjoy the great outdoors, wind in your hair, and all that. And when it's dark or nasty outside, you're good to go on a bike that's more comfortable to spend a long time on than standard stationary bikes. With a little dedication and a lot of good music or a couple of your favorite TV shows, it's not too hard to get used to spending an hour at a time on an indoor bike.

If you want to cross-train with cycling, you better be pretty committed to it. Ride at least two days a week so that your legs remain accustomed enough to the activity to allow your heart to reap the benefits.

Speaking Elliptically

Some of the most coveted pieces of equipment in fitness centers these days are elliptical trainers. Many runners now name them as their cross-training equipment of choice, both when healthy and when injured.

FOOTNOTES

Steve Holman, the best American miler of the 1990s and an Olympian, relied solely on elliptical trainers to maintain his fitness when he was injured. Before the 2000 Olympic trials, Holman started running only three weeks before the trials, but was able to place fifth because of the work he had done on elliptical trainers.

Elliptical trainers comprise foot-sized plates atop moving levers. The degree to which you adjust the slope of the levers determines how much your leg motion simulates that of running—a steeper slope moves your legs in a round-and-round motion (either forward or backward) that more closely resembles cycling, while a lower slope moves your legs in a back-and-forth motion that more closely simulates running. I bet you can guess which one I recommend, especially if you're using an elliptical trainer while waiting for a running injury to heal.

Probably the biggest reason for their popularity among runners is that, by using the back-and-forth motion, you can come pretty close to simulating not only the feel of a run, but also that nice post-workout sense of accomplishment. Put in a good 45 minutes on an elliptical trainer, and you won't be spending the drive home wondering if you put in a hard enough effort. Another nice thing about them is that, regardless of what slope setting you use, your feet never leave the platforms, so there's no real pounding involved.

Because you're working so hard but staying in place, expect to sweat buckets while on an elliptical trainer. Most runners do a simple trade of usual running time for time on the trainer.

Other Options

The four best remaining aerobic alternatives for runners are in-line skating, cross-country skiing, stair machines, and hiking. Studies have shown that a similar effort between in-line skating and running requires you to skate twice as fast as you run. In other words, as with cycling, if you don't coast and have lots of room to roam, this can be a good option for you.

Cross-country skiing has been touted as the best all-around exercise because you simultaneously use just about all of your major muscle groups in a nonpounding activity. You and I don't live in Finland, however, so to plan it as a regular part of your program is going to mean hopping on a NordicTrack or similar indoor machine a few times a week. That's a tough routine to sustain for any appreciable amount of time.

Stair machines have similar pluses and minuses. They can provide a great workout, assuming you take deep enough steps and don't lean against the rails. They're also *low impact*. But they, too, can require Herculean efforts of will to stay on for at least half an hour a few times a week. That's why most people on them read, listen to music, or watch TV while waiting for the clock to run out.

DEFINITION

An activity that has substantially less pounding than running is considered **low impact.** Such activities include walking and stair climbing.

Hiking offers the great benefit of being outside in beautiful surroundings without the pounding of running. And a mile covered on foot burns roughly the same number of calories whether you run it or walk it. But it's tough enough to find the time to run for short periods a few times a week. For hiking to make sense as part of your regular program, you're going to need at least a block of a couple hours a few times each week.

The Least You Need to Know

- Doing another aerobic activity in addition to running will help you to lose weight, stay motivated, and remain injury-free.
- Cross-train with a sport that you'll do at least twice a week.
- Cross-training should supplement, not replace, your running.
- Every minute spent cross-training at an intensity similar to your usual running effort gives roughly the same aerobic benefit as spending that time running.
- The best cross-training options for most runners are swimming, cycling, and using an elliptical trainer.

For Women Only

Chapter 15

In This Chapter

- The few ways that running is different for women than men
- Running and the menstrual cycle
- Special dietary needs of women runners
- Running and the pill
- Running before and after pregnancy

As I mentioned in Chapter 1, women have traditionally been discriminated against as much in running as in most other parts of our society. Although a men's marathon was included from the get-go when the modern Olympics began in 1896, a women's marathon wasn't added until 1984. But as I also said in Chapter 1, things are changing for the better for women runners, and for a simple reason: more of them are ignoring the barriers that still exist and are joining the sport. Women in the 20 to 29 age group are among the fastest growing segments in running.

A lot of the old discrimination was blatant sexism. But as is often the case with discrimination, a lot was based on misunderstanding. Running for women was somehow thought to be different than it is for men. In most cases, it's not. When women start running, they get fitter, just as men do. But there are some female-only running issues, and that's what I'm going to deal with in this chapter, based on what I've learned from talking to women runners, such as Olympic gold medalist Joan Benoit Samuelson, as well as from reading.

Are Women Runners Different from Men?

Yes and no. Yes, if you're asking from the standpoint of "Can they run as fast?" But more importantly, no, if you mean, "Does running affect women differently?"

FOOTNOTES

The Boston Marathon didn't officially allow women to enter the race until 1972. To enter that year, women had to meet the same qualifying standard then in place for men, 3:30. Eight women ran, led by Nina Kuscsik in 3:10:26.

If the two are equally well-trained, the average woman is going to be slower than the average man, from the 100-meter dash on up to the marathon. Women have certain disadvantages when they compete against men:

- Women have smaller hearts than men, so the heart pumps less blood with each beat. To run a given pace, a woman's heart rate has to be higher than a man's.

- Women have lower *hemoglobin* levels than men, so less oxygen is sent to working muscles.

- Women have higher essential body fat stores than men.

- Women's lower levels of testosterone mean that women have less muscle mass than men.

DEFINITION

Hemoglobin is a protein in red blood cells that carries oxygen from your lungs to your muscles. With less hemoglobin, women have less oxygen per unit of blood.

Working together, these unavoidable physical factors make women, on average, 10 to 12 percent slower than men at all commonly run distances.

So on the whole, women are always going to be slower than men. I suppose it's easy for me to say this, but I wouldn't make that big a deal out of it. Although women are not as fast as men, running has the same effect on both genders. Women used to be discouraged from running as much or as hard as men, but there's no basis for this practice. Studies have consistently shown that women who train at the same level as men see the same amount of increase in their fitness.

FOOTNOTES

The women's world record for the marathon is 2:15:25, by Great Britain's Paula Radcliffe. In 2008, only one British man ran faster for the distance!

Remember that strange phrase, VO_2 max, from Chapter 2? It's your body's ability to use oxygen while working and is the most important measure of your cardiovascular fitness. Six months to a year after starting to run, previously sedentary people can expect their VO_2 max values to increase by 20 to 30 percent. That's equally true for women and men.

What you probably care about a whole lot more than maximum speed is your running—how to get fitter, how to find the time for it, how to stick with it, and so on. The answers to those questions are the same for all runners. That's not to say that women runners aren't going to want answers to questions that we men never have to think about. The following sections examine some of the most common areas of concern.

Running and the Menstrual Cycle

Just as the effects of menstruation itself differ greatly from woman to woman, the effects of menstruation on running performance vary greatly as well. Some women notice no difference in performance; others notice a great deal of difference.

TRAINING TIP

Be sure to drink a lot of water if you have bloating during your premenstrual phase. You might think that drinking water will only make you more bloated, but that bloating is caused by sodium retention. Drinking enough water will flush that sodium out of your system and will help you to feel better on your runs.

If your period is going to affect your running, it's most likely to occur during the premenstrual and early flow phases of the cycle. The good news is that many women runners find that their running helps to ease cramps, bloating, headaches, fatigue, and all of those other friendly monthly visitors. To best deal with the effects of menstruation, track how your cycle affects your running in a training log, and then plan accordingly. For example, if you notice that running often seems harder during your premenstrual phase, accept that and don't try runs that are longer or harder than usual during this time.

On the not-so-good side, running can lead to increased bleeding. Some of the pain-killers, such as ibuprofen, that help with other side effects can also reduce bleeding. The increased bleeding usually isn't so great that it's visible. But if you're worried about this, do what Olympic gold medalist in the marathon, Joan Benoit Samuelson, does and run with a tampon in a plastic bag pinned inside of your shorts or tights.

Women runners sometimes don't have periods. This condition is called *amenorrhea*, and although it might sound like a dream come true, it's not good. It usually means that little or no estrogen is circulating in your body, which can lead to your bones becoming weaker, as well as short-term infertility.

DEFINITION

Amenorrhea is the absence of regular menstrual cycles. The main cause seems to be not eating enough to meet your energy needs. It can lead to weakened bones and should be avoided.

The causes are complex, but most experts think that amenorrhea is caused more often by not eating enough than by exercising too much. Running alone can't be named as the cause, given that some women train more than 100 miles a week and still have regular periods. If your periods stop or become irregular (more often than every 25 days or less frequent than every 35 days), see a doctor. Just don't let him or her convince you that running is solely to blame.

Women of Steel: Iron Needs

Women runners should be more careful than men runners about preventing low iron stores. Iron is used to produce hemoglobin in your red blood cells. As mentioned before, one of the reasons that women are, on average, slower than men is because women have less hemoglobin. This condition is made worse if your iron stores are low, because then your hemoglobin levels become lower. When hemoglobin levels decrease, less oxygen reaches your muscles when you run, so running your normal pace feels harder.

Why are women runners more susceptible to low iron stores? For starters, all women lose iron through menstrual blood. On top of that, women runners tend to be more careful about their diet than sedentary women. That's usually good, except that one of the things that women runners often get more selective about is eating meat.

Limiting meat can be a good way to cut fat out of your diet, but it also can mean too severely limiting your iron-rich food choices.

Good food sources of iron that aren't high in fat include the following:

- Lean red meat and dark poultry

- Dark green, leafy vegetables

- Legumes

- Dried fruit

- Whole-grain or enriched cereals and bread

 TRAINING TIP

You'll absorb three times as much iron from a breakfast of cereal and toast if you drink orange juice rather than coffee with it.

You can increase how much iron you absorb from a food by eating foods rich in vitamin C at the same time. Using cast-iron cookware also helps. On the other hand, you decrease how much iron you absorb from foods when you drink coffee or tea with meals. Premenopausal women runners should shoot for an iron intake of at least 15 milligrams (mg) per day; postmenopausal women need 10.

Other reasons that women runners might have low iron stores apply to men, too: loss through sweat and urine, increased blood volume with training (which lowers iron concentration in the blood), and what's known as footstrike hemolysis, which is the breakdown of red blood cells from your feet repeatedly hitting the ground. When you have blood tests done, ask for your hemoglobin and serum ferritin (a measure of your body's iron stores) levels to be checked. Normal hemoglobin concentration for women is from 12 to 16 grams per 100 milliliters of blood. Because of the increased blood volume that comes with running, a reading of 11 can be considered safe for a woman runner, but anything below that is asking for trouble.

The "acceptable" range for serum ferritin is 10 to 200 milligrams per milliliter of blood. I say "acceptable" because a reading at the low end of that range is not at all acceptable for runners. A serum ferritin reading below 25 will harm your running—you'll feel like you're dragging all the time, because you're operating in an iron-deprived state. Most experts recommend doing what's necessary to get your serum ferritin level up to at least 50 to improve your running.

Running and Birth Control

Obviously, birth control is an incredibly personal choice. I just want to tell you what some women runners have experienced. A few studies have found that women runners are less likely than sedentary women to take birth control pills. Many women report that they just don't feel as good while running when they're on the pill. Fatigue and nausea are common side effects of being on the pill, as is weight gain.

Because the pill eliminates the premenstrual and early flow phases of a period, the pill can be a good birth control choice for women runners who feel that their running suffers at these times. Overall, though, most women runners who have found a successful alternative to the pill prefer to avoid oral contraceptives.

Two for the Road: Running and Pregnancy

In June 1995, while 8½ months pregnant, Sue Olsen ran a marathon in 4:00:50. The next week, she gave birth to a healthy son who weighed 7 pounds, 3 ounces. How healthy was her son? Well, in 2008, they returned to the same marathon they had run "together" when Olsen was pregnant and finished the race together! Okay, so Olsen is a bit on the extreme side. But I thought you should know about her because she, and her healthy son, are evidence that being pregnant doesn't necessarily mean lying on your back for nine months eating chocolate-covered pickles.

Play, Don't Labor: Running While Pregnant

Pregnant women used to be told any exercise beyond even the most low-key, minimal exertion would endanger both their health and that of their fetus. The main concern was that the mother and fetus wouldn't gain enough weight to produce a healthy baby come birth. It was also thought that when a pregnant woman runs, the fetus would be harmed because of less oxygen and blood flow going to the uterus.

Because of fears like these, the American College of Obstetrics and Gynecology (ACOG) used to say that pregnant women shouldn't work out strenuously for more than 15 minutes and that they should keep their heart rates below 140 beats per minute. In other words, don't really run. A lot of faithful women runners chose to ignore those recommendations when they became pregnant. As they did, and seemed to produce normal, healthy babies, more studies were done about running and pregnancy.

Among other good things, these studies found that the fears of damage to the fetus by running moms-to-be were unfounded. The pregnant body has compensatory mechanisms for decreased oxygen and blood flow to the uterus. It's been shown that both the woman and fetus have all the fuel they need when the woman runs, even in the late stages of pregnancy, when fetal growth really takes off. Hey, Sue Olsen had to get energy somewhere during that marathon, after all.

In terms of birth and after, studies have shown no real difference between sedentary pregnant women and active ones in these important matters:

- Complications of pregnancy, labor, and delivery
- Type of delivery (C-section versus vaginal)
- Circumference of the baby's head
- Overall health of the baby
- Weight of the baby at birth

As for weight gain during pregnancy, one study found that active pregnant women put on about 30 pounds each, compared to 39 to 42 pounds for nonexercisers. ACOG recommends that most women gain 25 to 35 pounds.

One study compared women who worked out vigorously, including running, to those whose only exercise while pregnant was walking. When the children of these women were five years old, those of the intense exercisers scored higher on tests of intelligence, coordination, and language skills.

Because of all of this evidence that vigorous exercise is safe, ACOG has revised its guidelines. Now it encourages women who are fit and active when they become pregnant to remain so as long as they can comfortably during pregnancy. So long as you keep in close contact with your doctor and use common sense, ACOG says, it's okay to run vigorously throughout your entire pregnancy.

RULES OF THE ROAD

Although the latest thinking encourages pregnant women to exercise vigorously, it's still important not to overdo it. Your body temperature shouldn't get above 101 degrees while running when you're pregnant.

Now whether Sue Olsen's exploits would get the ACOG seal of approval, I'm not sure. But I bet they wouldn't have any problem with Joan Benoit Samuelson, who ran 5 miles on the morning before she gave birth to her second child, and remembers the run as one of the favorites of her whole life. Remember, this is a woman who won the Olympic Marathon!

Sue and Joan are among the luckiest ones. No matter how many green lights ACOG gives you, and no matter how dedicated you are, there comes a time when intensive weight-bearing exercise like running becomes too uncomfortable to be worth doing for most pregnant women. If and when that occurs will vary from woman to woman and even from pregnancy to pregnancy for repeat moms. That's where the common sense part of ACOG's current guidelines come into play.

 TRAINING TIP

When you're pregnant, don't compare your running to your pre-pregnant days. If you go to races, forget your usual goals and just participate to have fun.

When running isn't an option anymore, many women runners turn to less-intensive cross-training options. My pregnant runner friends have met their activity needs through swimming, walking, riding a stationary bike, hiking, doing yoga, etc. Swimming is an especially popular choice. The key is that they sensed when the running wasn't worth doing anymore, accepted that temporary situation, and found other, more comfortable, ways to stay fit and active.

Post-Partum Expression

The answer to how much and how fast to run after giving birth, just like how much and how fast to run before giving birth, differs from woman to woman. A lot of it has to do with how tough your pregnancy and delivery were. A standard guideline is to wait about six weeks after a vaginal delivery, a bit more for a C-section. Again, though, those are just general guidelines. Part of being a runner is being in touch with your body, and you should have a feel for when it's right to get going again.

As some women runners have pointed out, you never know until it's too late if you tried to come back too soon. In this sense, starting to run again after giving birth can be a lot like starting again after an injury. You're always going to be wondering if it's okay to try to progress, and you're going to feel a lot different running than you used to. That's especially the case for new mothers who are probably trying to run with more weight than they had before being pregnant.

FOOTNOTES

Some women return to running after pregnancy with few problems. In 2007, Britain's Paula Radcliffe won the New York City Marathon just 10 months after giving birth!

Your joints and ligaments remain loose for about nine months to a year after delivery. This looseness makes you especially susceptible to injury during this time, so you should avoid hills and uneven terrain. Put all those factors together, and most women runners who have been through the process, even highly motivated ones, think it's a good idea to err on the side of caution.

Some women say that once they return to their regular running program after giving birth, they feel much stronger. Of course, there's a psychological side to this. As a lot of my female friends have told me about being a running mother, there's nothing like a forced nine months off to get you really motivated.

The Least You Need to Know

- In terms of the effects of training, women runners are no different than men.
- The average woman is slower than the average man because of physical differences.
- Although a great variation among women exists, most women runners find that running helps during their menstrual cycle.
- Women runners should consume more iron-rich foods than sedentary women.
- Moderate running during pregnancy is safe for both the mother and the fetus.

Weathering the Elements

Chapter 16

In This Chapter

- Why it's harder to run in heat and humidity
- How to run safely in hot weather
- Why winter running is better than you think
- When the weather is too bad to run
- Skin care for runners

I've run through more than 40 New England winters. I've run in Arizona in the spring, in New York and Ohio in the fall, and even run a marathon in Vietnam in the summer. Let's just say I get around.

So I always laugh a little when, on a slightly cloudy day, someone asks me, "You're not going to run *today*, are you?" People ask this because, in our society, most inactive people have no real exposure to the elements—they're almost always in a house, a car, or an office. Running regularly gets you outside. In fact, finding a certain beauty in all kinds of weather, and living in harmony with Mother Nature, is one of the great appeals of running.

I'm not going to lie to you and say that I always love running in all kinds of weather. You have to respect the conditions and plan accordingly, or it can get pretty frightful, rather than delightful, out there. Once you learn how to do that, though, you'll be good to go pretty much anytime, anywhere. You'll see autumn sunsets, winter wild-life, summer showers, and spring blossoms in ways that most people never do. In this chapter, I'll explain how to cope with some of the more extreme weather conditions that you'll face as you stick with a year-round running program.

A Hot Time in the City

You know that you tire more quickly when it's 90 degrees rather than 50 degrees, even if you're just taking a leisurely stroll. And you know that the harder you work, the more tired heat makes you. But why is that? And what can you do about it?

When you run in the heat, your body sends more blood to your skin to cool you via evaporation. As a result, less blood, which carries oxygen, goes to your leg muscles, and they have to work harder just to maintain your usual pace. Also, the warmer it is, the more you sweat. This is good, because sweating helps to cool you as your perspiration evaporates. But it's also bad, because your blood volume decreases. With less blood returning to your heart, your heart has to pump more often to keep the same amount of blood circulating throughout your body. And when your heart rate increases, you're working harder.

FOOTNOTES

Even the best runners in the world slow significantly in the heat. At the 1976 Boston Marathon, where the temperature reached 101 degrees, Jack Fultz won in 2:20:19. This is the slowest winning time there since 1968. Two years later, when it was 47 degrees at the start, Fultz ran 2:11:17. (I won.)

Running is even tougher on humid days. You generate all that sweat, and it's supposed to cool you down, but the air is so moist that it can't absorb much more water. So your sweat stays on your skin rather than evaporating, and your body just keeps producing more and more sweat, and you just keep getting more and more tired. That's why it's a lot tougher to run on a 90-degree day in the humid mid-Atlantic part of the country, like Washington, D.C., than in someplace like New Mexico. Out in the desert, it's hot but dry, and your sweat can cool you like it's supposed to.

The Dangers of Dehydration

The upshot of all this dripping sweat is a dropping pace. One study found that for each 1 percent of body weight that you lose because of dehydration, your running performance falls by 3 percent. Bear in mind that 1 percent of body weight isn't much—if you weigh 150 pounds, that's only 1.5 pounds, or 24 ounces. It's not unusual to lose 3 or 4 pounds of water in an hour of running on a hot day. This loss causes your performance to sag by more than 5 percent, which can be as much as a minute slower per mile. Are you starting to see why it's so tough to feel comfortable while running in the heat?

You also need to consider cumulative dehydration. Cumulative dehydration is what happens when it's hot for several days in a row, and you don't replace all the fluid you lost after each run. Suppose that during a hot week, a 150-pound runner doesn't rehydrate himself completely each day. By the end of the week, he has a cumulative loss of 2 pounds of water—that's more than 1 percent of his weight. As a result, his performance is off by more than 3 percent by week's end, but he may not make the connection to dehydration. A lot of runners, myself included most summers, go through the hottest parts of the year chronically dehydrated. As a result, our running suffers.

RULES OF THE ROAD

If you feel dizzy while running in the heat, stop, get out of the sun, and drink water. You're probably suffering from heat exhaustion. If you stop sweating, stop running immediately. You're probably suffering from the more serious heat stroke. This condition requires immediate medical attention.

Beating the Heat

Now that I've completely turned you off on running in the heat, what can you do to fight dehydration? Drink, drink, then drink some more. Your thirst mechanism is imperfect; by the time you're thirsty, you're dehydrated.

How do you know if you're staying on top of staying hydrated? First, weigh yourself before and after runs in hot weather. However much lighter you are at the end of the run, drink at least that amount of water within the first two hours of your run. Remember, a pint's a pound the world around, so for every pound you lost on the run, drink 16 ounces.

RULES OF THE ROAD

Besides weighing yourself before and after runs, watch your urine during the day. It should always be clear in color and frequent. If it's dark or infrequent, you need to drink more water, even if you're not thirsty.

Don't cheat on this method if one of the reasons you're running is to lose weight. The weight that you lose on a run in the heat isn't fat. It's water and needs to be replaced if you want to keep running. Your blood and other body fluids help to remove waste products and to carry nutrients to muscle tissues, so the faster you replace lost fluids, the more quickly you'll recover from run to run. Replacing water doesn't have anything to do with how many calories you burn on a run, which is what counts in determining how much fat you lose. If anything, quickly replacing water weight loss will *help* you lose weight because you'll feel better from day to day, and you'll be more likely to stick with your running in tough conditions.

Make it easy to drink water often throughout the day. One coach I know tells his runners to keep a 2-liter bottle of water at their desks at work. They're supposed to finish it at least once from when they get to the office until they go home. I also know runners who are in the habit of stopping for a drink at every water fountain they pass during the day, regardless of whether they're thirsty. It's also a good idea to keep a bottle of water by your bed.

 TRAINING TIP

Most people can absorb only about 7 ounces of fluid every 15 minutes. That's why it's better to drink small amounts of water throughout the day and during your runs instead of drinking a lot at once.

Not only is it important to drink water before, after, and between runs, it's important to drink during them as well. I keep a water bottle hidden in the woods a few miles from my house. When I run by it, I stop and drink, and then restash it. When it's empty, I carry it home, refill it, and drive it back to its hiding spot. Here are other ways to conveniently get drinks on the run:

- Plan your route so that you'll pass schools, gas stations, and other places that have water fountains.

- Plan your route so that you pass your home once or twice. Have a water bottle waiting for you at the end of the driveway.

- The night or morning before a longer run, drive over your route, stashing bottles along the way.

- On the hottest days, carry water with you. Many runners prefer fannypacks that hold bottles to keep their hands free and their arm action normal.

- If you don't mind running with a fannypack, store money in it to buy drinks at convenience stores.

If you can use some of these methods to make sure you get some fluid every 15 to 20 minutes during your run, you'll last a lot longer in the heat. I also like to drink two or three glasses of water a few minutes before I run. Sometimes the water sloshes around in my stomach at the start, but I know it will help me by the end of the run.

Nothing beats water for pure hydration. But you're more likely to drink enough if you enjoy a variety of fluids. What are other good options for just before, during, and right after a run? Studies have shown that sport drinks that are 4 to 8 percent carbohydrate, like most of the commercially available ones, are absorbed as quickly as water. They have the added plus of providing energy. Fruit juices aren't absorbed as quickly; dilute them by half with water. Carbonated beverages aren't a great idea because they might upset your stomach and because they make you feel full. If you drink a carbonated drink, you might think that you're more hydrated than you are.

TRAINING TIP

If you drink caffeinated drinks or alcohol, drink at least an equal amount of extra water for each drink to balance the dehydrating effect. For example, if you have two beers with dinner, drink at least an extra 24 ounces of water.

The Winter Wonderland

One of the main reasons that running in the winter can be so nice is because running in the summer can be so tough. With all the heat that you generate after a few minutes of running, you can be warmer running outside in 40-degree weather than inside your 68-degree home. So you stay warm enough to stay comfortable, but don't get so hot that you get really dehydrated. The best of both worlds!

RULES OF THE ROAD

When running, you generate up to 11 times the amount of heat that you do when at rest. If you're warm at the start of a cold-weather run, you're going to be too hot later on. Dress for how warm you'll be 10 minutes into your run.

You can't get away with running in just anything in the winter. As explained in Chapter 8, some necessary items of clothing will help you stay comfortable when it's cold. The key is wearing the right gear for the right conditions, which usually involves layering.

The Freeze-Your-Lungs Myth

Except for the few hottest days of the year, most people aren't going to question your sanity when you're out running in July or August. But keep running through the winter, and eventually someone is going to ask you, "Aren't you afraid that you'll freeze your lungs?"

Even my dad used to ask me this when I started running in high school. I was taught to respect my elders, so I didn't laugh in his face or anything, but this question is one of the silliest I've ever heard. Have you ever met someone who has frozen a lung? Of course not. As the air you breathe works its way into your lungs, it's warmed more than enough to keep it from freezing anything.

I bet you have met someone who was in pretty good shape, but stopped working out when it got cold, and started the spring with more weight and less fitness. That's a shame, and an unnecessary one, because winter running can be some of the best of the year. And I'm a New Englander, so it's not like I'm sitting here espousing the joys of winter running from my house in Los Angeles.

Running in the winter involves a bigger mental aspect to it than running during the rest of the year. I admit that after doing this for 40 years, I still sometimes have a tough time getting psyched to run when there's only been eight hours of daylight for the last couple of months. You just need to keep focused on your goals. After a while, you'll learn how to get out the door and through those tough first few minutes until you start getting warmed up. I can usually do this by reminding myself how much better I'll feel after my run. Also, ask yourself if you would be so ready to bag your run if it were sunny and 70 degrees.

Footing, Short Days, and Icy Roads

The lack of light, not the potential freezing of your lungs, is the biggest threat to your well-being when you run in the winter. Watch your footing. Try to run on level surfaces that you're familiar with and choose the most well-lit routes. Be extra careful after snow or ice storms. Snow on the ground can often help your night vision, because it reflects what light there is. But under that snow may be patches of ice.

 TRAINING TIP

On windy days, plan your route so that the wind is primarily at your back on the way home. You don't want to build up a bit of a sweat, and then get too cold when you're facing a head wind on the return trip. It's also not much fun to fight a head wind when you're tired toward the end of your run.

Also, watch traffic even more than you usually do. Don't assume that cars can see you or that, if they do, they can get out of the way quickly. Just as snow and ice can make you slip around during your runs, they also can cause cars to careen out of control. Fortunately, most good winter running apparel made these days has reflective features. If yours doesn't, you can buy reflective strips, a reflective vest, or a lightweight head-lamp at most running stores. Almost all good running shoes have reflective elements built into their design. These elements are a must if you want to run safely in the dark.

Neither Sleet, nor Hail: Foul-Weather Running

Along with the frozen-lung query, one of the other most common weather-related questions I hear is, "What do you do when it rains?" The answer: get wet. What I mean, without being too much of a martyr about it, is that part of being a runner is coping with the hand that Mother Nature deals. Again, most people in our society have lost their connection to the outdoors. The only running in the rain they can imagine is from their office building to the car.

But what do you do after a run? You get in the shower; you get wet. Why is it so horrible to get wet *during* your run? Unless the rain is cold, running in the rain can be incredibly enjoyable. Think about when you were a kid and how you splashed in puddles or how good it felt to be in the rain in the middle of summer.

RULES OF THE ROAD

When running after a snowstorm, wear darker clothing so that drivers can see you better against the white backdrop. If you have more than one pair of running shoes, wear the one with the most studded outsole so that you'll have better traction.

Of course, running in the rain isn't always ideal. As I said, a cold rain is not that fun. You have to be extra careful, especially if you're running near a lot of traffic. Cars aren't going to be able to see you as well. But most times, putting on the right gear (see Chapter 8) and a baseball or painter's cap is the only added step you need to take to have a great run. When you get home, just be sure to change into dry clothes as soon as possible.

The only other weather I really fear is lightning. I just don't go out when it's striking. Fortunately, you can usually wait for it to pass and get in a nice poststorm run.

Made in the Shade: Sun Protection

People used to think that a great tan was one of running's main side benefits. Now we know better. There are almost a million new cases of skin cancer every year in the United States. My grandfather died from a melanoma, and my mom has had skin cancer, so I'm especially aware of this problem. But it's not just those of us with a family history of these problems who need to be careful. These days, smart runners can take a few easy steps to lower their risk of overexposure to the sun.

The major one is to wear a waterproof sunscreen. It should have an SPF (sun protection factor) rating of at least 15. Ten to 15 minutes before your run, apply it liberally to any body parts that are going to be exposed.

RULES OF THE ROAD

A hat provides good sun protection, but can also trap a lot of heat on warm, sunny days. To keep the sun off of your face, but also stay cool, wear a visor.

Other steps to lower your sun exposure while running include the following:

- Wear something on your head to shield your face.
- Wear sport sunglasses to protect your eyes.
- Try not to run when the sun is strongest, from 10 A.M. to 2 P.M.
- Run in the shade. (You'll also stay cooler if you do.)

If you're lucky enough to be running during daylight hours in the winter, don't forget the sunscreen. The sun isn't as strong then, but it can do its work nonetheless, especially when it's reflecting off snow.

The Least You Need to Know

- For every 1 percent of your body weight that you lose to dehydration, your running performance suffers by 3 percent.
- If you're thirsty, you're already dehydrated.
- The best way to prevent dehydration is to drink small amounts of water throughout the day, rather than a few big drinks all at once.
- If you have the right gear, winter can be one of the best times of the year to run.
- To prevent skin cancer, wear sunscreen with an SPF of at least 15 when you run.

Join the Human Race

This part is about going to races. I've always been a racer, from my first race in 1963, to my last four Boston Marathon victories in 1980, up to today, now that I'm in my 60s. Racing is the icing on the running cake, and it's sweeter than any dessert I've ever had.

Find out why so many runners race, and where they go to do it. You'll experience basic workouts that will improve your running, even if you decide never to attend a race. Then I'll detail more specific training for the most popular race distances, from 5K to the marathon to trail running.

The Finish Line: Why You Should Race

In This Chapter

- Why runners attend races
- How racing for time helps to keep you motivated
- How people help others by running marathons
- Why separate age groups for older runners are good

More than 15,000 running races are held in the United States every year. This chapter explores some of the main reasons that people like to go to races. Most of those reasons might not be what you think, and they don't all involve killing yourself to shave one second from your 5K time.

People Pay to Do This?

The average road race is held early on a Sunday morning. A standard road race with T-shirts, awards, postrace refreshments, and so on, costs $20 to $30 to enter. In other words, most people running in them have gone to bed early on a Saturday night, gotten up at least as early on a Sunday morning as on a regular workday, and then handed over the cost of a nice dinner for the opportunity to inflict pain on themselves. Sounds like they're the idiots, huh?

They're far from it, and I'm not just sensitive to that charge because I go to 25 to 30 races a year. At some level, these runners realize that far from being masochists, they're indulging themselves. That's right—indulging themselves! Racing is the proverbial icing on the running cake.

Your regular training gives you the big health and fitness benefits that are the most important thing about running for most people, but experiencing only that part of running can get a little tedious. You need some excitement and some variety in anything that you do regularly, no matter how much you love it. In running, that excitement and variety most often comes from going to a race. You don't even have to try to run harder than you do when you run on your own. There's just something about lining up with your fellow runners and experiencing the same course together that adds an element to your running that's impossible to find otherwise.

Say you really like to cook. Which would you rather do: Always cook for just you and your spouse, making pretty much the same types of dishes at the same time of day? Or would you rather use those daily cooking sessions as the main way to enjoy your hobby, but also throw a dinner party once in a while where you get to put it all on the line and let yourself and others see just what you're capable of? Most people would choose the second option, and that's why you see so many people at races.

 RULES OF THE ROAD

For races up to 10K (6.2 miles), your weekly mileage should be at least three times the distance that you want to race. For example, you should be running at least 15 miles a week before attempting a 5-mile race.

Let's continue that dinner party analogy just a bit farther. Say you invite a few friends over for dinner. You don't worry about how your culinary skills compare to Martha Stewart's, do you? No. You do the best you can given your background and ability, and afterward you're rewarded with the feeling of a job well done.

The same is true of nearly all of the people in any race. They know that they don't have to look like the winner of the Boston Marathon to race. They know that races give their running a focus and are a great source of motivation for getting out the door most days. Preparing for a race that's a few months away is one of the best examples of setting the challenging, specific goals that were discussed in Chapter 6.

Many beginning runners have a sense that their running would be more exciting if they went to races, but they're afraid that they'll finish last and be embarrassed. Here's why they shouldn't be: first, most races have at least a few hundred runners in them. Just like only one person is going to finish first, only one person is going to finish last. The odds of that being you are pretty long, believe me.

More important, if it is you, so what? No one has ever been shot or even booed for finishing last in a road race. In fact, some of the loudest applause from spectators in races are for those near the back of the pack. The spectators recognize the extra effort that these runners are putting out. Adding to that applause are often many of the runners who have finished their races, and then hung around the finish area to cheer on their fellow runners. That kind of camaraderie with your fellow runners is one of the main draws that races have.

Racing's Best-Kept Secret: It's Fun!

People who haven't been to races aren't going to know this, so you'll just have to take my word for it until you see it for yourself: you'd be hard-pressed to find an event more filled with smiles and unambiguous goodwill than your local road race. Put another way, why should you race? Because it's fun!

A road race is the closest thing to a mobile party that I can think of. (Well, the closest legal thing.) Everywhere you look, there are smiles, cheers, laughs, and heartfelt congratulations from one runner to another. There's music before and after (sometimes even during), there's great food after, prizes are given out, and kids are roaming all around—sounds more like a circus than someplace where a bunch of skinny masochists gather to be miserable together, doesn't it? Or think about it this way: how many other times do you see hundreds or thousands of people gathered in public without the slightest worry by anyone about crowd control, police protection, that sort of thing?

 TRAINING TIP

> After a race, talk to the people who finished near you. These people are good potential training partners because you're currently at roughly the same level of ability as they are.

Of course, most people aren't laughing it up and smiling during the race; they're working pretty darned hard. But that effort explains the festive atmosphere afterward. The runners have pushed and challenged themselves, and now they're all celebrating the sense of accomplishment that doing so brings.

In life, isn't one extreme of something usually more enjoyable if you've recently been near the other extreme? Isn't a sunny day more special when it's been raining for a week than when it's the tenth bright day in a row? Doesn't your easy chair feel best when you've been working your hardest? That's why races are so much fun. Once you've experienced a race, you'll agree with me that there's a certain kind of fun that comes from challenging yourself within sharply defined parameters while others around you are doing the same.

Personal Bests

I've always been a competitor, ever since I was the fastest kid in a run during gym class in school. Seeing how fast I can run has long been my primary motivation to be a runner. Oddly enough, that's why I stopped running for a few years after college. My goal then had been to break 9:00 for 2 miles, and I did. I didn't see the point in racing anymore, so I didn't see the point in running anymore. (Now, of course, I know better. What's that about youth being wasted on the young?)

I was fortunate to be able to win races when I was younger. I'm not going to lie to you and tell you that doing so wasn't incredibly satisfying. Let me tell you, if you ever need motivation to get out the door for a run on a tough New England winter day, try telling yourself that you'll be defending your title at the Boston Marathon in a couple of months. It worked wonders for me.

> **FOOTNOTES**
>
> I ran my first organized race in 1963. It was a five-lap-to-the-mile race put on by the Newington, Connecticut, Parks and Recreation Department as part of its summer games program when I was in high school. I won in 5:20.

But even when I raced for place, I was also always focused on my finishing times in races. Now that I don't win races anymore, I'm even more fanatical about them. I'm certainly not alone in that regard. For many runners, setting personal records, or getting under a certain barrier for a distance, or seeing how their time at a race this year compares to what they ran there last year, or any of the million other ways that you can look at your running times provides the biggest reason to race. There's something intoxicating about racing against yourself.

Your race times provide an objective record of your accomplishment on that day. There's just no way around it—your race time is how long it took you to run this course on this day. Unlike other sports competitions, races are about unadulterated human performance. In other sports, you're maneuvering against your opponents and trying to finesse some piece of equipment. When you race for time, it's just you, the elements, and the clock.

Nothing else I've found in sports gives you that yes-or-no sense of accomplishment that racing for time does. Suppose you play on a softball team. How do you know whether you've had a good game? There are so many variables that you don't have primary control over. Did you get two hits because you swung the bat well or because the other team's pitcher stunk? What about when you made that nice play at third base, but the first baseman flubbed your throw, or the umpire made the wrong call? There's none of that uncertainty when you race for time.

RULES OF THE ROAD

Many races these days are timed using small devices you attach to a shoe or wrap around an ankle. These items record when you cross the start and finish lines, so you receive a time based only on how long it took you to cover the race course, not how long it took you to get to the start line and then cover the race course. Because it can take a minute or more for many runners to cross the start line in big races, you should count your net time as your real time in a race.

Earlier in this chapter, I told you how aiming for a race is one of the best ways to set the short-term goals I keep recommending. On top of that, aiming toward a race and having a time goal for it helps to keep you running even more. It lends a logic to your training—with the race as your goal, you have a better idea of what types of running you should be doing. Those time goals are a great answer for that little voice in your head that's occasionally going to say, "Why are you doing this?"

Charitable Contributions

Races have long been venues for raising money for charities. I've always liked being able to tie in doing something good for myself with helping others. Most of the people running these kinds of races would probably have participated in them anyway; the money raised for charity is a nice side consequence of them doing so.

However, one of the biggest trends in American racing is charity running that works the other way around—people enter races (usually marathons, but also, increasingly, half-marathons) solely for the purpose of raising money for charity. This approach to running is different than activities like AIDS rides or walkathons, because the runners use races that already exist, rather than events that are created specifically for them. But the great benefits for society are the same.

The biggest of these types of programs is called Team in Training, run by the Leukemia Society of America. Runners sign up to participate in one of the many marathons that Team in Training sends people to. In exchange for raising a specified amount of money (usually in the neighborhood of $3,000) in pledges, program participants receive free entry, travel, and lodging at their chosen marathon. The locales can be pretty exotic, such as the program's most popular race, the Mayor's Midnight

Sun Marathon in Anchorage, Alaska. Other big Team in Training sites are Bermuda, Honolulu, San Diego, Dublin, and Paris.

> **FOOTNOTES**
>
> Charity runners have had an incredible impact on the size of the field in some marathons. In 1994, just more than 300 people ran the Mayor's Midnight Sun Marathon in Anchorage, Alaska. In 2009, more than 3,000 people ran the race, almost all of them charity runners.

Runners in the program receive free coaching from knowledgeable runners in their area. Most groups meet once a week for a long run and a prerun clinic from their coach. The usual training program lasts for six months so that the runners gradually build up to being able to finish the marathon.

> **RULES OF THE ROAD**
>
> Although some people run a marathon just six months after starting to run, I think you should wait until you've been running regularly for at least a year before you attempt this most demanding of distances. Give yourself a chance to build a solid base of endurance, and you'll be better able to increase your training toward a marathon.

Team in Training has been phenomenally successful in meeting its goals; in 2009 alone, it raised $69 million for leukemia research, and now is the source of more than half of the Leukemia and Lymphoma Society's revenue. Similar groups have sprung up that raise money for arthritis research (Joints in Motion), cancer research (Fred's Team), and other causes.

Many runners join these groups for emotional reasons—they know someone who suffers from the disease that their fundraising will battle. Almost all of the participants in these programs are first-time marathoners. In some cases, they're even first-time runners, having started to run only after deciding to finish a marathon to raise money for charity.

Charity runners care mostly about finishing their marathon to raise money, not how fast they can run the marathon. They've added an important new element to the sport and have helped running to continue to grow. (It's no accident that the most popular running magazine, *Runner's World*, sponsors the program, because all those new runners mean potential new readers.) Because of the good coaching they receive, nearly all of them complete their marathon. See Appendix C for more information on running-related charities.

Mastering the Possibilities

Now that I'm in my 60s, I can no longer run a single mile at the same pace that I used to be able to maintain in a marathon. But that doesn't depress me. Why? Because like a lot of runners, I've been reborn since I became a *masters runner.*

DEFINITION

A **masters runner** is a runner age 40 or older.

No matter how long you've been running, once you're 40 or older, you'll be called a masters runner. For longtime runners like me, the phrase makes a certain amount of sense—after all those years of putting in the miles, you've mastered how to keep at it and with enough interest that you're still showing up at races.

TRAINING TIP

Many big races have clinics or expos the day before. These clinics often feature expert speakers on running, so they're worth attending if you want to learn more about running.

What's so great about masters running? There must be something to it because I know I'm not alone in finding my running revitalized by the turning of the clock. Competition for the top prizes in the masters category are among the toughest in running.

Masters racing recognizes that no matter how intelligently you go about your running, it's a lot tougher to run fast when you're 45 than when you're 25. That's especially so for people who have been at it for a long time. Most runners reach their best performances in the first 8 to 12 years of running, regardless of the age at which they start. So if you start at a young age, by the time you're 40, your times in races are almost assured to be slower than they were in your early 30s.

This inevitable slowing with age can be pretty depressing if you don't have a way to deal with it. Say there were no age-group awards in races, but just prizes for the top 10. Who would ever have a chance to take home a trophy except for the young and the breathless? Even if you were never an award winner in your youth, how would you go about setting goals when you know that no matter how hard you work, you're never going to run as fast as you once could?

RULES OF THE ROAD

For races of 10 miles and longer, you should run at least two thirds of the distance at least once in the 3 weeks before the race. For example, before a half-marathon (13.1 miles), you should run at least 9 miles at least once in the preceding 3 weeks.

Enter masters running. With awards given out in five-year brackets, you're not forced to fight it out with the young bucks if taking home loot is part of the appeal of racing to you. Instead, it's just you and your contemporaries, who are more likely to have the body and schedule that you do than some just-out-of-college hotshot is. The age-group categories level the playing field.

More importantly, masters running does a tremendous job of keeping runners motivated enough to keep attending races by giving you a way to set goals. In the last few years of my 30s, I was a little bit adrift. I was no longer fast enough to duke it out with the top guys in most races, and I wasn't running as fast I used to, even though I was training as hard. It was tough to know how to assess my performances and how to set goals for future ones.

But when I turned 40, suddenly there were all these masters records to aim for—I got to see how close I could get to what other runners past the age of 40 had done. Mentally, I wiped the slate clean. I concentrated on setting masters personal records and took each personal record as a new standard, rather than comparing it to my faster times from my 20s and 30s. I start fresh every time I enter a new five-year age group.

That kind of attitude helps to explain why in some races, more than half the runners are past the age of 40. They've figured out that they can continue to find meaning in their race performances by comparing them to what they have achieved recently. Racing gives them a fresh outlook and new goals to shoot for every few years. When you do that, you've found the fountain of youth, regardless of how old your birth certificate says you are.

The Least You Need to Know

- Going to races adds excitement and variety to your running.
- The challenge of racing for time provides focus and motivation for your running.
- An increasing number of runners in half-marathons and marathons participate more to raise money for charity than to get a good finishing time.
- Comparing results within five-year age groups helps to keep a lot of runners coming back to races.

The Racing Circuit

In This Chapter

- The different types of races
- The cost of entering road races
- Finding races in your area

Arriving at a race can be an eerie experience. You may have been driving through early morning darkness for an hour, following directions you printed off the web that have taken you places you've never been before. When you get to the end of the directions, you start looking around, and you see them: emerging from their cars, other runners are walking purposefully into that old school or that tent across the field. They've all somehow found their way from their homes to this one spot, where all of you will work together to get the best from yourselves. In this chapter, I'll show you how to join the party.

A Race to the Start: Types of Races

The different types of races are defined mainly by the type of surface they're run on. (Within each type are races of various distances.) You either race on the roads, on the track, or on dirt and grass. You rarely see a race that combines surfaces. Each of the different types of races has a feel all its own.

Takin' It to the Streets

More than 90 percent of the nonscholastic races held in the United States are road races. If you know someone who has run a race, it's almost guaranteed that he or she ran in a road race. There are road races of pretty much every distance you can imagine from the mile to the marathon. The most popular distances are 5K (3.1 miles), 8K (about 50 yards short of 5 miles), half-marathon (13.1 miles), and marathon (26.2 miles).

The size of the fields in road races runs the gamut, too: you can find small rural affairs among 15 people all the way up to the country's biggest road race, the Bay to Breakers, a 12K (7.4 miles) in San Francisco that had almost 65,000 official finishers in 2009. (The race has even more unofficial entrants, making for close to 100,000 running the streets of San Francisco.) A typical road race, in which runners wear race numbers and receive T-shirts, will have anywhere from a few hundred to 1,000 runners in it. Races with more than 1,000 runners are major productions.

I'm obviously biased toward road races, having earned the nickname "King of the Roads" in the 1970s. I like how the course of each road race has its own quirks that you have to master. I also like the (usually) firm footing and long stretches so that I can get in a good rhythm. The party atmosphere that I told you so many races have is almost exclusively at road races.

 TRAINING TIP

Arrive at the site of a race 45 minutes to an hour before the start. This will give you time to park, register, find a bathroom, and warm up with plenty of time to spare and without worrying that you're going to miss the start.

Another cool aspect of road races is that they are one of the few, if not the only, instances in sports where an average participant competes at the same time on the same course as the best in the world. Want to play baseball with Derek Jeter? Good luck. But line up with the 50,000 runners who run the Peachtree 10K in Atlanta every Fourth of July, and some of the fastest runners around are at the front of the field. Sure, you're not going to be going head to head with them, but running is different because you're experiencing the race exactly as the elite runners do. It's fun to see how your time compares to theirs. You can't do that in baseball, football, basketball, or almost any other sport.

Choose Your Road

For the most part, road races basically fall into two main categories: those put on by various community organizations and those put on by local running clubs. The most popular time for both types of road races to be held is early on a weekend morning. Start time is usually 9 A.M. in the cooler months, 8 A.M. in the warmer months. More races are held on Sundays than on Saturdays.

FOOTNOTES

Does this race count as a morning or evening race? Every year at midnight on New Year's Eve, more than 5,000 runners take part in a 4-miler in New York City's Central Park.

Races in the first category are usually held in conjunction with a local event or as a once-a-year fundraiser for a charity. The people involved in organizing the race are usually volunteers from whatever organization will benefit from the race. The organizers usually pay a professional finish-line coordinator to handle timing, scoring, and other race day logistics. In these races, you almost always wear a number during the race, and you almost always get a T-shirt as part of your entry fee. There's probably also going to be nice postrace refreshments, decent prizes for the top runners, and other amenities.

TRAINING TIP

Many large races offer a way to pick up your race number on the day before the race. If doing so isn't a major hassle for you, this is a good way to avoid long lines on race day. Avoiding the long lines gives you the time and mental energy to focus on your race.

Local running clubs also put on races as part of their regular schedule of events. These races are usually more low-key and have smaller fields. Most of the people running them are members of the club, although all runners are certainly welcome to take part. Organization and logistics are handled entirely by volunteers lined up from the club. These races sometimes cost only a few dollars to enter, because there are no T-shirts or other major costs to cover. (These races often take place in more rural areas, so the organizers don't have to pay as much, if anything, for permits, police, and so on.)

Show Me the Money

A typical 5K costs $25 to enter. Marathons can cost $100 or more. Why do road races cost that much? I mean, aren't you just running down a public road? Who's getting rich off of these things?

Nobody is. The entry fee that races charge usually covers only about one third of the costs of putting on races. Events are a lot more expensive to stage than they used to be. Local governments didn't used to charge for the police who are often necessary for traffic control. Municipalities are also increasingly requiring races to pay for permits to stage events, even though there's really not a whole lot of demand for the space by others at 8 A.M. on Sundays. San Francisco's Bay to Breakers race shells out several hundred thousand dollars to the city to cover police, park, and other fees.

RULES OF THE ROAD

Races don't just get put on by magic. Any runner who attends races should volunteer at a race at least once a year. Volunteering at races is a good way for injured runners to stay connected to their sport.

Most of the expenses to put on a race are picked up by the race sponsors. Donations also go a long way to keeping race costs down. Because most races are to benefit some charity or nonprofit group, the organizers can appeal to the goodwill of local merchants to donate food and prizes. Given all that goes into putting on a race, a $25 entry fee is quite a bargain.

Some runners try to rebel against what they think are high entry fees by being *bandits*. They run the race, but don't sign up for it. Bandits are bad. Not only do they sometimes mess up the timing of the race because they're not wearing numbers, but they leech off of the majority of the runners who paid the entry fee. If everyone acted that way, then there wouldn't be any races for them to be mad at. If you think that a race charges too much, then voice your disagreement with a letter and by staying away, not by being a bandit and thinking that you're accomplishing anything more than ripping off fellow runners.

DEFINITION

Bandits are runners who participate in races without paying to register for them. Bandits like to think that they're protesting the high cost of races, but they're really cheapskates who hurt their fellow runners.

You can usually save money on races by registering a month or more before the race. Race day entry fees are usually about $5 higher than early registration.

Get on Track

Races held on the track can be hard to find once you're out of school. But especially during the summer, many local running clubs will put on one or more *all comer's meets*. In some parts of the country, you also can find indoor track meets open to all runners during the winter. These track meets are usually sparsely populated events, with less than 100 runners taking part. There are no T-shirts, and the entry fee is nominal. All comer's meets have an intimate atmosphere that's hard to match at a big road race.

DEFINITION

A track meet that encourages runners of all speeds and ages to participate is an **all comer's meet.**

Whereas road races are often about doing the best you can on the course you find yourself on, there's no such mystery in track races. Seen one, you've seen them all. Because of this universality of tracks, most runners are going to be there to chase after a time goal. As a result, many runners are intimidated by track races because they associate racing on the track with something that only really fast people do. That's a shame, because I think all racers should experiment with different types of races occasionally.

Track races are usually shorter than road races; 5K (12.5 laps of the track) is usually the longest race. Many runners gravitate to the longer distances because that's what's available on the road. But by running track races in addition to road races, you might find that you have a talent for speed-based events such as the mile.

Track races are also a good place to develop a strong sense of pace. Because there's no variation from lap to lap, you do best by getting in a rhythm. Learning how to get in a rhythm can help you on flat road courses as well. You also develop the ability to concentrate when you compete on the track frequently because churning lap after lap can get so boring.

RULES OF THE ROAD

If it's 80 degrees or warmer at the start of a race, start the race slower than you had planned. The heat is going to take its toll on you regardless, so it's better that you be in control of the situation rather than overheating and slowing down even more.

Over Hill, Over Dale

The most elemental of races is *cross-country*. These races take place on grass and dirt, usually through woods, on golf courses, or in other pleasant settings. Cross-country races are usually from 5K to 10K in length and are usually held in the fall. (Trail runs, of course, are also technically cross-country races, but because they're usually much longer, feature difficult footing, and have their own feel, I'm treating them as their own baby. See Chapter 23.)

DEFINITION

A race that's held on dirt or grass is a **cross-country** race.

Like track races, cross-country races are usually put on by local running clubs and have, at most, a couple of hundred runners. They usually are low-key affairs with no T-shirts and a small entry fee. Cross-country races are often team races, and many people like that aspect of them. Times are pretty meaningless in cross-country, so runners concentrate on feeling that they ran strongly.

How to Find a Race

Where can you find details on races in your area? The best place to start is with a local running club. Don't worry if you don't know anyone in the club or even how to contact them. If you don't know any runners in your area who you can ask about local clubs, contact the Road Runners Club of America at www.rrca.org. Ask for the name and number of the club nearest to you. Once you know the club in your area, check it out. Most clubs maintain a website with a calendar of upcoming events; even the smallest club will have a telephone hotline you can call to find out what's up the road.

If you know of a running store near you, visit it. Ask the salespeople (who are usually local runners) if they know where you can find information about local races. Many areas have local running publications that do a fantastic job of listing all of the upcoming races in a locale. Most running stores are also depositories for race flyers. Look through them to see if any of them interest you.

The web is a great way to find races, either in your area or if you want to try a race while you're on vacation or traveling for work. Appendix C lists some of the best running websites. Because of the nature of this book, most of those websites are national in scope, but many have links to local running websites.

The Least You Need to Know

- The three main types of races are road races, track meets, and cross-country races.
- Road races are by far the most popular type of race.
- The average road race is between 5K and 10K long, costs $15 to $25 to enter, and is held early on a weekend morning.
- The best sources for information on races in your area are local running clubs, the web, and running stores.

Basic Training for Racers

Chapter 19

In This Chapter

- Reasons to vary the length and pace of your runs
- Tips on how to schedule different runs within a week
- Advice on how to run fast and relaxed at the same time
- Guidelines for speed-building workouts

Getting out the door for 30 or so minutes of steady running a few times a week brings you most of the health benefits. But if you want to run faster in races, you need to add some extra elements to your training. In this chapter, I'll show the types of workouts that I and other racers do to improve our performance, and I'll show you how to fit them all together into a sensible plan.

I'm going to be throwing a lot of lingo at you in this chapter. Just like on a hard run, don't feel bad if you need to slow down and catch your breath. At the end of this chapter, even if you never do any of these workouts, you'll at least be able to hold up your end of the conversation with any running geek.

Adding More Structure

Nobody needs to do the workouts in this chapter. You can run the same distance at the same pace every day for the rest of your life, and I'll gladly call you a fellow runner. Certainly no one has ever been barred from entering a race because they hadn't done hard workouts on the track for the last several weeks.

But if you want to run faster in races and your running is at the moderate, steady pace that I've been urging, you need to make a few changes in your training. You'll race better if once a week you include a few miles of running at race pace or faster. You'll have more strength for these fast workouts if you boost your endurance by occasionally running longer than usual.

 TRAINING TIP

When you add more structure, plot your training a week at a time so that you're sure to allow enough time between your hardest efforts. Be realistic about when you'll have the time and energy to do which workouts. A common plan is to do your longest run of the week on Saturday or Sunday and your fastest workout in the middle of the week.

I think all runners, even those who aren't going to race, should at least dabble in the different types of workouts covered in this chapter. Including runs that are faster or longer than usual is just part of training more completely, like stretching and strengthening exercises are.

The Hard-Easy Principle

In Chapter 3, I told you that you progress in your running by applying a stress, allowing enough recovery time for your body to rebuild itself a little stronger, and then applying a slightly higher stress. When you start adding different types of workouts, apply that principle to your training as a whole. You want to start training by the hard-easy principle—you run faster or longer than usual on one day, and then follow that day with a run that's shorter or slower than usual.

The hard-easy principle helps you in two connected ways. Say I have a fast track workout planned for Wednesday. On Tuesday, I'll be sure to run very easy. This might mean running a bit less than usual, and it definitely means running at a slow pace for the entire run, no matter how good I feel. This slow pace reserves my body's strength for the next day and allows me to have a better workout than if I had gone into it more tired. By running easy before a hard effort, you progress because you're able to get more out of yourself on your hard days.

For at least one day after my fast workout on Wednesday, and more often two days, I'll take it easy again. After a hard workout, it's usually easy to go slow enough because I'm beat from the previous day's work. Taking it easy allows me to consolidate the gains from my hard workout and helps me to avoid injury. If you run too fast or long on the day after a hard workout, then you're risking injury or staleness later on. Your body needs that chance to rebuild itself.

Remember that the general rule is to plan an easy day the day before a hard workout and allow for at least one or two easy days after a hard workout. By hard workout I mean either a run that includes at least a couple of miles at race pace or faster or a run that's much longer than usual. What counts as an easy day varies among runners. For some runners, an easy day means a day of no running—that's certainly a good way to make sure you don't work too hard! In running terms, an easy day means making sure that you can pass the talk test the entire run.

On the days before and after a day of fast running, it's okay to run your usual distance, as long as you keep the pace easy. Before and after runs that are longer than usual, you should not only keep the pace easy, but also run a shorter distance than usual. The longer runs drain your glycogen stores. The day before, you don't want to run too far because you might start your long run low on glycogen. The day after a long run, your muscles will still be a little low on fuel, so you're risking injury if you ask them to go too far.

Smooth Striding

One of the best ways to introduce fast running into your program is by doing *striders*. Striders are good because they're fast enough to teach your muscles and nervous system how to run smoothly at a fast pace, but they're so short that they don't fatigue you.

DEFINITION

Striders are runs of 100 yards or so done at close to top speed. Striders help you learn how to stay relaxed when you run fast.

Striders don't really count as a hard workout. Still, I think that all runners should do them once or twice a week. Striders move you through a fuller range of motion than regular moderate runs. They also feel great—it's fun to run at close to top speed, knowing that you're only going to be doing so for 20 seconds or so.

Most runners do striders at or near the end of a normal run. When you do striders, do 8 to 12. You can do them anywhere you can run smoothly for 100 yards at a time on a flat, level surface. A good day to do striders is the day before a fast workout or a long run. Striders wake up your body from the usual plodding. That's why most serious runners also do a few striders just before starting a fast workout or a race.

The key to doing striders is to stay relaxed. Watch the top sprinters in the world, and you'll see that although they're running faster than 25 miles per hour, their entire bodies, especially their shoulders, neck, and face, are incredibly relaxed. Shoot for this lack of tension when you do striders. Accelerate smoothly to what feels like the fastest pace you could maintain for half a mile. Try to reach that speed by halfway, hold that speed for a bit, and then gradually slow down. Wait a minute or so, and then start your next strider.

Striders are a great way to improve your running form. By learning to run smoothly when you're running at close to top speed, you become better able to do so at all speeds. On each strider, concentrate on one aspect of good running form. For example, concentrate on keeping your shoulders low and relaxed during one strider. On the next, think about maintaining a quick, smooth turnover of your feet. On the next, concentrate on keeping your hands cupped, relaxed, and passing your body at about your waist. Pretty soon, you've done your 8 to 12 striders.

The Long and Short of Long Runs

When I was training to be the best marathoner in the world, my *long run* was the focus of my week. But you don't have to be a marathoner to benefit from long runs, and your long runs don't have to be 20 miles or more, like mine were. What counts as a long run is relative to how much you usually run. Marathoners need to build up to at least a couple of runs of 20 miles or more before they should try to cover 26.2 miles. But for a 5K runner, a long run could be as short as 6 miles.

DEFINITION

A **long run** is a run that's at least one and a half times longer than your second longest of the week. For a runner who usually runs 5 miles at a time, 8 miles is a long run. Most runners do a long run every one to two weeks.

There's no set standard for what constitutes a long run, but here's a good guideline: two out of every three weeks, do a run that's at least one and a half times longer than any other run you do that week. If your normal run is 3 miles, then 5 miles is a long run for you. If you measure your runs by time, the same standard applies. If you usually run for half an hour, then going 45 minutes or more would be a long run for you.

Many runners do a long run every week, but you don't have to. Two out of every three weeks is a good goal. This frequency is enough to progress in boosting your endurance, but the occasional week off gives you a chance to recoup physically and mentally. A plan that many runners use is to do a long run on weekends that they're not racing. This plan mixes things up nicely.

What do you get from doing long runs? Obviously, marathoners need to train their bodies and minds to be out there for a long time. But every runner, even ones who aren't going to race, should incorporate runs of varying lengths into their training. When you do a long run, you deplete your muscles' glycogen stores more than usual. During your recovery from the long run, your muscles develop the ability to store more glycogen. This means that the next time you run as far, your muscles won't get tired as soon.

FOOTNOTES

Other things happen in your muscle cells when you do long runs that help you on all of your runs. Capillaries, the tiniest blood vessels, border every muscle fiber. Their job is to deliver oxygen and fuel to your muscles and take away waste products. Long runs increase the number of capillaries per muscle fiber, which improves their efficiency. This increased efficiency makes all of your runs feel easier. Also, long runs increase the number and size of mitochondria in your muscle cells. (Mitochondria are the little aerobic energy factories in your muscles.) With more mitochondria, you can produce more energy, so you can maintain a faster pace at a given level of effort.

Psychologically, long runs help your usual runs seem easier. When you're used to being out there for almost an hour once a week, then your normal 30-minute runs don't seem as daunting. And obviously, the longer you run, the more calories you burn, and the longer you'll burn calories at an accelerated rate after your run. Long runs are great for losing weight.

Do your long runs at your normal training pace. These runs count as hard workouts because of the increased distance, not because you maintain a faster pace. You should be able to finish your long runs at the same pace you start them. If you have to slow dramatically at the end, then you've prematurely depleted your glycogen stores by starting too quickly.

The key to successfully increasing your long run is progressing gradually. When you can comfortably complete a long run at a given distance, try going 1 mile farther the next time. This is the approach I take. After my racing season ends in the fall, I take it easy for a while. My longest run for a month will be 10 miles or so. Starting in December, I'll go 12 miles or so once a week, and then start adding 1 mile per long run until I'm at my target distance.

If you've been nursing a slight injury but are still going to try a long run, create a course that keeps you close to home, such as several different small loops. That way, if your injury flares up, you can cut your run short more easily.

Make your long runs special. Try to do them in a nice setting, and try to do them with friends. These factors will make these runs more enjoyable, and the miles will pass more easily.

Warming Up and Cooling Down

You should start all of your runs at a gentle pace and spend the first 5 to 10 minutes of the run building to your normal training pace. This gradual building allows your muscles, heart, and lungs to warm up and work better when you want to get going. You also should ease off during the last bit of a run to allow your heart rate to return to normal more gradually. When you start doing races and fast workouts like the ones in this chapter, you need to make your warm-up and *cool-down* much more pronounced.

DEFINITION

A **cool-down** is running very easily for 1 to 3 miles after a fast workout or race. A cool-down helps to remove some of the waste products that build up in your muscles when you run hard, so cool-downs help you to recover from a hard run more quickly.

Most people know that they should warm up before trying to do something hard, whether it's running fast, lifting a heavy weight, or what have you. The best way to warm up for any activity is by doing that activity at a low level of effort. So a weight-lifter might do a few bench presses at a very low weight, and runners might run 1 to 3 miles very slowly before they try to run fast.

Where many runners fall short is on the other end of the workout. They neglect to do a good cool-down after a hard effort. Usually that's because they're exhausted, and think that more running is just going to exhaust them more.

But cooling down (you'll also hear runners call it warming down, but that's really the opposite of what you're doing) helps you recover more quickly from your hard efforts. When you finish a race or a hard workout, your heart rate is near its maximum, and waste products have built up in your muscles. You're tired, so you plop down and consider yourself done for the day. The next time you run, your legs are still sore because those waste products have pooled in your muscles. A good cool-down flushes those waste products out.

Cool-downs don't have to be long. One mile is often plenty. After catching your breath, run very slowly for at least 10 minutes. A cool-down run should be at a much slower pace than your regular runs. By the end of the cool-down, I guarantee that you'll feel better.

On the Fast Track: Speed Work

Speed work is the best way to train the physiological systems that are stressed when you race. Your regular daily runs give you the base to cover the distance; striders help you to run fast smoothly; long runs give you a little extra boost of endurance so that you can keep running strong when you get tired. But to boost your performance in a race, you need to do some running at the pace that you hope to maintain in the race or even a little bit faster.

DEFINITION

Speed work is running a workout of several runs of a mile or shorter at race pace or faster, with slow recovery jogs between the hard runs.

Running fast works in the same general way as running long does. After you do a long run, your body rebuilds itself so that it's better prepared the next time that you try to do such a silly thing. Same thing with running fast—your leg muscles get used to turning over quickly, your heart gets used to working at a higher rate for a sustained time, and your lungs get used to processing a lot more oxygen. Just as important, your mind gets used to putting up with a certain kind of pain, but persisting nonetheless.

Aim for one speed workout a week when you're building toward a race. The best ways to make speed work more bearable are to stay focused on your race goal to remind yourself why you're doing it and (does this sound familiar?) to do speed work with others of similar ability (see the figure on the following page). Many runners who run on their own every other day of the week seek out people to do speed workouts with. They know that they'll be less likely to bag the workout when they're running with others, and they know that sharing the effort with others helps the workout to pass more quickly.

Speed workouts are easier when you do them with other runners.

A Decent Interval

The most popular place to do speed work is at a standard 400-meter outdoor track. Such a track is precise and unvarying, so you get objective feedback about how fast you're running. When you do speed work on the track, you're doing *intervals*.

DEFINITION

Intervals are structured speed work in which you run fast for a specified distance, run very slowly for a specified time or distance to recover, and then repeat the process a specified number of times. Different interval workouts are best to prepare for different races.

An interval workout has a defined structure. First, you run fast for a specified distance (usually 1 to 4 laps, which equals just under ¼ to 1 mile). You have a rest interval of a set length, expressed either in distance or time, during which you jog very easily to recover from the fast run. At the end of that interval, you run fast again. You repeat this process for the number of times you had planned at the start of your workout.

Technically, the term "intervals" refer to the recovery portion of the workout, but everyone has his or her own usage for this term. Some people call the fast runs the intervals, as in, "I'm going to do mile intervals today." (I will use the term this way in this book.) Other people don't use the "intervals" term at all; they call the fast runs repeats, as in, "I'm going to do half-mile repeats today." Don't let them confuse you. If they talk about doing intervals, that refers to the workout as a whole; it means they're doing speed work on the track. (Some runners just say they're "doing a workout," meaning that they're going to do intervals as opposed to a normal training run.)

RULES OF THE ROAD

If other people are on the track during your speed workouts, do your recovery jogs in the outside lanes so that you don't get in their way.

How do you structure an interval workout? What's best depends on what race you're training for. If you're concentrating on 5Ks, then you're better off running shorter intervals at a slightly higher intensity. If you're getting ready for a half-marathon, you should do longer intervals at a bit slower pace.

In the next three chapters, I'll show you what interval workouts are best for the most popular race distances. Here are some general guidelines:

- Aim for a total of 15 to 20 minutes of hard running in your workout. This range means that the shorter your intervals, the more you should do of them. Don't do more than 25 minutes total of hard running in a single workout.

- For intervals that take longer than five minutes to complete, allow a recovery time of about 50 percent of the time it took you to complete the interval. For example, if you run a fast mile in eight minutes, recover for four minutes before running hard again.

- For intervals that take from three to five minutes to complete, allow a recovery of about 75 percent of the time it took you to complete the interval. For example, if you run a fast half mile in 3:30, recover for 2:30 before running hard again.

- For intervals that take less than three minutes to complete, allow a recovery time that lasts roughly as long as it took you to complete the interval. For example, if you run a fast quarter mile in 1:40, recover for 1:40 before running hard again.

- Have the workout planned before you start. If you make it up as you go along, you're more likely to quit too early.

- Figure out what your goal pace for an interval is in terms of time per lap, and then try to hit that pace on each lap. For example, if you want to run each of your interval miles in eight minutes, try to run each lap as close to two minutes as possible.

- Your time from interval to interval shouldn't vary by more than 10 seconds per mile. If you run two interval miles in 8:00 each, and then a third one in 8:30, you did the first two too quickly.

How fast to run depends on how long your intervals are. I'll show you how to figure that pace for specific workouts in the next three chapters.

 TRAINING TIP

Bring water with you to the track on hot days. Taking a small drink between your hard efforts is a nice mental break and will help you feel better on your intervals.

Fartlek: Not an Intestinal Disorder

Some runners thrive on track workouts. They love the precision and the ability to objectively compare their workouts from week to week. A lot of runners get burned out when they do speed work on the track frequently, however. They just don't like going around and around in circles. Also, many runners don't have easy access to a track, or they have to train when it's dark, or the track is covered with snow. How can these runners get in their fast running?

They can do a *fartlek*. That's not what you do on a run after having a burrito; it's a Swedish word that translates as "speed play." Fartlek workouts are done away from the track. Many runners prefer them because the change in scenery makes them less mentally grinding, and they find that they can concentrate of running fast.

 DEFINITION

Fartlek is a Swedish word that means "speed play." When you do a fartlek workout, you alternate fast and slow running, but you do the workout on roads or trails rather than the track. Fartlek workouts are usually less structured than track workouts.

Fartleks can be a lot less structured than speed work on the track. You might plan a fartlek on your usual 5-mile course. After running easily for a mile, you might run hard to that telephone pole way down the street, and then jog easily until the end of the next block, and then pick up the pace again until the school, and so on, until you had a mile left in your run, when you would run easy the rest of the way home as your cool-down.

Some runners make fartleks more structured. They might head out on one of their loops and, after warming up, spend the bulk of their run alternating running hard for two minutes with running easy for two minutes. Runners who don't have access to a track often use this approach. (It helps to have an alarm on your watch for this type of workout.) This approach is also good when the weather is bad, and you know it would be hard to reach your usual times on the track. In this situation, do a fartlek on the roads and get in a good workout without the weather-induced slower times bumming you out.

The Least You Need to Know

- You'll progress more in your running if you regularly vary the lengths and paces of your runs.
- A long run once a week builds your endurance and makes your regular runs easier.
- Alternating very fast running with slow recovery jogs is speed work.
- To race your best, you need to do speed work regularly.
- You can do speed work on a track, road, or trail.

Short but Sweet: 5Ks to 10Ks

In This Chapter

- Maximizing your aerobic capacity
- Learn why you should run at an even pace in your races
- Prerace eating guidelines
- Training schedule for 5K races
- Training schedule for 8K/10K races

More people run 5K (3.1 miles) races than any other distance. Some of the biggest races in the country are 10Ks (6.2 miles). In recent years, an intermediate distance has become increasingly popular—8K, or about 50 yards short of 5 miles.

What's so great about these races? You don't have to train like a marathoner to run them, and they're not going to leave you walking downstairs backward for days afterward, but they're still very challenging distances. You're running right at the limits of your aerobic capacity, seeing whether you can hang on for just a bit longer until the finish line comes into view.

If you want to know how to improve your performance at these distances, this chapter is for you. I'll show you how to set goals for these races and give you an eight-week schedule leading up to a target race.

How Far Is a K?

What's the deal with all these "K"s runners are always talking about? I mean, everyone trains all week by measuring their miles, and then they go off on the weekend and race 5Ks and 10Ks. "K" stands for kilometer, as in a 5-kilometer race. A kilometer is a metric standard of distance equal to 1,000 meters. One kilometer equals .621 miles.

Europe is the epicenter of the international track and field circuit. Every summer, the best runners in the world spend June through August traveling to track meets throughout Europe to race each other. World-class track meets in Europe are like the Super Bowl is here. They often sell out more than a year in advance, with some stadiums holding more than 50,000 fans.

> **FOOTNOTES**
>
> When this book went to print, the men's and women's world records for 5K on the track were 12:37, by Kenenisa Bekele of Ethiopia, and 14:11, by Tirunesh Dibaba of Ethiopia. That's 4:04 per mile for Bekele and 4:34 per mile for Dibaba. The American records are 12:56, by Dathan Ritzenhein, and 14:44, by Shalane Flanagan.

I ran a few of these meets in the late 1970s, and it was an incredible experience. The fans are really knowledgeable. They spend most of the distance races clapping rhythmically, stomping their feet, cheering wildly. You can't help drawing from their energy. You just don't see that happening at track meets in this country, which are usually more sparsely attended than a shoe-sniffing contest.

As a result, European track meets set the agenda. Because tracks are measured metrically, being 400 meters around, almost all races are in metric distances. (The main exception is the mile, which fans all over the world love.) The two main distance races are 5,000 meters, or 5K, and 10,000 meters, or 10K. Usually when people talk about track races, they give the distance in meters; when they talk about the same race on the roads, they describe it in kilometers. So a 5,000 on the track is the same distance as a 5K on the roads. Wacky, eh?

Racing 101

The first step to running your best in any race is being able to cover the distance. I don't care how fast Usain Bolt can sprint; if 5K is a long run for him, he's not beating me (or many other people, for that matter) in that race. The longer a race is, the more being able to negotiate the distance becomes a limiting factor. That's why 5Ks to 10Ks are so popular. You don't have to run all that many miles each week to be able to finish the race.

But when you want to do more than just finish the race, then you need to alter your training. How? Here's a simple training principle that many runners ignore: different races have different physiological demands; that is, they stress different systems of your body. It's impossible to effectively train all of the systems of your body in a short period (say, a few months). Therefore, to reach your potential, you should pick a race distance that you want to focus on for a racing season, and then train to meet the physiological demands of your target race.

In other words, you can't train to be a miler and a marathoner at the same time. The demands of the distances are so different that you have to choose, and then structure your training accordingly. If you want to be a miler, then do a lot of short, very fast speed workouts, and don't worry about how many miles you run each week. If you want to be a marathoner, don't worry about how fast you can run a quarter-mile; concentrate on increasing your endurance with long runs.

FOOTNOTES

When this book went to print, the men's and women's world records for 10K on the track were 26:17, by Kenenisa Bekele of Ethiopia, and 29:31, by Wang Junxia of China. That's 4:13 per mile for Bekele and 4:45 per mile for Wang. The American records are 27:13, by Mebrahtom Keflezighi, and 30:22, by Shalane Flanagan.

This focused, seasonal approach is what the best runners in the world do, but many recreational runners are all over the place. They run a 5K one weekend, a half-marathon the next, then another 5K, then a 10K. That's not to say that you can't or shouldn't race at a variety of distances. But within any period of a few months, you'll do better if you focus on a group of distances that have similar physiological demands. That way, you'll be able to train more effectively because you can concentrate on developing the type of fitness needed for your target races.

This principle underlies the workouts that I recommend in the next three chapters. After all, 5Ks and 10Ks place different demands on you than marathons do. Therefore, the workouts that you do to prepare for them should be different. Otherwise, you're wasting valuable training time.

VO₂ to the Max

The key to training to become faster at 5Ks, 8Ks, and 10Ks is to improve your aerobic capacity, or VO_2 max. That's because you run these races at very close to your aerobic capacity—an all-out 5K is run at about 95 percent of your VO_2 max, a 10K at about 92 percent. To run those races better, then, you need to max out your VO_2 max. The best way to do that is to do one workout each week in which you run intervals at a pace that's roughly at your VO_2 max.

But wait a minute. Didn't I tell you early on in this book that steady, comfortable running increases your VO_2 max and that it will increase by 20 to 30 percent within a year of running? Why would you need to do anything more to race a good 5K? Early on, you don't. You're getting fitter by leaps and bounds just by running easy. But after those initial gains, you have to work harder to keep improving. It's like learning a new computer program—you make the greatest improvements in the beginning, when you go from complete unfamiliarity to a basic working knowledge. It's only after more extensive experience that you learn all those little tricks of the program that allow you to make that small but significant leap from a basic user to the one in the office who everyone asks for advice.

 TRAINING TIP

It's common to feel suddenly tired soon before you have a speed workout planned. That feeling is almost always just nerves and anxiety about the hard work in front of you. Just go through a good warm-up, remind yourself how the workout will help you to reach your goals, and start the first interval.

In the training schedules at the end of this chapter, I'll have you do one speed workout each week that will focus on boosting your VO_2 max by having you run your intervals at roughly that pace. In your case, I'm making them a bit faster, because I'm assuming you haven't done systematic speed work before, so you have more room for improvement than a longtime runner. It's important to run them as close as possible to that pace to get the greatest improvement.

In these workouts, harder isn't necessarily better. Most runners think that if they can run a workout of 3 interval miles in 8:00, then running them in 7:40 will be that much more of an effective workout. But it doesn't always work that way. In these workouts, the important thing is to work right at the limits of your VO_2 max. But that's not the same as your max.

Remember, you run 5Ks very close to your VO_2 max. But obviously you can run shorter races faster; you can maintain a quicker pace for 1 mile than you can for 3.1 miles. In races shorter than 5K, a bigger percentage of your energy is supplied anaerobically, independent of the oxygen that you breathe in. So it's possible to run faster than your VO_2 max for a short distance, stop running until you catch your breath, and then run anaerobically again.

Unfortunately, many ambitious runners do their speed workouts this way. They run each interval as hard as they can. When they do that, they're definitely training hard, but they're not training very effectively. By training faster than their VO_2 max pace, their workouts are more anaerobic, so they're training their anaerobic systems. But then they go and race 5Ks, 8Ks, and 10Ks, which rely almost entirely on their aerobic systems. In their races, they'll often not perform up to their expectations. They'll think, "Gee, I ran three mile intervals the other night in 7:00 each, but I could only average 7:20s in the race." To make matters worse, they'll then often think that this means that they should train that much harder, and the next week they'll push themselves to run their mile intervals in 6:50.

See how they're making their workouts less and less effective the farther that they stray from doing them at their VO_2 max pace? Don't let it happen to you. Train at the right intensity, and you can pass them in the races, leaving them to wonder why you're behind them in speed workouts, but ahead of them in races.

RULES OF THE ROAD

You need to do a good warm-up before races of 5K to 10K because you're going to go almost immediately to near your top aerobic speed. Jog 1 to 2 miles, finishing 10 minutes before the start. Put on your race gear, and then do four to six striders up to race pace. Get in place in the pack just a few minutes before the start.

The Proper Pace Prescription

I've convinced you that you'll run faster in 5Ks to 10Ks by doing a weekly speed workout at your VO_2 max pace, and I've convinced you that you'll improve more if you do them at this pace instead of as fast as you possibly can. Now you have just one question: How do you know what that pace is?

If you've run a 5K race at a solid effort within the last few months and have been running consistently since, use that pace as your current VO_2 max pace. Better yet, hop in a 5K race soon, run hard the entire way, and figure out your average pace per mile. In both cases, make your 5K goal pace (what, you hope, will become your new VO_2 max pace) about 15 seconds per mile faster. If you haven't run a 5K in a while (or ever), you can still figure out the proper pace. If you're running at least 15 miles per week and know your average training pace, subtract 1 minute per mile to get a reasonable 5K goal pace.

The 5K and 10K training schedules later in this chapter include speed workouts that are based on your 5K goal pace. The intervals in the 8K/10K schedule are a little longer and a little slower to better meet the demands of the longer races. If you're decently trained, you should be able to run an 8K or 10K within 10 to 15 seconds per mile of your 5K race pace.

These workouts will help you to know what pace to try to reach in your race. You'll be used to running hard while tired. After a while, the pace will become second nature. That's not to say that it will feel easy, but that you can launch into it and be confident that you're at your goal pace until you get your first split time.

You should try to run as even a pace as you can in races of 5K to 10K. Many runners like to blast through the first mile much faster than their goal pace. This is a bad idea. Their reason behind doing this is to build a cushion to allow for when they slow later in the race, and their strategy becomes self-fulfilling. They have to slow in the second half of the race because they've gone into *oxygen debt*. Oxygen debt doesn't demonstrate how mentally tough they are; it is an unforgiving physiological fact of life. As a result, their overall time is slower than if they had run at an even pace.

DEFINITION

When you run so fast that you can't take in enough oxygen to meet your muscles' needs, you've gone into **oxygen debt.** When this happens, you either have to slow down or stop running. You can avoid going into oxygen debt by having the right goal pace, and then running that pace from the start of the race.

Running the second half of a race faster than the first half is called running **negative splits.**

Your finishing sprint in the last few hundred yards of a race is your **kick.**

In races of 5K to 10K, when you're working right at your VO_2 max, you have a very small margin of error. If you run more than 10 seconds per mile faster than your VO_2 max pace, then you're running at a pace that you can sustain for at most 2 miles, usually much less. Trouble is, you still have at least a mile to go. So you're going to have to slow way down, and you're really going to hurt. It's not uncommon for runners to have to slow by more than 30 seconds per mile in the last mile of a 5K when they've started too quickly.

In these short races, I sometimes start out a little bit more slowly than my goal pace. I give myself the first few minutes of the race to build gradually. For the first few minutes, I might be running at 5 to 10 seconds per mile slower than my goal pace. This slower start helps my heart and muscles better adapt to the sudden shock of running so quickly.

Then when all systems are firing, I can take off. Running an even pace is physically the most efficient way to race, but trying to run *negative splits* provides a tremendous psychological boost. You're passing other runners pretty much the whole way.

If you've ever run a race and been passed by someone in the last mile, you know how disconcerting it can be. You're trying as hard as you can, and this runner is just blowing by you. There's nothing you can do. When I run negative splits, I like to key on a runner about 100 yards ahead of me. I'll focus on chasing him down and pulling him in gradually, and then I pass him quickly to demoralize him and move on to my next target.

Running at an even pace or at negative splits leaves you better prepared for your *kick*. How good a kick you'll have at the end of a 5K, 8K, or 10K depends a lot on how intelligently you ran the race. If you haven't gone out too quickly, then you'll still be running aerobically. This means that you can start your kick from farther out than if you've gone into oxygen debt. If you have good natural speed, you can shave several seconds from your finishing time with a good, long kick.

Your body can run anaerobically for about 300 yards, so that's the farthest away from the finish line that you should launch your sprint. If you've started the race too fast and have slowed during the second half of the race, you're going to have a tough time kicking for more than 50 to 100 yards.

Sample Eight-Week 5K and 8K/10K Training Schedules

Following are two training schedules, one for building up to a 5K and one for building up to an 8K or 10K. Here's the fine print on these schedules:

- They assume that you can manage the first week's training. If you're not at that level yet, build your mileage until you are.

- Don't run so much or so hard the rest of the week that you can't complete the listed workouts. They are the ones that will spur your improvement.

 TRAINING TIP

During your recovery between intervals, keep moving rather than standing bent over. Moving around helps to clear some of the waste products that built up when you were running hard, so you'll be more ready for the next interval. Jog slowly or at least walk.

- Try not to miss any of the key workouts, but don't try to "make up" missed ones. Just keep going through the schedule.

- If you miss the key workouts two weeks in a row, postpone your goal race by two weeks, and pick up the schedule where you left off.

- The speed workouts are in terms of meters. If you don't want to run speed work on the track, translate miles to minutes, and do the workouts on the road or trail.

- The schedules include races before your goal race. Enter these to get used to what racing feels like.

- Don't run to exhaustion within five days of your goal race.

RULES OF THE ROAD

When should you not complete a speed workout? Stop immediately if you have sharp pain anywhere below your waist. Also, if you do the first half of a workout and are running 15 seconds or more slower per mile than usual and there's no obvious reason why, such as bad weather, you're probably overly fatigued from your training.

The speed workouts are in runner shorthand, specifying the number, distance, and pace for the workout. For example, 4 × 800 meters at 5K goal pace means to do 4 intervals of 800 meters each at your per mile goal pace for 5K, with the proper recovery between the intervals. Remember, a standard outdoor track is 400 meters around, so 800 meters equals 2 laps. Also, keep in mind that an 8K/10K goal pace is 10 to 15 seconds per mile slower than a 5K race pace. Finally, before starting these training schedules, your minimum weekly mileage should be 15 miles for the 5K and 25 miles for the 8K or 10K.

Eight-Week 5K Training Schedule

	Day 1	Day 2	Day 3	Day 4	Day 5	Day 6	Day 7
Week 1	Rest	Short easy run, followed by 8–12 striders	Short easy run or cross-training	4 × 800 meters at 10 seconds slower per mile than 5K goal pace	Rest or cross-training	Rest	Long run: 4 miles
Week 2	Rest	Short easy run, followed by 8–12 striders	Short easy run or cross-training	4 × 800 meters at 5K goal pace	Rest or cross-training	Rest	Long run: 5 miles
Week 3	Rest	Short easy run, followed by 8–12 striders	Short easy run or cross-training	3 × 1200 meters at 5K goal pace	Rest or cross-training	Rest	Long run: 5 miles
Week 4	Rest	Short easy run, followed by 8–12 striders	Short easy run or cross-training	3 × 1600 meters at 5 to 10 seconds slower per mile than 5K goal pace	Rest or cross-training	Rest	Long run: 6 miles
Week 5	Rest	Short easy run, followed by 8–12 striders	Short easy run or cross-training	3 × 1600 meters at 5K goal pace	Rest or cross-training	Rest	Long run: 6 miles
Week 6	Rest	Short easy run, followed by 8 striders	4 × 800 meters at 5K goal pace	Rest or cross-training	Short easy run	Rest	5K Practice Race
Week 7	Rest	Short easy run, followed by 8–12 striders	Short easy run or cross-training	2 × 1600 meters at 5K goal pace	Rest or cross-training	Rest	Long run: 5 miles
Week 8	Rest	Short easy run, followed by 8 striders	4 × 800 meters at 5K goal pace	Rest or cross-training	Short easy run	Rest	Goal 5K Race

Eight-Week 8K/10K Training Schedule

	Day 1	Day 2	Day 3	Day 4	Day 5	Day 6	Day 7
Week 1	Rest	Short easy run, followed by 8–12 striders	Short easy run or cross-training	4 × 800 meters at 5K goal pace	Rest or cross-training	Rest	Long run: 5 miles
Week 2	Rest	Short easy run, followed by 8–12 striders	Short easy run or cross-training	3 × 1,200 meters at 8K/10K goal pace	Rest or cross-training	Rest	Long run: 6 miles
Week 3	Rest	Short easy run, followed by 8–12 striders	Short easy run or cross-training	3 × 1,200 meters at 5K goal pace	Rest or cross-training	Rest	Long run: 7 miles
Week 4	Rest	Short easy run, followed by 8–12 striders	Short easy run or cross-training	3 × 1,600 meters at 8K/10K goal pace	Rest or cross-training	Rest	Long run: 8 miles
Week 5	Rest	Short easy run, followed by 8–12 striders	Short easy run or cross-training	2 × 2,000 meters at 8K/10K goal pace	Rest or cross-training	Rest	Long run: 8 miles
Week 6	Rest	Short easy run, followed by 8 striders	4 × 800 meters at 5K goal pace	Rest or cross-training	Short easy run	Rest	5K Practice Race
Week 7	Rest	Short easy run, followed by 8–12 striders	Short easy run or cross-training	2 × 2,400 meters at 8K/10K goal pace	Rest or cross-training	Rest	Long run: 6 miles
Week 8	Rest	Short easy run, followed by 8 striders	4 × 800 meters at 5K goal pace	Rest or cross-training	Short easy run	Rest	Goal 8K/10K Race

The Least You Need to Know

- To race your best, pick a target distance, and do workouts relevant to the demands of that distance.
- The most important aspect of running a faster 5K or 10K is boosting your VO_2 max.
- Speed workouts at about your 5K race pace are the best way to improve your VO_2 max.
- If you start 5Ks and 10Ks by running faster than your race pace, you'll have to slow dramatically in the second half of the race.
- The best race plan is to run an even pace until near the end, then kick to the finish.

Middle Ground: 15Ks to Half-Marathons

In This Chapter

- Why more runners should consider 15Ks and half-marathons
- What your lactate threshold is and why it matters
- Prerace eating guidelines
- A 10-week training schedule for 15K and half-marathon races

Back when I tried to win the Boston Marathon every year, an important part of my preparation involved a trip to Washington, D.C. No, it wasn't so that I could ask President Carter to deny the visas of foreign runners who I thought might beat me. I went there to run the Cherry Blossom 10-miler two weeks before the Boston Marathon to get a good gauge of my race fitness.

Now that I don't race the marathon anymore, races of 10 miles or more have become my marathons. They're the longest races I run in a year, and I build up to them like I used to prepare for marathons. In this chapter, I'll show you why I think more runners should strike this middle ground of 15Ks and half-marathons, and I'll show you how to train for these races.

The Rodney Dangerfields of Races

Races of 15K (9.3 miles) through the half-marathon (13.1 miles) get no respect. Even though the half-marathon is growing in popularity more than any other distance, it doesn't even get its own name; it's just half of another distance. Imagine if people called 5Ks "half-10Ks."

This range of races, which also includes 10-milers and 20K (12.4 miles), is almost never the focus of a runner's races. Runners usually use these races as *tune-up races* a month or so before a marathon. Or some runners will run one of these races at the beginning of a racing season to build strength, and then drop down in distance to 5Ks and 10Ks for the rest of the season. But you almost never hear a runner say, "This fall, my goal is to be the best 10-mile runner I can be."

> **DEFINITION**
>
> **Tune-up races** are shorter races that you use as part of your training for a longer race. Marathoners tune up with 10-milers, 10K runners tune up with 5Ks, and 5K runners tune up with 1-mile races.

That's too bad. These hybrid distances can be some of the most satisfying in running. They're plenty long, so you're not going to get through one by running a few miles a few times a week, as you could with a 5K. But they're not so long that they're going to knock you down for too long. Most of the soreness and lingering fatigue that people have from marathons comes from what happens after 18 or 20 miles.

> **FOOTNOTES**
>
> The fastest times for distances from road races are officially called world bests, rather than world records, because of the great variation among road race courses. When this book went to press, the men's and women's world bests for 10 miles were 44:23, by Haile Gebrselassie of Ethiopia, and 50:54, by Lornah Kiplagat of Kenya. That's 4:26 per mile for Gebrselassie and 5:05 per mile for Kiplagat.

Should you try a 15K, 10-miler, or a half-marathon? Why not? For people who are thinking about trying a marathon someday, building up to one of these races is a good idea. You learn the routine of training for longer distances by gradually extending your distance. Anyone running a marathon should have experience with other races first. These longer races will give you a better idea of what you're going to experience if you try to tackle a marathon.

If you usually don't run farther than 5 miles, keying on one of these races is a good motivation to extend your distance. In this case, ignore the training schedule at the end of this chapter and make finishing the distance respectably your goal the first time around. To do that, increase the distance of your long run by 1 mile 2 out of every 3 weeks. For 15Ks and 10-milers, work up to running that far 2 weeks before the race. Take it easy for the next two weeks, and then run the race at a strong but reasonable pace that you know you can maintain to the end. If you're going to do a half-marathon, then build up to 10 to 12 miles at a time, again doing your last long run 2 weeks before the race.

But if you've been running a bit more and think that you can not only cover the distance, but also run a good notch faster than on your usual training runs, you can improve your performance at these distances by entering the strange world of the lactate threshold.

Beyond the Lactate Threshold

Put on your lab coats: it's time for a little science lesson. As you know by this point in the book, glycogen, a form of stored carbohydrate, is your body's preferred source of fuel for aerobic exercise. The faster you run, the more glycogen your body burns compared to how much fat it burns. Like any chemical-burning process, the process of burning glycogen generates by-products. Burn paper, and you get smoke. Burn glycogen, and you get lactate. Lactate is the by-product of your body burning carbohydrates.

You've probably heard about lactic acid. For our purposes here, that's the same thing as lactate. Have you ever tried to sprint all-out for more than a few hundred yards? Remember how at the end of the sprint your muscles felt as though they were on fire? That's because there was a lot of lactate circulating in your system from all the carbohydrates that were suddenly being burned to power you down the track. So much lactate was being produced that your body couldn't clear it from your blood, so your muscles stung.

Some people think that you're damaging your muscles when you expose them to lactate. That's wrong. You're always producing lactate—when you're running easy, when you're walking, even when you're sitting. When you burn carbohydrates, as you almost always do, you produce lactate. Your muscles don't ache at these low levels of effort because the rate of lactate entering your blood is equal to the rate at which it's removed.

As you move up the intensity scale from walking to easy running, you produce more lactate, but your body also increases the rate at which it removes lactate from your blood. When you exercise above a certain intensity, however, the rate at which you produce lactate is greater than the rate at which your body can clear it. The lactate concentration rises in your muscles and blood, and suddenly your effort feels much harder. At this point, you've reached your *lactate threshold*.

DEFINITION

The exercise intensity at which you produce more lactate than your body can remove is your **lactate threshold.** Having a high lactate threshold means that you can maintain a faster pace for a longer distance before you have to slow. An experienced runner's lactate threshold is approximately his or her 15K to half-marathon race pace.

You're probably thinking, "Thanks for the biochemistry lesson, but what does this have to do with running a 10-mile race?" Remember the basic race-training principle that I laid down last chapter: if you want to complete a race, you have to be able to cover the distance. If you also want to *race* the distance, then you should do workouts that improve your capacities to handle the limiting factors on your performance in that distance. For 5Ks and 10Ks, that meant doing workouts to max out your VO_2 max. For 15Ks to half-marathons, that means improving your lactate threshold.

Once you get past the hump of being able to cover the distance without great fatigue, the limiting factor on how fast you can run the 15K to the half-marathon is your lactate threshold. In fact, your race pace for the 15K to the half-marathon is roughly equal to your lactate threshold. Go faster than that, and you'll start accumulating lactate in your blood. You can exceed your lactate threshold in shorter races, such as an 8K, but 15Ks to half-marathons last 1 to 2 hours for most runners, and you just can't run that fast for that long.

To improve, then, you need to increase your lactate threshold. When you do that, your lactate threshold occurs at a higher percentage of your VO_2 max. So with the right training, you can push your 15K to half-marathon pace closer to that of your 5K pace; that is, you can make better use of your basic aerobic fitness. You can run faster before you start accumulating lactate.

Timing Is Everything: All About Tempo Runs

Improving your lactate threshold is pretty straightforward: you train at or slightly above your lactate threshold. In the training schedule, I call this speed your LT (lactate threshold) pace. Training at your LT pace pushes back the point at which lactate accumulates, allowing you to maintain a faster pace for these midrange races.

FOOTNOTES

When this book went to press, the men's and women's world bests for the half-marathon were 58:33, by Sammy Wanjiru of Kenya, and 1:05:44, by Susan Chepkemei of Kenya.

How do you know what this pace is for you? If you already race in 15K to half-marathons, your race pace for those races is your LT pace. If you haven't raced much, you can still approximate what your LT pace is. If you've run a 10K, your LT pace will be about 20 seconds slower per mile than your 10K race pace. If you've only run a 5K, your LT pace is probably around 30 seconds slower per mile than your 5K race pace is, but you should go run a 10K first anyway before trying to race a 15K to half-marathon.

Regardless of what pace you choose to shoot for, keep this guideline in mind: your effort during LT workouts should feel "comfortably hard." You should feel as though you're working at a high level that you can sustain. If you were to increase your pace by 10 seconds or more per mile, you would have to slow within a few minutes.

It's important to run as close to the right pace for as much of your LT workouts as possible. Remember what I told you in the last chapter about training to improve your VO_2 max: the biggest gains come from doing the workout in that small window where you're most stressing the systems that you want to improve.

 TRAINING TIP

A good way to know if you're at the right intensity during an LT run is a modified version of the talk test. You should be able to say a few words coherently at a normal conversational speed. If you can only blurt out a word at a time, you're going too fast. If you can speak in complete sentences, you're going too slow.

When you do LT workouts, you'll probably think in the first mile that you should be going faster. After all, you're not all that much out of breath. Stick to your pace. The point of the workout is to run it all at your LT pace. That's different than starting out too fast, and then slowing in the second half of your LT workout. In that case, you might average the right pace for the whole workout, but never run any part of it at the right intensity. That kind of workout won't improve your LT as much.

The classic workout to improve your lactate threshold is the *tempo run*, a continuous run of 20 to 40 minutes at LT pace. An example of a tempo run workout is a 2-mile warm-up, a 4-mile run at your LT pace, and a short cool-down jog. You can also do

LT intervals. In these workouts, you do two or three intervals of a fairly long distance at LT pace, jog easily for 25 to 50 percent of the duration of the interval, and then repeat the sequence. For example, after warming up, you would run 2 miles at your LT pace, jog for 5 minutes, run 2 miles at your LT pace, and then do a cool-down jog.

DEFINITION

A **tempo run** is a run of 20 to 40 minutes at about your 15K to half-marathon race pace. It builds your ability to sustain a hard pace for a long time.

In the training schedule, I start you with LT intervals to get you used to the workouts and to help you learn what your LT pace feels like. Once you're familiar with your LT pace, I have you do tempo runs. Tempo runs are better because you become more accustomed to concentrating for an extended period while you're running hard. This kind of training helps you mentally in your races.

At first, you should do LT workouts on the track or other accurately measured courses so that you have a way of checking your pace. After a few LT workouts, you should have a feel for the pace. Studies have shown that most runners can accurately produce that "comfortably hard" level of effort on their own once they have learned it. This frees you to do your LT workouts on the roads or trails. Doing a 5-mile tempo run on the track can get pretty boring, after all. Doing some of your LT workouts away from the track is an especially good idea if you'll be running a hilly race because you'll be more used to running LT pace over a variety of terrain.

TRAINING TIP

If you do your tempo runs with someone else, take turns sharing the lead. Switch positions every mile. If you're sore the day after a tempo run, then you ran it too fast.

Prerace Noshin'

Before a short race like a 5K, what you don't eat is often more important than what you do eat—you're not at risk of depleting your muscles' fuel stores, but too much grub in the gut can cause you stomach trouble in the race. Things get a little more complicated with races in the 15K to half-marathon range.

After all, even in a 15K, you're going to be out there for more than an hour; in the case of a half-marathon, you might be on the road for two or more hours. That's a long time to be working at a high level of effort. So you need to start the race well fueled. I'm not saying you need to go through the elaborate dietary manipulations that marathoners do in the last days before their race (see Chapter 22), but if you want to run your best in one of these races, you can't be nonchalant about what's going 'round the training table. Be sure for the few days before to emphasize the sort of high-carbohydrate diet I detailed in Chapter 13. (That is, save the trip to the all-you-can-eat sushi bar for another time.)

On the morning of these races, I always eat a light, complex-carbohydrate breakfast, just to be sure my glycogen reserves are topped off. Toast with Smart Balance buttery spread is my first choice for one of these prerace meals. I'm also a Cheerios eater, with skim milk. When I'm traveling to races, I may rely on bagels or bananas. Most people can get away with eating plain, high-carbohydrate foods like toast or a bagel two to three hours before the start without encountering stomach problems during the race. Plenty of water and 8 to 16 ounces of sports drink in the two hours before the race helps you avoid dehydration and the resulting muscle fatigue.

RULES OF THE ROAD

Be sure to drink plenty of fluids during your 15K to half-marathon races. You're going to be out there for more than an hour and can get dehydrated easily.

Sample Ten-Week 15K/Half-Marathon Training Schedule

Before starting this training schedule, be sure to review the long list of training advice that I gave before the training schedules in the last chapter. Everything I said there about how to structure your training weeks for 5K and 10K races applies here, too. Here are some additional guidelines for races of 15K to the half-marathon:

- The schedule assumes that your weekly mileage is at 30 miles when you begin the schedule.

- The schedule assumes that you have already completed a 15K to half-marathon race and now want to improve your time.

- The schedule assumes that you have run a 5K to 10K race within a few months of starting the schedule so that you have a way of setting a 15K/half-marathon goal pace. Remember that your LT pace is equal to your goal pace for the 15K/half-marathon, 20 seconds per mile slower than your 10K race pace, or 30 seconds per mile slower than your 5K race pace.

- The schedule assumes that you can complete the first week of training without it killing you.

- You run four workouts in the schedule faster than LT pace. You'll run these workouts at fairly close to 10K race pace. These workouts will help to improve your VO_2 max, which is also important for racing a good 15K or half-marathon.

- The schedule includes two tune-up races, the first either a 5K or 8K and the second either an 8K or 10K. These races will also improve your VO_2 max. Use these races to practice your race routine and to monitor your progress. Don't worry if your 5K time isn't what you think it should be. The focus of your training is on improving your lactate threshold, not your VO_2 max.

- On race day, warm up with half a mile to a mile of easy jogging and a few striders at LT pace to remind yourself what the pace feels like. Finish your warm-up no more than 10 minutes before the start, and then keep moving to keep your heart rate elevated.

- Run as even a pace as you can in your race. Starting too quickly will push you beyond your lactate threshold and not allow you to use your training. From the start of the race, try to get in that pace that you've run so many times in your workouts.

After your race, run easily for one to two weeks, and then pick a new goal to start working toward.

FOOTNOTES

The world bests for 15K are 41:29, by Felix Limo of Kenya and Deriba Merga of Ethiopia, and 46:28, by Tirunesh Dibaba of Ethiopia.

Ten-Week 15K/Half-Marathon Training Schedule

	Day 1	Day 2	Day 3	Day 4	Day 5	Day 6	Day 7
Week 1	Rest	Short easy run, followed by 8–12 striders	Rest or cross-training	2 × 3,200 meters (2 mi.) at LT pace	Short easy run	Rest	Long run: 8 miles
Week 2	Rest	Short easy run, followed by 8–12 striders	Rest or cross-training	2 × 4,000 meters (2.5 mi.) at LT pace	Short easy run	Rest	Long run: 10 miles
Week 3	Rest	Short easy run, followed by 8–12 striders	Rest or cross-training	6,400 meters (4 mi.) at LT pace	Short easy run	Rest	Long run: 12 miles
Week 4	Rest	Short easy run, followed by 8–12 striders	Rest or cross-training	4 × 1,600 meters at 15 seconds faster per mile than LT pace	Short easy run	Rest	Long run: 10 miles
Week 5	Rest	Short easy run, followed by 8–12 striders	Rest or cross-training	8,000 meters (5 mi.) at LT pace	Short easy run	Rest	Long run: 13 miles
Week 6	Rest	Short easy run, followed by 8 striders	2 × 1,600 meters at 15 seconds faster per mile than LT pace	Rest or cross-training	Short easy run	Rest	5K or 8K Practice Race
Week 7	Rest	Short easy run, followed by 8–12 striders	Rest or cross-training	8,000 meters (5 mi.) at LT pace	Short easy run	Rest	Long run: 15 miles
Week 8	Rest	Short easy run, followed by 8 striders	2 × 1,600 meters at 15 seconds faster per mile than LT pace	Rest or cross-training	Short easy run	Rest	8K or 10K Practice Race
Week 9	Rest	Short easy run, followed by 8–12 striders	Rest or cross-training	3 × 1,600 meters at 15 seconds faster per mile than LT pace	Short easy run	Rest	Long run: 10 miles
Week 10	Rest	Short easy run, followed by 8 striders	3,200 meters (2 mi.) at LT pace	Rest or cross-training	Short easy run	Rest	Goal 15K/Half-Marathon Race

The Least You Need to Know

- More runners should consider doing races in the 15K to half-marathon range.
- If you haven't run one of these races before, run one to complete it before you try to race it.
- Your lactate threshold is the pace at which you begin to accumulate lactic acid in your blood.
- When you race a 15K to half-marathon, you're running at your lactate threshold.
- The best way to improve your performance in 15K to half-marathon races is to improve your lactate threshold.
- The best way to improve your lactate threshold is to do runs of 20 to 40 minutes at your lactate threshold pace.

In It for the Long Run: The Marathon

In This Chapter

- History of the marathon
- Deciding whether the marathon is right for you
- How to train for your first marathon

The marathon is the crown jewel of running. Some have called it the ultimate race. I made it the focus of my running—okay, the focus of my life—for 15 years. The challenge of running 26.2 miles is something that no other race can provide.

You can't roll out of bed and run a marathon. Finishing one is a lot of hard work, not just during the race, but in all those miles you log just to get to the starting line. And yet, almost anyone can finish a marathon. Grandmothers do it; cancer patients do it; Oprah Winfrey, Will Ferrell, and U.S. presidents and vice presidents have done it. It's not easy, but it's simple. In this chapter, I'll show you the basic training that you need to complete if you want to proudly wear those crown jewels.

A Little History

I told you before about how your body can usually store only enough glycogen to fuel about 20 miles of running. And yet marathons are 26.2 miles long. What gives?

The legend of the origin of the marathon goes like this: in 490 B.C.E., a Greek messenger named Pheidippides ran the 24 miles from the Plains of Marathon to Athens to announce that despite great odds, the Athenian army had defeated the invading Persians. Upon reaching Athens, Pheidippides said, "Rejoice. We conquer!", collapsed, and died. When the modern Olympics began in Athens in 1896, organizers included a 24-mile race from Marathon to Athens to honor this great moment in Greek history.

FOOTNOTES

When this book went to press, the men's and women's world marathon bests were 2:03:59, by Haile Gebrselassie of Ethiopia, and 2:15:25, by Paula Radcliffe of Great Britain. That's 4:44 per mile for Gebrselassie and 5:10 per mile for Radcliffe. The American record for men is 2:05:38, by Khalid Khannouchi. The American record for women is 2:19:36, by Deena Kastor.

Did this really happen? No one knows for sure, but the general consensus is that like any good story from antiquity, there's some embellishment stirred into the truth so well that it's hard to separate the two, and it's more fun not to bother anyway. There was a Greek messenger of the time named Pheidippides, but no contemporary record of him producing such a great deathbed quote exists. Nonetheless, the legend has its own resonance. At the 20-mile mark of his first marathon, Frank Shorter turned to a runner next to him and said, "Why couldn't have Pheidippides have died at 20 miles?"

The long race caught on after the 1896 Olympics. The first Boston Marathon was held the next year. Early marathons weren't standardized—they were 24 or 25 miles, depending on how long a course turned out to be. Early in the twentieth century, the starting line of a marathon in England was moved back so that the queen could watch from Windsor Castle. The resulting distance was 26 miles, 385 yards, or 26.2 miles, which is now the official distance for a marathon.

Caveat Runner

Even if you're all fired up to run a marathon, you have to tread carefully. You're going to be doing training runs that are substantially longer than anything you've ever done before. If you don't become an expert at listening to your body's response to the training, you might not even make it to the starting line on race day. It's not uncommon for runners to have to postpone or give up their marathon hopes because the training necessary to do one is too much for their current level of fitness.

I think you should be a regular runner for at least a year before starting to train for a marathon. You need that amount of time for basic strength building to get your muscles, tendons, bones, and ligaments used to the stress of running. You also need to be in a good training routine, having figured out how best to make your running work with the rest of your life.

A lot of the new breed of marathoners, the ones who do them to raise money for charities, don't meet this general guideline. Many of them, in fact, haven't even started running when they sign up for a marathon six months away. And despite this lack of background, many of them meet their goal of finishing a marathon. But just because you *can* do something doesn't necessarily mean you *should* do it. (Otherwise, for example, why not stay out partying until 3 A.M. every night this week and go to work at your normal time?)

These new runners' enthusiasm is admirable, even enviable. But I stand by my one-year-of-running rule. You're going to get so much more out of your marathon experience if you start the training with a solid base. More important, it's just not good for your long-term running career to have your initial exposure to it be training for one of the most challenging distances in the sport. One thing that's not often mentioned about runners who finish a marathon six months after taking up running is that they're more likely to become former runners than those who take a more gradual approach.

After all, if you've climbed Mount Everest soon after becoming a mountaineer, why waste your time on Little Round Top afterward? My main point in this book is that running is a lifetime sport, not something, like learning to tango, that you cross off your Bucket List and then move on to the next item. If you take the time to build your base and remain open to the many challenges that running affords, you're more likely to want to sample all the racing distances at some point. And you'll be better prepared for them. Trust me on this one—there will still be plenty of marathons a year from now if you decide you want to try one.

A Run or a Race?

The fastest male marathoners in the world run 26.2 miles at faster than 5:00 per mile. The fastest female marathoners in the world run 26.2 miles at faster than 5:30 per mile. I think we can safely say that these people are racing the marathon. That was certainly how I went about it. For me, the challenge wasn't just running 26.2 miles; it was seeing how fast I could run 26.2 miles. When I ran marathons at 5:00 per mile, I was running about a minute faster per mile than my usual training pace.

Most people, however, are running the marathon just to conquer the distance. I'm all in favor of that approach. Remember the basic principle from Chapter 20: the first step to participating in any race is being able to cover the distance. The longer the race, the more that negotiating the distance becomes a limiting factor in performance. Almost anyone can run 1 mile faster than their regular training pace. Almost no one can run 50 miles faster than their regular training pace.

For your first marathon, your goal should be to finish. Trust me, that's more than enough challenge for one race. If you define a race as trying to run the best that you can for a set distance on a given day, then just finishing your first marathon is a race. After you've done one or two marathons, then you can try to reduce your time.

Don't Hit "The Wall"

You might hear a runner explaining why she dropped out of a 5K by saying, "I hit The Wall." Well, now she's got two strikes against her: not only did she not finish her race, but she's misusing runner lingo. Get her a copy of this book, and quick! When you get tired in a short race because you're breathing so hard, that's fatigue. When you're doing a run of 90 minutes or more and you're feeling fine, and then all of a sudden, bam, every step is a major production and your pace gets way slower, that's *The Wall.*

DEFINITION

When you've run so far that you've depleted your muscles' glycogen stores, you hit **The Wall.** Most runners crash into it at about the 20-mile mark of the marathon.

Most people can store enough glycogen in their muscles to fuel about 18 to 20 miles of running. When you run long distances, your body senses that it's getting low on glycogen. It wants to preserve that glycogen, so it starts to burn more fat. At this point, you're able to maintain your pace, so you keep running. Your body has to keep doling out its precious glycogen stores, and it starts burning more and more fat.

By now, you can keep up your pace, but you have to work a little harder to do so because fat doesn't burn as efficiently as glycogen when it comes to fueling your running. But you keep running because you were idiotic enough to listen to me when I told you how great the marathon is. Now your glycogen stores are getting very low, and you're burning more and more fat.

That wouldn't be all bad, except for this fact: fat burns on a flame of glycogen. To keep running at your normal pace, you need at least enough glycogen to help burn the fat. But you've pretty much used it all up. You're primarily burning fat, and fat takes a lot more oxygen to burn than glycogen does. As a result, you have to slow down dramatically, sometimes by more than two minutes per mile. You will want nothing more than to lie down by the side of the road.

To top it off, you've also depleted the small amount of glycogen that's stored in your liver. Your liver is supposed to feed this glycogen into your bloodstream to maintain your blood sugar well enough to feed your brain glucose. When this process starts breaking down, you feel woozy, light-headed, uncoordinated. Great! You want to lie down by the side of the road, and now you're getting so uncoordinated that you just might have your wish fulfilled. You've got as many as 8 miles to go. Unless you've got incredible willpower, you're a leading candidate to join the *DNF* list.

DEFINITION

If you did not finish a race, you're a **DNF.** DNF is also a verb, as in, "How did you do?" "I DNFed."

So how do people ever survive marathons? First and most important, they train. Long runs improve your body's ability to store glycogen. Runners who do marathon training can store more than twice as much glycogen in their muscles as untrained people. Your body can get more fuel from the food that you eat when you train properly.

Also, marathoners start their marathons at a pace they know that they can maintain to the finish. The faster you run, the more glycogen you burn. Going out too fast in a marathon is a huge mistake, because even at a reasonable pace you're going to need every last bit of glycogen that you can get. One trick that runners do to make sure that they don't go out too fast in the marathon is to run the first mile one minute slower than the pace that they hope to average for the distance.

TRAINING TIP

Do your long runs at your normal training pace. A good habit is to do the second half of your run 10 seconds per mile faster than the first half. This strategy helps you to start the run slow enough so that you'll be able to finish it, and picking up the pace a bit at the end teaches you how to concentrate when you get tired.

Even if you do the right training and pace yourself well in the marathon, The Wall can be pretty daunting. But what you do in the few days before the marathon can push it past the finish line.

The Rest Is Easy

If you look closely at the training schedules in the two previous chapters, you might have noticed that I have you doing less work as your goal race nears, not more. That's especially the case in the marathon schedule—your last long run is three weeks before your marathon. Whatever happened to use it or lose it?

Preparing for a top effort isn't like cramming for a test or meeting a deadline at work. It takes time for your body to get the benefits of a training session. The day after a long run, you feel tired. But two weeks later, you feel stronger. The longer your race, the more important *tapering* is.

DEFINITION

When you cut back on your training before an important race, you're **tapering.** This reduction in training allows your muscles to be able to perform on race day.

In the marathon, tapering is especially important because of the whole glycogen-storage issue. When you taper, then obviously you're not draining your glycogen supply as much. But because of your long runs, you've tricked your muscles into thinking that they had better be ready anytime, anywhere to fuel you for hours. So even though you're barely running, they're still suspicious that something is up, and they keep stockpiling glycogen at a high level. This gives you a larger gas tank on race day.

Notice what I said—when you taper before a race, you're barely running. That's a lot different than not running at all. If you follow the tapering plan in the marathon schedule, you'll maintain the benefits of your hard work. Once you become fit, you don't have to do as much running to maintain that fitness, at least for a while. So in the three weeks before your marathon, you can, and should, gradually reduce your training.

RULES OF THE ROAD

Postpone your marathon if in the last two weeks before it you develop a cold that lasts for more than three days. Your immune system is depressed after a marathon anyway, so the two things together could really knock you back.

Spaghetti for Dinner Again?

In Chapter 13, I told you that eating isn't the key to running well. That's true. A good diet merely allows you to get the most from your running; it doesn't take the place of running. But I also told you that there's nothing you can eat to make you a better runner. Confession time: that's not entirely true. In the few days before a marathon, you can help to push The Wall a few more miles back by *carboloading*.

DEFINITION

Increasing the percentage of your calories that comes from carbohydrates to more than 65 percent in the few days before a long race is **carboloading.**

Carboloading is often misunderstood. It doesn't mean looking at the last three days before a marathon as an excuse to hit every all-you-can-eat buffet in town. You're running less; you don't need to eat much more than you usually do. What matters is increasing the percentage of your calories that come from carbohydrates to more than 65 percent, not just chowing down on everything in sight.

Carboloading works for the same reason that tapering works. Your muscles have become trained to store more glycogen. You're tapering, so you're not running much. Good—you're barely dipping into your fuel stores. Simultaneously, you're eating more carbohydrates than usual. Your muscles love it! They soak up the stuff. Do it right, and you can store an additional few hundred calories. That's worth an extra 3 miles of running!

TRAINING TIP

If you can, avoid the spaghetti feeds held the night before marathons. You'll use up a lot of mental energy at these loud, boisterous affairs. Have your prerace dinner in a quiet setting with family and friends. You'll have several hours the next day to spend with the runners.

The key to carboloading is to emphasize the right foods. Concentrate on basing all of your meals in the three days before a marathon on high-carb foods, especially the complex ones. Most runners eat pasta when they're carboloading, but rice and other grains are good, too. As I pointed out in Chapter 13, be sure that what you think is high carb really is. Fettuccini alfredo is pasta, but it's pasta in a heavy cream sauce. If you're going to eat pasta, go with the light red sauces.

On the morning of the race, you definitely want to eat a light breakfast a few hours before the start. Yes, this will probably mean getting up ridiculously early. But you're probably not going to be able sleep all that well, anyway, because of nerves. Guess what? It's carbs again! A few hundred calories of easily digestible high-carb foods, such as a bagel and a banana, will top off your liver glycogen stores and help you maintain a better pace in the last few miles.

 TRAINING TIP

Use your long runs to experiment with what prerace foods work best for you. Because you'll probably be doing your marathon at around the same pace as your long runs, if you find a food or foods that agree with you before a training run, they'll work fine for you on marathon day, too.

Sample Twelve-Week Training Schedule for First-Time Marathoners

To finish a marathon, the least you need to do is still pretty darned much. There's no way to get around the necessity of long runs—that's why they're the focus of this marathon training schedule. As a first-time marathoner, your goal should be to cover the distance. The way to do that is to gradually build the distance that you can cover without having to slow dramatically in the last few miles.

These long runs are probably longer than you've ever run. They're all the training stress that your body needs, so this schedule doesn't include any speed workouts. At this point, they'll just get in the way of recovering from your long runs. But you will be doing striders. Most weeks, you'll be doing them twice. That's because when you do nothing but train for marathons, it's easy for your form to deteriorate. You're always just shuffling along, not moving through a full range of motion. Striders will help you to improve your form, and they're a fun contrast to the long runs.

The schedule doesn't have you running a long run every week. That would be too much because your long run starts getting up there in distance. On the weeks when you're not going long, I want you to do a hilly 10-mile run on the day that you usually do your long run. This run will help to build leg strength and will give your VO_2 max a bit of a boost.

With two weeks to go, try to run a 15K to half-marathon race. Don't worry so much about your pace as about experiencing a race atmosphere. A lot of first-time marathoners train in isolation for months, never enter a race, and freak out when suddenly they're surrounded by thousands of others in a marathon.

RULES OF THE ROAD

After you finish your marathon, keep moving so that you won't get as stiff and sore. Get something to drink. Put on dry clothes. If you can, go for a walk later in the day. You'll feel better.

As with the training schedules in the previous two chapters, this one assumes that you can handle the first week's training. If you've gone on a 12-mile run within the last 2 weeks, you can. If you haven't, take your time building up to that level, and then report back when you're ready.

Twelve-Week Training Schedule for First-Time Marathoners

	Day 1	Day 2	Day 3	Day 4	Day 5	Day 6	Day 7
Week 1	Rest	Short easy run, followed by 8–12 striders	Rest or cross-training	Medium run: 7 miles	Short easy run, followed by 8–12 striders	Rest	Long run: 14 miles
Week 2	Rest	Short easy run, followed by 8–12 striders	Rest or cross-training	Medium run: 7 miles	Short easy run, followed by 8–12 striders	Rest	Long run: 15 miles
Week 3	Rest	Short easy run, followed by 8–12 striders	Rest or cross-training	Medium run: 8 miles	Short easy run, followed by 8–12 striders	Rest	Long run: 16 miles
Week 4	Rest	Short easy run, followed by 8–12 striders	Rest or cross-training	Medium run: 8 miles	Short easy run, followed by 8–12 striders	Rest	Long run: Hilly 10 miles
Week 5	Rest	Short easy run, followed by 8–12 striders	Rest or cross-training	Medium run: 7 miles	Short easy run, followed by 8–12 striders	Rest	Long run: 18 miles
Week 6	Rest	Short easy run, followed by 8 striders	Rest or cross-training	Medium run: 9 miles	Short easy run, followed by 8–12 striders	Rest	Long run: Hilly 10 miles
Week 7	Rest	Short easy run, followed by 8–12 striders	Rest or cross-training	Medium run: 7 miles	Short easy run, followed by 8–12 striders	Rest	Long run: 20 miles
Week 8	Rest	Short easy run, followed by 8 striders	Rest or cross-training	Medium run: 9 miles	Short easy run, followed by 8–12 striders	Rest	Long run: Hilly 10 miles
Week 9	Rest	Short easy run, followed by 8–12 striders	Rest or cross-training	Medium run: 9 miles	Short easy run, followed by 8–12 striders	Rest	Long run: 20–22 miles

continues

Twelve-Week Training Schedule *(continued)*

	Day 1	Day 2	Day 3	Day 4	Day 5	Day 6	Day 7
Week 10	Rest	Short easy run, followed by 8 striders	Rest or cross-training	Medium run: 7 miles	Short easy run, followed by 8 striders	Rest	15K/Half-Marathon Practice Race
Week 11	Rest	Short easy run, followed by 8–12 striders	Rest or cross-training	Medium run: 9 miles	Short easy run, followed by 8–12 striders	Rest	Long run: 10 miles
Week 12	Rest	Short easy run, followed by 8 striders	Rest	Short easy run, followed by 8 striders	Rest	Rest	Marathon

The Least You Need to Know

- You don't have to run a marathon to consider yourself a runner.
- Your goal in your first marathon should be to finish.
- The key to finishing a marathon is building your weekly long run to at least 20 miles.
- Training, tapering, and carboloading help you avoid hitting The Wall.

Roots, Rocks, and Ruts: Trail Running

In This Chapter

- Why trail running is so popular
- How to run trails
- Special trail running considerations
- The difference between trail running shoes and regular running shoes
- Responsible trail running

Thanks to a few magazine covers long ago, I've been called "King of the Roads" for a couple of decades now. When people think about my running, big-city marathons and other road races come to mind.

Don't let the nickname fool you, though. Yes, nearly all of my races in the last 35 years have been on asphalt, but I started as a cross-country runner, going over hill and dale. And as I've said in earlier chapters, one of the great appeals of running for me has always been being in close touch with nature. I've long sought out trails in training. These days, a lot of other people are, too. In this chapter, I'll tell you why so many runners are turning to trails, and what you can do to make your time in the woods more rewarding.

Trees, Not Traffic

It's a sad statement that words like "sprawl" and "road rage" have become part of our everyday vocabulary. As more and more of our country gets paved over with look-alike strip malls and prefab houses, more and more people want ways to get back to nature, if only for a little while. We increasingly want the mental, even spiritual rejuvenation that the natural world brings. One offshoot of that desire is that trail running is one of the fastest-growing segments of the running scene. Trail running has enjoyed double-digit growth in participation every year for more than a decade now, and its popularity shows no signs of waning. Participation grew by more than 12 percent between 2008 and 2009. The first National Trail Running Day was held in August 2009. There's even a magazine, *Trail Runner*, devoted solely to off-road running.

What do I mean by trail running? Let me start with what I don't mean—running around the fields at your local high school or maybe on a dirt path alongside an asphalt bike path. As I said in Chapter 4, I'm all for running on soft surfaces as often as possible, but those types of "trails" aren't what I'm discussing in this chapter. Rather, I mean trails that have been cut through forests, along mountain ridges, beside streams, and so on, for the specific purpose of allowing people some refuge in natural beauty. As with some trails out in the western United States, they might be miles from civilization; or, as with some in the eastern United States, they might be located in the middle of dense cities. But they're all similar in that when you're on them, you know you're someplace special, someplace where the cars and cacophony can't touch you.

Because trail running is so distinct from "regular" running, this chapter is located in the racing section of this book. Trail running has its own ethos and its own feel. As with running a race, trail running entails special preparation if you're going to get the most from the experience. There are people who consider themselves first and foremost trail runners in the same way that other runners consider themselves first and foremost marathoners. Some of these people not only do almost all of their training on trails, but also almost all of their races off-road.

FOOTNOTES

The Western States 100-miler, held in California on the Western States Trail, is probably the most prestigious trail race. Trail runners talk about Western States with the same awe that road racers talk about the Boston Marathon.

Of course, you don't have to run trail races to be a trail runner, just like you don't have to run marathons to be a road runner. In fact, the low-key nature of trail running is another big explanation for its growing popularity. A lot of people who are really into trail running now were hard-core road runners a decade or more ago. As they aged and slowed, the appeal of seeing how fast they could run for a set distance on a road lessened. Mastering trail running has offered a new set of challenges for these runners, in an inviting atmosphere that provides even more stress relief than "normal" running does.

> **TRAINING TIP**
>
> Hills on trails are often steeper than on roads. To maintain good, erect form while running uphill on trails, imagine that you're pulling yourself up by a rope that runs right into your sternum. Swing your arms so that your hands pull this imaginary rope, and your legs will follow with the proper cadence.

Trail Technique

What's this about "mastering trail running"? Running is running, right?

My co-author, Scott Douglas, used to think so, until he took a friend up on an invitation for a 17-mile run along the Appalachian Trail. Scott was faster in road races than his friend, so he figured that, if anything, he would be holding back the entire run. Or at least that's what he figured until they got to the first downhill, and Scott tentatively baby-stepped his way down. Meanwhile, his friend looked like he had hit warp speed and was suddenly at the bottom of the hill. On the uphills, Scott got dropped almost immediately, as he struggled bent over at a near 90-degree angle while his friend smoothly glided up and over the ascent. Throw in a few momentum-stopping ankle twists (and accompanying Anglo-Saxon words), and you can start to see why Scott changed his mind. His superior fitness was no match for his friend's honed trail running ability.

> **TRAINING TIP**
>
> One way you can prepare yourself for trail running is by doing quick feet drills. These exercises will train your legs to move quickly while your feet stay close to the ground. After an easy run, run in place on a soft surface while concentrating on achieving as quick a stride cadence as you can. Build up to 4 sets of 20 seconds each.

The Glide Stride

The biggest difference between trail running and road running is the ever-changing surface on trails. Uneven ground, ruts, leaf beds, rocks and pebbles, loose dirt, hidden puddles, mud aplenty—these and other stride breakers can await you around every turn. And about those turns—they come with a lot more frequency and severity than the nice right angles you encounter when making turns on roads. All this means that you're probably going to want to alter your stride a bit when running trails so that your feet, not your face and hands, are what hit the trail.

Watch experienced trail runners, and you'll see that most of them sort of glide across the earth. They're not using the high knee lift or strong back kick successful road and track runners often employ. Instead, they're staying low to the ground so that they're better able to stabilize themselves every time their feet hit the ground.

 TRAINING TIP

Because of the extra challenges of trail running, especially the long, steep hills you're likely to encounter, establish your aerobic base first before hitting the trails. If you run on a regular basis for at least three months before doing any serious trail running, you'll be better able to run under control on trails and still enjoy the surroundings.

This adjustment to your stride, plus the curvy nature of and obstacles found on most trails, means that you're almost certainly going to run slower on trails than on roads. Don't worry about it. As I said earlier, one of the reasons that a lot of people are turning to trail running is its low-key nature. People take to the trails for a great aesthetic experience, not to set land speed records. If anything, you're likely to be so captivated by the scenery that you'll run farther than usual. And when you're making your way up a steep, rocky hill, you'll have no doubt that you're working hard enough.

Vision Quest

The other big adjustment to make in going from road running to trail running is where you look. If you're like me, when you run on the roads, you're looking around constantly, checking out the sky, other people, or maybe some interesting architecture you're running past, all the while remaining mindful of cars and scanning the road for anything that might merit a detour. Even if you're always looking straight ahead, you're probably looking at the road 15 feet ahead of you rather than straight down to where your contact with the ground is going to be.

 RULES OF THE ROAD

When you're running trails with others, stay farther away from each other than you would when running on roads. You need that extra distance between you so that everyone in the group can see and make adjustments for what the next little stretch of the trail has to offer.

On trails, you need to be a lot more disciplined about where you look. This can be tough, when you consider that one of the main attractions of trail running is the chance to see great natural beauty. But if you allow your attention to wander too much, you'll soon find yourself hugging, not just looking at, Mother Nature.

The key is to look no more than 10 feet ahead of you. You definitely don't want to stare at the ground right in front of you because then you're not going to see that tree root up ahead until you've tripped over it. But you also don't want to look too far ahead. Experienced trail runners look just far enough ahead to anticipate their next few strides. Over time, it becomes almost second nature to them to simultaneously see that their next landing will be problem-free but that in three steps they're going to want to go slightly to the left and up to avoid that pointy rock just up the trail. (This sense of constant vigilance is another reason that you're likely to run slower on trails.)

From Trail to Road

The immediate experience of trail running is more than enough reason to get off the roads on a regular basis. But trail running has benefits that also help you be a better runner on all surfaces.

For starters, regular trail running will help your *proprioception*, which is your body's ability to react and adjust to external forces such as uneven or undulating surfaces.

DEFINITION

Proprioception is your body's system for reacting to external forces. Maintaining your balance despite obstacles and changes in terrain is an important part of proprioception, and improves with regular trail running.

Experienced trail runners seem to glide over the ground at least in part because their proprioceptors are highly developed—even if they hit a rock or a root, they're able to adjust quickly enough to maintain forward motion. This ability is helpful on all surfaces because other than when you're running on a treadmill, there's always going to be some variation in your running surface, and you're always going to be making slight adjustments.

TRAINING TIP

You can increase your proprioception, and thereby make yourself a better trail runner, with balance exercises. While standing on one foot, raise your other leg to a 90-degree angle. Now close your eyes. Work up to being able to stay erect in this position for 30 seconds at a time for each leg.

Another carryover benefit from trail running comes from the frequent, steep uphills you encounter on trails. Some runners like to think of running uphill as "weightlifting for the legs." Competitive track runners often seek out hills for hard workouts because they want the increased power in their legs that comes from overcoming gravity to that much greater of a degree. Regular trail runners get that increased power while going about their business.

And from the what-goes-up-must-come-down department, the steep descents you'll encounter on trails can also help you in the rest of your running career. Once you get the hang of running downhill on trails, you'll have developed a quicker turnover that yields benefits at all distances on all surfaces.

Plants and Birds and Rocks and Things

As you might have noticed by now, trail running has its unique challenges. The most important ones have to do with the more treacherous footing you're going to encounter. That's especially the case when you're running on *single-track trails;* that is, trails that are cut just wide enough for one person to pass through at a time.

DEFINITION

Single-track trails are paths cut just wide enough for one person to pass through at a time. Most often, you'll find them on trails that cut through dense forests.

But there are other things you should be mindful of when trail running. Does the phrase "Leaves of three, let it be" mean anything to you? Poison ivy, poison oak, and poison sumac are just three plants that can turn your bucolic peak experience into a bitter itchy memory. As much as possible, avoid coming into contact with any unknown greenery. (And certainly don't do what one runner I know did, which is grab a handful of the nearest leaves for make-do, on-the-run toilet paper. Let's just say that this runner had reason to remember this run for more than a week.)

RULES OF THE ROAD

One good way to minimize your encounters with undesirable plants and animals is by not getting lost. Many trails are marked with frequent paint splotches on trees. A single marking means that you're on the right track. If you see two markings, that means a turn is coming up soon. (If you realize you haven't seen any markings for a while, do a U-turn.)

Be alert for fauna as well as flora. Bears look great at the zoo, but they aren't so cute and cuddly when you've disturbed their berry gathering. Your best bet is to stay at least 25 yards away from all wild animals. Yes, they're likely to be at least as frightened by you as you are of them, but they might have a funny way of showing that fear, such as by charging you. Many wild animals are most active at sunrise and sunset, so be especially mindful of the critters if you're trail running at those times.

The Dirt on Trail Running Shoes

In Chapter 7, I told you about the basic types of running shoes and how to know which type is best for you. I was describing shoes designed to be used on the surfaces most runners cover most of the time—roads, tracks, treadmills, obstacle-free dirt paths, and so on. What's the difference between them and *trail running shoes*, which are designed specifically for running on treacherous trails?

DEFINITION

Trail running shoes are trainers built with the hazards of trail running in mind. They're usually heavier and sturdier, with more protective features on the uppers, than road running shoes.

One of the first things you'll notice when comparing a trail shoe with a road shoe is the outsole of the trail shoe (see the figure on the following page). On road shoes, the outsole (the bottom part that hits the ground) is relatively smooth. Sure, there might be some sort of nubs to provide a little traction, but mostly, the outsoles are designed to help speed you down the road. After all, other than the occasional slight divot or loose gravel, there's not a lot of surficial variety on the streets of your town.

Contrast that with an average trail. The ground is probably uneven, rocks and roots might pop up at any time, leaves might be covering the path, and so on. Any one step is seldom like the one before it. A shoe with a more lugged outsole—that is, a lot of little grippy things—is going to give you better traction so that you don't spend your whole run slip sliding away.

Trail running shoes are almost always heavier and sturdier than road shoes. Because even with the best balance, you're still likely to get tossed around a bit on such an uneven surface, trail shoes have stiffer heel counters to help minimize side-to-side motion (and in severe cases, sprains).

A trail running shoe (bottom) has a more lugged outsole to provide better traction than a road running shoe (top).

Added weight also comes from the extra materials laid over the uppers. These extra materials are meant to protect you from jutting rocks and sticks, as well as other parts of nature that might be nice to look at, but don't feel all that great when they scrape across the top of your feet. Finally, most trail shoes have waterproof materials added to the uppers, for the puddles and streams you'll inevitably encounter. These, too, increase the weight of the shoe.

Do you need special trail running shoes if you're going to run on trails a couple of times per week? Unless you're running on highly technical trails (a lot of twists and turns and obstacles), and unless you twist your ankles just walking down city streets, probably not.

Many runners believe that a good running shoe is a good running shoe, period, and that one with a decent amount of traction will work just fine on the types of trails that most of us are likely to encounter. Some runners go further, saying that trail shoes are so stiff that they inhibit, not increase, your feet's ability to react quickly to the varying surface of a trail. Trail shoes are certainly not as castlike as when they first became popular about 10 years ago, but they still are usually unnecessarily bulky. Among many runners, trail shoes have the same reputation as SUVs—made for the rugged outback, but most often used for expeditions to the suburban grocery store.

If you have your heart set on trail running shoes, I recommend starting with one of the hybrid road/trail shoes that most manufacturers offer. These are a little lighter, and they're a lot more useful in situations in which you'll be running to a trail via a road.

Leave Only Footprints ...

As I said earlier, trail running is becoming so popular because it gives you a chance to get away from cars, concrete, and commotion. As more and more of our landscape is taken over by sprawl, people really relish the chance to be surrounded by nature.

Not to get too finger waving here, but when you run trails, it's important to help maintain that natural beauty. As the old saying goes, leave only footprints, take only memories. (Yeah, yeah, I know some people say "take only photographs," but trail running can be tricky enough without toting a camera.)

For starters, don't litter. Now I know *you* would never do such a horrible thing, but somebody out there sure seems to drop a lot of energy bar wrappers, gel containers, and sport drink bottles while running. If you can carry it in, you can certainly manage to carry your leftovers out.

RULES OF THE ROAD

No matter how pristine an area you're trail running in, don't drink from streams. You can't tell by looking whether they contain any of several organisms that might cause you to become ill.

But being a responsible trail runner involves more than not being a litterbug. It might not seem like it when you're slipping on wet leaves and wondering whether you made a wrong turn 10 minutes ago, but trail maintenance is hard work. Somebody—almost always a volunteer—has put in many hours to create and tend to your chosen running path. As a user, you can help to keep their upkeep time down by being environmentally sensitive. This includes avoiding overly muddy or dry trails, because running on them can lead to erosion. In the same way, as tempting as direct routes might be, help to keep erosion down by sticking to *switchbacks* (trails that zig and zag up or down a hill rather than taking the shortest route). And of course, obey "No Trespassing" signs and other indicators that you're about to traverse an area not meant for running.

DEFINITION

Switchbacks are back-and-forth trails that gradually make their way up and down hills. Their design helps to cut down on erosion.

Finally, be nice out there. Sure, seeing others on a trail can cut in to your reverie, but they have a right to use it, too. (Unless, that is, they're flagrantly violating a rule such as "No Bikes"; in which case, you might want to gently point out the regulations.)

Give plenty of warning when you're approaching someone from behind, such as by shouting "On your left!" If you're running uphill and someone is running down, yield to them. These little acts of kindness go a long way toward keeping the trails a refuge for all sorts of people seeking a temporary escape from the rush and noise of modern life.

The Least You Need to Know

- Trail running is one of the fastest-growing segments of running because it puts runners in such close contact with nature.
- Good trail running form involves a low-to-the-ground stride and careful monitoring of the ground a few feet in front of you.
- Regular trail running can help you be a better runner on all surfaces.
- Special trail running shoes usually aren't necessary.
- Stick to marked trails to minimize erosion of sensitive lands.

Running Through the Ages

By now, I hope that I've gotten across to you that running is a lifetime sport, even a way of life. Running isn't just for fast, lean 25-year-olds. Children run, teens run, old geezers in their 60s like me run, and great-grandparents run.

Most of what I've said in this book applies to all runners. But in this part, you'll find out what runners at the two extremes of the age scale should know. I'll explain what kind of running is right for children and whether it's safe for senior citizens to start running. (Can you guess what the answer is?) Finally, in this part you'll discover how your running changes over the years when you stick with it, as well as what to do to keep running the sport of your life.

Kidding Around: Running for Children

In This Chapter

- Introducing children to running
- How much children should run
- Making fitness a family affair
- The best races for children
- Special advice for high school runners

One time my co-author, Scott Douglas, came over to my house. My younger daughter was in the driveway when Scott pulled up and asked him, "Are you here to see my daddy?" "Yes," Scott said. "Tell him Frank Shorter is here to see him." Erika ran into the house and told me that Frank had arrived. This was news to me—I was expecting Scott, not an impromptu visit from an old rival who lives on the other side of the country! I dashed out to the driveway and saw only Scott and realized that toying with a gullible five-year-old was his idea of a joke.

The reason that Scott's lame little ploy worked was because Erika didn't know Frank Shorter from Frank Sinatra, Barney Frank, or Frankenstein. That's good. Erika was in elementary school at the time, and at her age, I wanted her to take part in as many activities as she enjoyed, not become some hard-core preteen running geek.

Encouraging children to be active without going overboard is what this chapter is about. I'll explain how much and why children should run and what types of races I think are good for them. I also have a few words for the older children out there who may have joined their high school cross-country or track team.

Should Children Run?

Of course children should run! Running should be as much a part of children's lives as walking, skipping, playing tag, and so on. It should be a normal part of their play. For preteens, play can and should be the major source of physical activity. Some researchers have estimated that when kids are left to their own devices, they'll cover as much as 6 miles a day on foot. Obviously, they don't cover this distance all at once, and it's a lot different from when an adult goes out for a 6-mile run or walk, but that's okay. At that age, most experts would agree, what you want is for your children to be active in a variety of activities that they enjoy.

Of course, many kids aren't active. The average American child spends close to six hours a day in front of some sort of screen, be it watching television, playing video games, texting, or surfing the web. Keep that in mind as you ponder these scary statistics: less than one quarter of children ages 6 to 17 meet minimum standards of cardiovascular fitness. Seventeen percent of all Americans age 12 to 19 are obese—not overweight, mind you, but obese, meaning that their body fat percentage was 25 percent or more. This is more than double the number two decades ago. Sixty percent of American kids already have one of the risk factors for heart disease I told you about in Chapter 2. Overweight children are being hospitalized at dramatically rising rates for diabetes, sleep apnea, and other diseases that obesity causes or worsens. While health authorities have long warned that obese children are much more likely to become obese adults, these recent trends are even scarier—these children's obesity is seriously sickening them *now*.

> **TRAINING TIP**
>
> Children running 10 or more miles per week need good running shoes as much as adults do. Because their bones, muscles, tendons, and ligaments are still developing, young runners do best in shoes with good cushioning that will absorb much of the impact shock.

Unfortunately, we can't look to the schools for much help. According to one survey of children in grades 4 to 12, 49 percent of boys and 62 percent of girls get nine hours or less of physical activity each week. When you consider that these estimates likely include a lot of time standing around on a ball field during gym classes, the figures seem even worse.

Now the question of whether children should run changes. Should children run in an organized way, for fitness, the way that adults do? That one's a bit trickier to answer.

Be a Running Role Model

You certainly shouldn't force children into running. Little League syndrome is as bad in running as it is in baseball. Children can sense when you're pushing them into an activity. They might not resist immediately, but eventually they will.

Having fun consistently ranks as the top reason that kids give for participating in sports. For preteens, fun almost always means the here and now. Most preteens haven't developed what psychologists call abstract thinking, the ability to set long-term goals and to see how doing something that might not feel good right now is worth it for the payoff later. In a certain sense, isn't that what a lot of running is about? A big motivation for getting out for a run today is because you know that doing so will benefit you later—you'll feel better the next day, or you'll be able to run faster in a race a month from now, or you're working toward a weight-loss goal, or you're making one of an ongoing series of contributions to fighting disease, and so on. When children don't come to running on their own terms, they're not going to like it because they don't yet have that sense of delayed gratification.

> **RULES OF THE ROAD**
>
> Young runners should follow the same safety rules as adults, as laid out in Chapter 4. Running with others is an especially good safety guideline to follow.

If a kid wants to run and can state why and seems to enjoy it, then I'm all for some low-level regular running. Children's attitudes toward running largely stem from what they notice about how the adults around them approach it. If you're always walking around the house before your runs moaning about what a horrible chore running is, then don't be surprised if your kids don't show much interest in it. But if your children see that running to you means getting outside and exploring and feeling good and being with your friends and having fun, they'll probably think otherwise. Running will seem like a form of play.

Keep It Enjoyable!

Even if your kids want to run for all the right reasons, I don't think that children under the age of 14 should look at their running as training. This advice doesn't mean that children under this age can't run as much as 20 miles a week. If they want to run that much, enjoy doing so, and don't get hurt, I think that's an acceptable upper limit of mileage for preteens. Three miles or 30 minutes are good measures of the farthest that young runners should go at a time.

But although kids may run as much as adults, running should remain a part of their play and one of many regular activities, not something that they plan and obsess about. Going for a run should be primarily about enjoying it on that day, not to build endurance so that they can try to run twice as far in a month. This book has emphasized that if you're going to make progress in your running, then you need to be consistent with it. Kids who run should ignore all of that. If they hit a spell where they don't feel like running for a month or two, don't force them to. If you do, you're sending the message that running is something that they have to do, not that they want to do.

 TRAINING TIP

A good way to introduce kids to running and to solve the child-care question during your running time is to run on a track while they play on the infield. After a while, they'll probably be interested enough to want to try to join you for a lap or two.

The Fun of Family Fitness

When my daughters were young, I tried to introduce them to as many activities as possible. Sure, running was one of them, and it was kind of hard for them not to notice that it seemed as though Daddy was always heading out the door for a run. But I never told them how running is the greatest sport, or how they were wasting their time when they were skating, dancing, boating, playing basketball or tennis, or doing any of the other activities that they enjoyed.

 TRAINING TIP

When running with children, let them lead the way. Run half a step behind so that it doesn't seem that they're always working to keep up with you. If you make them follow you, running will seem to be more of a chore than a form of play.

What I wanted to do was get across the idea that fitness is a lifestyle. I wanted to show them that being active and healthy and feeling good while using your body on a regular basis should be the norm. Children are much more likely to develop good fitness habits for the rest of their lives if they see that fitness is important to you. That's a much better message to send than presenting fitness as an occasional intrusion that you have to tend to out of obligation.

In terms of running, this approach means that if your child expresses an interest in it, explore that interest together. Go for a run with your kid. Take him or her to your races, not so much to run, but to show the festive atmosphere that races have. Do what you can to expose your child to those elements of running that are going to have the most appeal to kids.

You might not think so, but one of the biggest appeals of running is going to be the chance to spend some quality time with you. Young kids, especially, will do almost anything to get adult attention. So if they want to run with you, indulge them. Running together can strengthen your relationship, because the child will see your runs as one-on-one, undivided attention time. Let these runs unfold on the child's terms. That might mean jumping through puddles, or stopping to look at animals, or heading home after just a few minutes. Let them set the pace and the course. Remember, it's supposed to be fun for them, which means feeling good right then.

The Right Races for Rug Rats

Back when I was winning marathons, a young runner named Wesley Paul ran faster than 3:00 for the marathon at age 9, the youngest that anyone had ever done so. This feat got him a lot of attention in the press, and one running magazine even speculated that he would grow up to break the world record. You don't hear about Wesley Paul these days, however. That's not surprising. For whatever reason, almost every child who is highly motivated to compete in races at a young age doesn't become a lifetime runner. It's probably the same reason that kids who are gymnastics dynamos aren't big on tumbling when they're 40 years old—the activity is associated with a lot of pressure, not fun, and we all have enough pressure in our adult lives as it is.

I'm not a big fan of age-group track meets for junior high and elementary school kids. There's just too much of a risk that the children are so serious at such a young age for the wrong reasons. Sure, some of the runners might be mature enough to be able to state why they're training hard toward meeting competitive goals, but I'd rather err on the side of caution. Kids who have the ability and interest to become top runners will have plenty of time to work on that goal later, when both their minds and bodies are more mature, and they can make fuller use of their potential.

The Boston Marathon doesn't allow anyone under the age of 18 to enter the race. I support this position. There's no real benefit to be had from runners younger than that doing marathons, and the risks of burnout and injury are too great, given how much you have to run to prepare for a marathon. Hey, it's hard enough for adults to articulate reasonably why they want to try to run such a crazy distance!

RULES OF THE ROAD

Young runners need to be especially careful in extreme weather. Children's bodies don't create as much heat as adults' bodies do, so they're at greater risk for hypothermia in cold weather. Children's cooling systems are similarly underdeveloped—they don't sweat as easily as adults, so they get hotter quicker in the summer.

So what kinds of races are good for kids who want to participate? I'm all in favor of the low-key, mostly noncompetitive children's fun runs that more and more road races have added. Both of my daughters have run in these types of events. The important thing to look for in these runs is that they're short enough that you know your child will be able to finish and that they encourage participation, not competition.

If the race is too long, it's going to be a frustrating experience for the child. Why would he or she want to fail? My older daughter's first event like this was 1 kilometer, or just more than half a mile, long. Anything more than 5K is asking for trouble. The child may stick it out and finish, but it sure won't be fun.

Kids are naturally competitive. Watch the start of these children's runs, and you'll see the term "youthful exuberance" defined. They just tear away from the starting line in a sprint! But to keep the events fun and worthwhile for all the young runners, children's races should give some kind of award to every finisher. At a young age, the top finishers are going to place first because they have more talent for running. Preparing for the event doesn't factor into winning as it does for adults, especially at short distances.

Acknowledging all of the participants, by giving them all identical finisher's medals, for example, gets across the idea that the most important victory is participating. This emphasis encourages the slower kids to keep coming back and to view running as a sport that's for everyone, not just the talented few. Kids see enough of the elitist view of sports as it is, with the overemphasis that school sports such as football and basketball receive.

Teen Angels: High School Runners

Once kids are in high school, it's okay for them to become more serious about competition. By this age, they'll be able to understand what training is and how sometimes you have to suffer in the present to have a better future. Racing might still be frustrating (it is for everyone at some point), but if they've freely chosen to compete, then a few bad experiences probably won't sour them on running for the rest of their lives.

Also, by this age, their bodies can handle the training better. Training for even the longest distances usually offered in high school (5K for cross-country, 2 miles for track) involves a lot of short, fast-speed work, usually on the track. By high school age, more runners are going to be able to do this type of training without breaking down.

FOOTNOTES

In the 2007–2008 school year, outdoor track and field was the second-most popular high school sport among boys and girls. In all, nearly one million high schoolers ran, jumped, or threw for the sake of school spirit.

The American high school record for the mile is 3:53.4, held by Alan Webb. For girls, the record is 4:35.2, held by Polly Plumer.

Most children who race the mile or 2-mile in outdoor track are going to top out at about 30 miles a week. Anything more than that and I'd get a little wary. Certainly, some teens can handle more running than that, especially if they started when they were younger. But even in high school, I think it's worth erring on the side of caution.

Some coaches are going to encourage members of the team to run more. It's not unheard of for cross-country team members to run 70 or so miles a week. Whether that's a good idea is going to be a judgment call. If a high school runner is doing that kind of mileage and understands why, then it can be okay, so long as the runners on the team are progressing and enjoying themselves. But if most members of the team aren't progressing, then the coach is trying to use methods that might work with older, more developed runners on younger ones who aren't ready yet for that high of a level of training. Because most high school runners are new to the sport, they should see steady progress in bringing their times down. If they've plateaued, it usually means that they're doing too much.

RULES OF THE ROAD

Young runners should learn from day one a fundamental bit of runner's etiquette—to shake hands with the runners who place just ahead and behind them immediately after the finish of a race. This action encourages good sportsmanship and reinforces the notion that everyone in a race competes against themselves and the conditions, as well as other runners.

I ran a few road races while in high school. Doing a few short ones a year is fine for high school runners, especially as a way to keep running interesting in the summer. But I'm not in favor of teen runners being serious road racers. They should concentrate on the shorter track races and work on developing their speed and good training habits. When they're out of school, they have the rest of their lives to plod around on the roads like the rest of us. Once you're out of school, it's tough to find good competitions at short races like the mile. So teen runners should take full advantage of the opportunity while they have it. If they choose to compete when they're older, they'll be that much more able to reach their potential at the longer races.

The Least You Need to Know

- Running should be one of many forms of children's play.
- Children will learn to view running favorably if they see it presented as something that's fun.
- The best races for pre–high schoolers are short, noncompetitive events that reward all of the participants.
- Children under the age of 18 shouldn't run marathons.
- It's okay for children to become more serious about training and competition once they're in high school.
- High school runners should focus on short races such as the mile rather than longer road races.

Late in the Race: Advice for Senior Runners

In This Chapter

- Why age doesn't matter
- Getting started after age 50
- Precautions for older new runners
- Special nutritional advice for older runners

When I turned 60 in 2007, people made a big deal about it. They thought it was incredible that I was still running at such an advanced age. Some people wanted to know when I was going to retire. Never, I hope. Our society has it all wrong about aging. Our bodies are meant to be used for our entire lives, not just when we're young.

But what if you didn't even use your body back then? What if you've been sedentary for a long time, but now want to start running? Is it for you? In this chapter, I'll tell you why you have nothing to fear from starting a running program, as well as give you some tips to make the transition from 50 and fat to 60 and sexy easier.

All Ages Welcome

It's never too late to get in shape. People who start running in their 70s will see the same kinds of gains that people in their 20s do. The principles that underlie why your aerobic capacity and strength increase when you start running have no idea how old you are.

That's not what older people have traditionally been told. People past the age of 60 were told to take it easy—maybe putter around the garden a couple of times a week or walk the dog (assuming the dog is no bigger than a dachshund). Get the old ticker going, and you'll be pushing up daisies, not pulling in Social Security. Getting sick and increasingly dependent on others is an inevitable part of getting old, we were told.

Now we know that that advice, like history, is bunk. As one of the leading researchers in this area likes to say, what most people think of as the natural consequences of aging are really the "atrophy of disuse." Our bodies are machines that like being used. Start them up at a good rate after years of practicing "atrophy of disuse," and they will thank you for it.

RULES OF THE ROAD

Don't forget what else I said in Chapter 3: if you're past the age of 60 and have been sedentary, see a physician before you start your running program.

One study started a group of sedentary men in their 60s on a walking and running program. They worked out 4 times a week for 30 minutes at 70 percent of their maximum heart rate. After only 4 weeks, their aerobic capacity had increased by 6 percent, and their heart rate at their training pace decreased by 10 beats per minute. After another 5 weeks, they had another 6 percent increase in aerobic capacity, and their training heart rate fell another 6 beats.

Older people can benefit from strength training as well. One of the main reasons that older people lose independence, and with it, quality of life, is because they've lost so much muscle mass that they can't perform basic daily tasks. Being unable to lift more than 5 pounds might not seem like much of a big deal until you do some quick math: half a gallon of milk weighs 3 pounds. Go to the store and buy that, a few pieces of fruit, and maybe some chicken breast, and you better be able to lift more than 5 pounds unless you want to rely on others to carry even the lightest groceries for you.

TRAINING TIP

Older runners can especially benefit from weight training. In general, older runners tend to get ankle and knee injuries and tendinitis around the joints. Weight training helps to protect joints by strengthening the tissues around them, which results in fewer injuries.

A famous study at Tufts University started frail people in their 80s on a serious weight training program. The old folks did repetitions at 80 percent of their one-rep maximum. That's hard work for anyone, believe me. In just eight weeks, their strength more than doubled.

The bottom line: not only can older sedentary people start an exercise program like younger people, but they should. The benefits of exercise, as well as the principles for obtaining these benefits, are the same no matter what your age.

Leaving Youth in the Dust

If you're over the age of 50 and have been sedentary for a long time, do you remember how you felt more than 20 years ago? Probably pretty darned good, huh? Even if you weren't brimming with vitality, you probably wouldn't mind feeling like that again instead of how you feel now, right? Well, if you start running, you can feel that way again.

FOOTNOTES

Think we old-timers can't duke it out with the young bucks? Mexico's Andres Espinosa placed fourth at the 2003 Berlin Marathon at age 40. His time of 2:08:64 is a world record for a masters runner. Russia's Ludmila Petrova has the women's masters world record of 2:25:43. She placed second overall at the 2008 New York City Marathon when she ran the record.

A study of runners age 50 and older compared them to healthy nonrunners in their 20s. The women runners had an average level of aerobic fitness the same as the sedentary 20-somethings, and the 50+ men runners had slightly higher aerobic capacities than the young couch potatoes. Based on these figures, you could say that running cuts 20 to 30 years from your age!

Retired Runners

In Chapter 5, I talked about one of the biggest barriers many beginning runners face—finding the time. We saw how simple it is to carve out a little time to run in a busy workday. But what about if you're in the opposite situation? What if you no longer work, and that old dream of hours of leisure time has become a bit of a nightmare? Throughout this book, I've shown how running is not just exercise; it's a lifestyle. No, you're not going to spend your entire day running, but it does help to center your day. Having this activity on your schedule has a way of organizing your day; there seems to be more of a purpose to what you do. I keep mentioning how running improves the quality of your life. This benefit is especially important for older people, who suffer from depression at a higher rate than young people.

I meet runners all the time who have had just this experience. With child rearing and their careers behind them, they found that running gave their days a little spark, a little structure. It certainly didn't hurt that they could head out the door almost any time they want! A lot of them tell me they're having the time of their life in what they playfully call "their second childhood." Wouldn't you like to join them?

Masterful Performances

Okay, so you're pretty fired up about all that running has to offer older people. Is there anything special you need to do besides rereading the chapters in the first section of this book? Yes, there is. Although the principles for getting fit are the same for everybody, they do require a slightly different application in an older body. How much is going to be different depends on how active you are. If the last time you got any exercise was when you hoisted beers in college, you're going to have to start much more slowly than if you've always walked places, played tennis once in a while, chased after the grandchildren, and so on.

RULES OF THE ROAD

Be mindful of old injuries from other sports. That knee that you wrenched playing football years ago might become a lot more noticeable when you start to run. See a good sports medicine doctor if you have an old injury site that bothers you when you start running.

What doesn't differ is the fact that all people should start their exercise programs with that basic 30 minutes, 4-times-a-week approach where you work hard enough to work up a sweat, but not so hard that you can't carry on a conversation. At what level of activity this occurs depends on how well you've taken care of yourself. Be honest about what it takes at first to reach the right workout intensity. Don't let visions of your former self cloud your perception of your current reality.

Some people in their 60s are able to start running right away, but a lot of older people have to walk at first. Whether you start off running or walking, you're getting the aerobic benefits of exercise, and you're building good workout habits. We older folks don't need instant gratification as much as the youngsters. We're used to working at something that has a promise of future reward. I hope by now that I've convinced you what a great reward is waiting for you if you stick with your running.

Slow and Steady

As I'll talk about in more length in the next chapter, one of the biggest changes that happens to your body as you age is that your ability to recover from a hard workout decreases. Most older runners find that they need to allow for extra time between hard workouts, or they'll risk injury. For longtime runners, making this adjustment is one of the trickiest aspects of getting older. When you were in your 30s, you had no trouble putting in long hours at the office, cranking out a good speed workout in the middle of the week, and racing or doing a long run on the weekend. So you wonder why doing so now takes so much out of you.

 TRAINING TIP

A lot of how you adapt to running has to do with your attitude. "The word 'training' is obnoxious to me," says New Zealand's Derek Turnbull. "When I run, it's for recreation. Fitness is half in the mind—if you enjoy your running, you'll get results." This is from a man who ran a 2:38 marathon in his 60s!

One of the beauties of beginning to run when you're older is that you don't have those memories. You don't have to worry about how to adjust the running schedule that used to work for you. But you still should be aware that all other things being equal, you're not going to recover from your workouts as quickly as new runners in their 20s. If they go overboard at first and get a lot sorer than they should, it's not that big a deal. They'll be fine in a couple of days. You, on the other hand ….

Be extra careful about running within your limits at first. Finish each of your workouts feeling that you could have kept going or that you could have done the workout at a faster clip. Try to maintain that little bit of extra conservatism for at least the first six months of your running program.

Be Flexible

Older beginners should also be extra diligent about a good flexibility program. Young new runners are limited mostly by their aerobic fitness. If they can't go faster, it's because their muscles, heart, and lungs need to develop the capacity to sustain a higher level of effort. But if they had to, they could launch into a full sprint and look pretty good doing it.

But older runners, especially ones who have been sedentary, have another limitation. They've probably lost a good deal of their range of motion over the years. One study found that older runners who did nothing to address the issue lost about 40 percent of their stride length in their 40s and 50s. If they tried to break into a sprint, they might very well trip over their feet, or at least risk pulling something.

> **RULES OF THE ROAD**
>
> If you used to work out, but haven't in more than a few years, you're starting from scratch. Don't try to match what you used to do, especially if you're comparing your current self to when you were in your 20s and 30s.

Running will help you to regain some of your range of motion as your muscles become used to working harder. But you can help them to help you by stretching regularly. For younger beginners, stretching is mostly going to maintain flexibility. But for older runners, stretching can improve your flexibility, helping you to regain some of that agility that you used to take for granted. This improvement can be exciting for older folks who have gotten used to not moving as well as they used to.

Aging Appetites

The basic nutritional lowdown that I gave you in Chapter 13 applies to all runners. No matter what your age, you should eat a low-fat, high-carbohydrate diet to get the most out of your running. That said, older runners can benefit from tweaking their diet a bit.

> **FOOTNOTES**
>
> The oldest person ever to break 3:00 for the marathon is Ed Whitlock of Milton, Ontario, Canada. Four months before his 70th birthday, he ran 2:52:47. That's about 6:30 per mile for 26.2 miles! Ed also holds the world record for 70-and-older runners with a 2:54:48 marathon.

As always, the most important advice has to do with fluids, not food. Everyone's thirst mechanisms are pretty lame at keeping them well hydrated. But as you age, your thirst mechanism becomes even less sensitive. To make matters worse, runners past the age of 40 have higher core body temperatures, heart rates, and overall loss of body water in the heat than younger runners do. It's a double whammy—if you're not careful, you start a run in the heat less hydrated, then have the heat take more out of you. So older runners should be even more zealous about staying hydrated than younger ones. Remember to drink some fluid every hour that you're awake, and check that your urine is frequent and clear in color.

Your stomach produces less acid as you age, which reduces your ability to digest protein. Most people find that a big steak just isn't as appealing when they're 60 as it was when they were 20. Overall, that's good, because, as I mentioned in Chapter 13, most people eat too much protein as it is. Still, older runners who don't have much of an appetite for animal products should make sure that they're getting their two to three servings of protein a day, or recovering from illness or injury is going to take longer.

Older women runners should be sure to get enough calcium. Yes, running helps to keep bones strong, but after menopause, estrogen levels plummet, and bones can become more brittle if you don't take in enough calcium. When this happens, you're more susceptible to stress fractures from your running.

Aging decreases your skin's ability to produce vitamin D. Many older runners, myself included, are rightfully concerned about skin cancer and wear sunscreen. Also, many older runners are more likely to find themselves running at nonpeak sun hours because of work and family responsibilities. All of this means that masters runners should take extra steps to get enough vitamin D through their diet, which works with calcium to keep your bones strong. Fortified nonfat milk is the best source.

The good news is that older runners get to eat more calories than their sedentary contemporaries. This means that you'll be able to eat enough of a variety of foods to take in the nutrients you need.

The Least You Need to Know

- New runners past the age of 50 get the same benefits from running as younger runners do.
- Older beginning runners should work out just as hard as younger beginners.
- Older runners should stretch diligently to regain range of motion.
- Older runners have a decreased thirst sensation and need to be extra careful about drinking enough water.

Running for Your Life

In This Chapter

- Running even when you become slower
- Maintaining strength and flexibility as you age
- Staying motivated as the years go by
- The greatest athlete in American history

I started running when John F. Kennedy was president. After dabbling in a summer track meet put on by the local recreation department, me, my brother Charlie, and my best friend, Jason Kehoe, went out for the high school cross-country team. We found out how much fun running is, so we didn't quit the team. Now 45 years later, you know what? We're all still running. We keep discovering new ways that running is fun. I don't think that any of us will be quitting the team anytime soon.

Running is a lifetime sport. In this chapter, I'll show you what changes happen over the years if you keep at it, and I'll show you how to make aging a positive thing, not a cause for despair. I'll conclude this book by telling you who the greatest athlete in American history is.

Do Not Go Gentle into That Good Night

What the Irish poet Dylan Thomas wrote to his aging father is good advice for all of us: "Rage, rage against the dying of the light."

Our notions of what getting older is supposed to be about are wrong. They're based more on observing what people do, not what they should do. Use it or lose it is certainly true concerning fitness in the short term. As we've seen, your aerobic capacity starts to decline after as little as two weeks of inactivity.

If that's the case, think about what happens over the years. People who say they want to "take it easy" now that they're getting older have a self-fulfilling goal. Take it easy, and trust me, that's all you'll be capable of.

Think about the more interesting older people whom you've met in your life. What did they have in common? They were active. Sure, they probably weren't out there banging out the miles every day, but they did *something*. They had something in their lives that they were passionate about, that they applied their mental and physical abilities toward. Talk to them, and you'll hear as much about the future, about what they still want to do, as you will about "the good old days." That's why they remained interesting people—they had found some pursuit that they enjoyed, that gave meaning and order to their lives.

It's not so much that they rebelled against our society's encouragement of giving in to inertia, but that they ignored it. They just went about their business, and happened to get older along the way. Haven't you ever noticed how so many classical music conductors are still leading orchestras at ages when most people have gone deaf to doing anything but sitting in a rocking chair?

You don't have to be a world-class musician to live this way, and you don't have to be a former world-class runner, like me. You just need to find something that you care about, then keep pursuing it, open to where it might take you. Do that, and incidentally, you'll stay physically and mentally sharp enough to rage against the dying of the light.

Don't know if you saw this coming, but if not, here it is: running is one of the best ways to live the rest of your life like this.

Through the Years: How Aging Affects Running

Going bald is a good analogy for what's going to happen to you if you keep running as you age. The changes are subtle, almost imperceptible from day to day. You can't point to one day and say, "That's when it all started." But a look in the mirror or the training log reveals that you're undeniably different. What you used to take for granted is now the stuff of fantasy.

If you're a performance-driven runner (and aren't we all to some degree?), you'll eventually find out the biggest change that happens to you when you get older: you slow down. You probably knew that already, but what you may not know is why that occurs and what you can do about it.

Recovering Performance Addicts

One of the first-noticed and universal changes that runners note with age is a decreased ability to recover after a long or hard run. When I was at my peak, I could get away with things that would destroy me now, like doing a two-hour run in the morning and a race in the evening. Thirty years ago, several hours was enough time to recover from the morning's long run. Now it's more like a few days. Intimately related to that need for greater recovery between runs is a drop in overall mileage. When I was training to be the best in the world, I cranked out 130-mile weeks with relative ease. (Don't let anyone tell you it's ever completely easy!) Now I run about half that much, but I sometimes feel twice as tired! Most longtime runners have a similar experience at their own levels of mileage.

Mileage aside, I just feel, well, older. I still have the energy to do the things that I want to do, but I'm more aware of being tired when doing them. When I get up in the morning, it takes me a while to get going. On days when I'm not pressed for time, I sometimes putter around the house for more than an hour before heading out for my run. I used to be able to start a run immediately, anytime, anywhere. Now I need to walk around a bit, loosen up, and make a more conscious effort to get myself out the door.

Most longtime runners find that they need to allow for more easy days in their training and that they need to put more easy days between their hard workouts. Instead of running 5 miles the day after a track workout, maybe they'll do some cross-training or not do any exercise. That way, they'll recover better in time for that long run in a few days.

FOOTNOTES

A study comparing 50-and-over runners with runners in their 20s found that the older runners had better training routines, such as regularly stretching, than the younger ones. Appreciate aging for how it motivates you and rewards you for good habits.

Another approach is to scrap the idea of looking at your training in week-long blocks. Instead of thinking that you have to get in a long run and a speed workout session every week and tweaking your easy days in whatever way is necessary to make that schedule fit, you could think in 10-day blocks, or 12-day ones, or whatever. You might just run easy after a hard workout until you feel ready to go hard again and not care whether that means three days, or four, or two.

There's a positive aspect about this reduced ability to recover from run to run. You become more conscious of the need to take care of yourself. You become better at finessing things in such a way to keep you on the roads. You probably acquire better habits, such as being diligent about stretching and maintaining a proper diet, because you have a better sense of how these things contribute to feeling better.

VO$_2$ Min?

Studies have found that after the age of 30, aerobic capacity drops by 1 percent each year. This means that everything else being equal, you're going to get a little slower each year. But not enough research has been done to distinguish how much of the decline that's observed in longtime runners is because of age and how much is due to training and living differently. My aerobic capacity is lower than it was 20 years ago. Some of that is inevitable, but how much of it is because I don't run as much as I used to? If my body would hold together at 130 miles per week, I bet my decline wouldn't be as great.

Aerobic capacity declines at a slower rate if you keep running. If you're running 20 miles a week now, that's a level that you will probably be able to handle 10 years from now. You can therefore duplicate the standards of your heyday a lot more easily than I can. Your drop isn't going to be as great as mine.

FOOTNOTES

Aerobic fitness drops more because of inactivity than because of aging. In 1968, Lou Castagnola was a 2:17 marathoner. After the Olympic Marathon trials that year, he stopped running completely. When he was retested just three years later, his aerobic capacity had decreased by more than 30 percent!

Remember, your aerobic capacity improves for the first several years of a running program. If you're starting out as a runner after the age of 30, your aerobic capacity is going to increase from your training a lot more than it will decrease because of aging. As explained in the last chapter, that can mean that runners in their 50s have the capabilities of average people in their 20s. Just remember that the more aerobic exercise you get, the longer your aerobic capacity will take to decline.

Fast Twitchin'

When you run fast, you're using your *fast-twitch fibers*. Everyone is born with a set percentage of fast-twitch fibers. If you have a lot of them, you'll be better at short races. If you weren't born with many (as I wasn't), then you have a higher percentage of slow-twitch fibers, the types that don't fire as quickly, but that can keep firing for a long time. If that's you, you'll be better at longer events. Differences in the percentages of fast-twitch and slow-twitch muscle fibers go a long way toward explaining why Usain Bolt is never going to run a good marathon and why I'm not a sprinter.

All muscle fibers degenerate with age, but fast-twitch fibers do so the quickest. Research indicates that if fast-twitch fibers aren't used regularly with age, their ability to fire is lost permanently. They kind of go into early retirement, and no amount of coaxing is going to bring them back. When this happens, you're going to lose your ability to move quickly, not just when running, but when doing daily activities.

DEFINITION

Fast-twitch fibers are muscle fibers that fire quickly to power explosive activities, such as sprinting or lifting weights. You're born with a set percentage of fast-twitch fibers, but you can keep the ones that you have activated by including fast running and strength training in your fitness program.

You can't increase the percentage of your fast-twitch fibers with training, but you can increase their ability to work hard. You do this by doing things that require them to fire, such as doing striders and lifting weights regularly.

Lift for Life

Related to the degeneration of fast-twitch fibers is the loss of muscle mass. This loss means that you lose strength, and that you're more likely to gain weight. The old saw about muscle turning into fat isn't true—biochemically speaking, they're different materials—but it sure can seem that way. What happens is that when you lose some muscle mass, your metabolism slows. When that happens, it's easier to eat more calories than you burn, so it's easier for your body to gain fat.

But as explained in the last chapter, people of any age can increase their strength and add muscle with weight training. One of the best things you can do to keep your running rewarding as you age is to become more diligent about lifting weights.

It's Not a Stretch to Say ...

Some decline in flexibility is inevitable. Muscles lose their resiliency over time. But most of why people are less flexible with age is because of their habits. As many runners age, they increasingly avoid running fast. Doing so feels tougher than it used to, so they stick with their easy daily runs. But this slower pace means that they're not working through a full range of motion like they should be. They're shuffling down the street, thinking about how much more difficult it is these days to run fast. But part of that is because they're shuffling down the street!

To combat this decline, do striders once or twice a week, even if you're not going to race. Striders are short enough that they're not going to tire you, but they require enough change in your running form that you're going to stretch your running muscles more than if you always run at just a moderate pace. (See Chapter 19 for a refresher course on striders.)

For many people, getting older means more days spent sitting behind a desk. Sitting all day shortens your hamstrings, tightens your lower back, and places tremendous strain on your neck. It detracts from your ability to move smoothly, especially in something like running where all of your body parts work in sync. A little regular stretching goes a long way toward keeping you from getting too creaky. Keep in mind that as you age, you have to keep doing your stretching routine just to maintain your flexibility.

Coping Strategies

When you're new to running, staying motivated is often easier than when you've been running for a while. If you follow some of the strategies in Chapter 6, you'll find ways to keep at it past your initial gains in fitness. Racing, especially, will help you to stay on track, so to speak, because you're likely to be fired up about chasing new personal records.

But what about when you realize that there won't be anymore personal records? Isn't running just going to depress you? Well, it's been almost 30 years since the last time I set a personal record, and in some ways, I'm enjoying my running more than ever. It's not that I don't care about my running times anymore. I do, fanatically. But I've broadened my appreciation of running.

 TRAINING TIP

When your times get slower, keep things in perspective. They might still be better than you think. When I was 49, I ran 52:22 for 10 miles. That's 5:14 per mile. When I was 15 years old, I ran a 1-mile race in 5:20. Three-and-a-half decades later, I was a better runner than when I was in my teens!

There's more to continuing to enjoy your running as you get older than doing striders and lifting weights. Much of your satisfaction (and therefore, motivation) is going to come from the right mental approach. Now that I'm in my 60s and have had the inevitable health challenges, I have a better sense of how running improves my life in ways that I pretty much used to take for granted. The health and fitness benefits of running have become more important to me. I realize now that if for some reason I was told I could never race again, I'd still run for an hour a day. I didn't think that way when I was younger. When I finished college, I wasn't motivated to race anymore, so I stopped running entirely. I didn't have that sense of how running improves all of the areas of my life that I do now.

As I said, I'm still pretty darned fired up about racing. One good way to stay motivated is to shift gears and take on different goals. For example, whereas the marathon used to be the focus of my racing, I've run only one marathon in the last 10 years. I moved away from the marathon because getting to the starting line in good enough shape to perform as I wanted was too taxing. The training that I wanted to do to race a good marathon was too much, and I kept breaking down. I realized that I would need to focus on other distances if I was going to keep at it.

This change has been good for me. All runners should become a different type of runner at different times in their running lives. I run a lot more 5Ks than I used to. Not being a fast-twitch kind of guy, this isn't my area of expertise, but I like the challenge. It emphasizes a slightly different way to train, and that variety helps to keep me interested. Many runners find that they have an increased appreciation for short races as they age. Some even turn to track meets and race distances of a mile or shorter. It's satisfying to give that brief, all-out effort and know that the race is short enough that it's not going to drain you for days.

At the other extreme, many post–personal record runners turn to increasingly longer distances. *Ultramarathons*, or races longer than 26.2 miles, are drawing bigger fields every year. People who have run marathons like the challenge of seeing whether they can extend their distance. Ultramarathons are so long that you can't run them faster than your usual training pace, so there's not that pressure to count every second. Many people find that they recover from ultramarathons more quickly than from marathons because you have to run them at so relaxed a pace. Older runners do exceptionally well in ultramarathons, because maturity is really rewarded in these how-long-can-you-last affairs.

DEFINITION

Races that are longer than marathons are **ultramarathons.** The most common distance for ultramarathons is 50 miles.

I'm not saying that everyone should go out and sign up for the next 50-miler. I've never run an ultramarathon, and I doubt I ever will. But you can get a lot of satisfaction out of testing the limits of your endurance. That might mean moving up from 5Ks to 10Ks or seeing whether you can work up to running 10 miles at a time if the longest run of your life is 5 miles.

As I mentioned in Chapter 17 when I told you about masters racing, another good way to keep a fresh outlook is to wipe the slate clean every five years. By comparing your efforts to those of your recent past, you can maintain that sense of excitement about your running. Changing your goals like this isn't giving in. You're in control of the process; it's just that you have to take different factors into consideration.

I've told you about how, when I first turned 50, I was chasing the American record for 10 miles in my new age group. I didn't get it, but in trying, I averaged 5:15 miles for 10 miles. Well, now that I'm in my 60s, I look back at that performance and shake my head at how good a mark that is. If only I were that young again! Think of what I could do!

That was then, this is now. I would be really psyched to run 5:15 for a single mile, even though I managed that pace for 10 miles just 10 years ago. That's not complacency, but reality. The key is that I appreciate what I accomplished, accept that I won't be able to do the same thing again, and refocus on a new challenging but attainable goal.

Finally, it helps to keep things in perspective. Not being able to run as fast as you used to might not be cause for elation, but it's not the apocalypse either. I hope by now you see that running has so much to offer that, like me, it's the thought of not doing it all, rather than doing it more slowly than you used to, that's the legitimate fear. Older runners sometimes point out that their running is the same as it used to be. They're still out there running for 30 minutes to an hour. They're covering less ground than they used to in that time, but that doesn't change the fundamental experience of their daily run.

The Greatest Athlete in American History

The greatest American athlete ever is Johnny Kelley. After he dropped out of the 1956 Boston Marathon, he thought that maybe it was time that he retired from running. Sure, he had won the race twice, in 1935 and 1945, and he had placed second seven times. But the last time that had happened was 10 years ago, in 1946. Since then, he had fallen farther and farther behind the leaders. Now he had dropped out.

He was 47 years old. He obviously wasn't going to win again. Why not just give up the whole thing and lead a normal life?

Kelley decided to stick with it, and he finished thirteenth at Boston the next year. The next year, he finished Boston again. And he kept finishing it, year after year. Kelley finished the Boston Marathon for the last time in 1991, when at age 83, he ran 5:42. It was the fifty-eighth time he had completed the race.

FOOTNOTES

Clarence DeMar won the Boston Marathon seven times, more than anybody else. He was 42 at the time of his last victory. When he was 50, he placed seventh. Even in 1954, at the age of 65, he placed seventy-eighth in a field of 153 runners.

Kelley is my hero. He's pure inspiration, a model for how we're supposed to live. He shows us that being an athlete isn't just being a young guy who gets paid millions of dollars to throw a football or hit a baseball for 5 or 10 years, and then let himself go to pot. Athletes keep at their sport their whole lives, always pursuing their passion, always striving to get the best out of themselves. Being an athlete isn't something that gets in the way of your life; it's something that gives meaning to your life. Kelley died in 2004 at the age of 97. Almost up until his passing, he still got out the door every day, rising early to trot along the ocean near his home in Cape Cod. I hope that this book has convinced you that that's a good goal for you. And I hope you see by now that it's a reachable one. Let's always run!

The Least You Need to Know

- Eventually, you're going to get slower as you age.
- Most of why people get slower is because of how they train, not just because they're getting older.
- Running striders and lifting weights regularly will help you to maintain your strength and range of motion.
- Getting older often means coming to appreciate your running more.
- Johnny Kelley, who finished the Boston Marathon 58 times, is the greatest athlete in American history.

Glossary

aerobic exercise   An activity, such as running, that you do at a steady level of effort for at least 20 minutes at a time and during which you're never completely out of breath.

all comer's meet   A track meet at which runners of all levels of ability are welcome to participate.

amenorrhea   The absence of menstrual periods.

ballistic stretching   Stretching that involves bouncing and sudden, jerking motions. It's the wrong way to stretch.

bandit   A runner who participates in a race without paying the registration fee.

body composition   How much fat you carry compared to how much of your weight is comprised of lean material (muscles, bones, ligaments, and so on).

calorie   A measurement of heat. Only food and drinks containing calories can be burned for energy by your body. A pound is equal to 3,500 calories. Walking and running burn roughly 100 calories per mile.

carbohydrates   Sugars and starches from your diet. Carbohydrates are your main source of energy when you run.

carboloading   Eating more carbohydrates than usual in the few days before a long race to boost your fuel stores.

cardiovascular fitness   The ability to sustain comfortably a moderate level of aerobic exercise. It's what people mean when they talk about stamina or endurance.

cool-down   A short, slow jog after a race or hard run that helps you to recover more quickly.

CoolMax   A fiber used in many running clothes that feels as soft as cotton but that keeps you more comfortable by not absorbing as much water.

core strength   How well your midsection stays stable and supportive when you're in motion.

course record   The fastest time run by anyone over a given race course.

cross-country race   A race that's held over grass and dirt.

cross-training   Doing other forms of aerobic exercise to supplement your running.

DNF   Stands for "did not finish." It describes a runner who drops out of a race.

drafting   This is when you run or ride behind someone else to save energy. In a 5K race on a windy day, drafting can make a given pace as much as 10 percent easier.

fartlek   A Swedish word meaning "speed play." It's an unstructured form of speed work that you do on roads or trails rather than on a track.

fast-twitch fiber   A muscle fiber that powers explosive actions, such as sprinting, but that tires quickly.

flexibility   The ability to move your body through a full range of motion.

fun run   An untimed, low-key run, often only a mile long, usually held as part of a longer race.

glycogen   The substance carbohydrates are turned into when they are stored in your muscles. It's your body's preferred fuel source during aerobic exercise.

heel counter   The back part of a running shoe that helps to make it more stable.

hemoglobin   A protein in red blood cells that carries oxygen from your lungs to your muscles.

iliotibial band   A thick band of tissue that runs from your hip along your thigh to the outside of your knee.

insole   The removable inner part of a running shoe that provides cushioning and offers arch support.

intervals   Short runs, usually from ¼ mile to 1 mile in length, that you run at faster than race pace to prepare for races.

junk miles   Miles that have no training purpose except to make your training log look more impressive.

kick   The all-out sprint that you do in the last few hundred yards of a race.

lactate threshold   The running speed at which your body can no longer clear lactate (a by-product of carbohydrate metabolism) from your blood as quickly as it produces it.

layering   Wearing light layers of clothing during cold-weather running to trap body heat.

long run   A run that's at least one and a half times longer than any other run that you do in a week.

low impact   An activity that has substantially less pounding than running. Such activities include walking and stair climbing.

marathon   A race that is 26.2 miles long.

masters runner   A runner age 40 or older.

maximum heart rate   The greatest number of times that your heart can beat in a minute.

medial post   A firm section in the inner heel of a running shoe that increases the shoe's stability.

microfiber   A broad classification of fiber that's used in a variety of running gear. It's tightly woven so that sweat vapor can escape from the inside while the fiber remains quick drying and wind and water resistant from the outside.

midsole   The part of a running shoe between the upper and outsole that provides most of the shoe's cushioning.

muscle imbalance   This results when opposing muscles don't have the right ratio of strength between them. This imbalance can harm your form and make you more susceptible to injury.

muscular strength   How much force you can generate doing one all-out repetition of a given exercise. This quality is important for runners, but not as much as muscular endurance, the ability to maintain a lower level of work for a long time.

negative splits   Running the second half of a race faster than the first half.

nonimpact activities   These are activities, such as swimming and water running, that involve no pounding.

opposing muscle groups   These are muscles in the same part of the body that work in opposite directions. For example, the biceps muscle in the arm flexes the elbow, and the triceps in the back of the arm extends the elbow.

orthotics   Devices placed in running shoes that help to prevent injury by fixing biomechanical problems.

outsole   The part of a running shoe that hits the ground and provides traction.

overpronation   When your feet roll in too much when you run. Overpronation is one of the leading causes of injury in runners.

overtraining   Running more than your body is prepared to for at least a few consecutive weeks. Overtraining can lead to injury and staleness.

overuse injuries   Injuries that result from repeatedly subjecting a body part to more force than it's prepared to handle. Most running injuries are overuse injuries.

oxygen debt   When you run so fast that your body needs more oxygen than you can take in. When you go into oxygen debt, you have to slow down.

plantar fasciitis   Inflammation of the plantar fascia, a thick band of fibrous tissue that runs along the bottom of your foot from your heel to your arch.

PR   Stands for "personal record"; it's your fastest time for a given distance.

progression principle   An important principle that says individual gains in fitness are small, but accumulate with consistency. That's why you can't go from being inactive to running a marathon; you have to gradually increase your endurance.

proprioception   Your body's ability to maintain its balance despite uneven surfaces and other distractions.

quarters   Intervals that are ¼-mile long or one lap around a standard outdoor track.

resistance training   This involves working a muscle or muscles against force. Common examples include lifting free weights, using an exercise machine, or using your own body to provide the resistance, such as doing push-ups.

resting heart rate   The number of times that your heart beats in one minute when you're still.

Runner's World   The world's most popular running magazine.

running stroller   A three-wheeled buggy you push while running that holds a child.

running suit   A pair of pants and a matching jacket that are warm enough for cold-weather running but not so heavy that they restrict your form.

single-track trail   A trail cut just wide enough for one person at a time to pass through.

singlet   A tank top worn by runners in hot weather and during races.

speed work   Mixing short, fast runs with slow recovery jogs to prepare for races.

splits   Your times at mile markers or other signposts along the way to the finish of a race.

sports bra   A snug-fitting bra made of the same materials as other exercise gear. You might also hear them called jog bras.

static stretching   Stretching that involves gradually lengthening muscles by holding the stretch for several seconds. Static stretching is the right way for runners to stretch.

stress/recovery principle   This principle says that you become fitter by subjecting your body to a stress, and then allowing recovery time before you stress it again. During the recovery time, the body rebuilds itself to be better able to handle that stress.

striders   Runs of 100 yards or so that you do at near full speed to develop quickness and improve your form.

supination   When your feet don't roll in enough after they've hit the ground when you run.

switchback trail   A trail that zigs and zags its way to the top of a long hill.

talk test   Seeing whether you're able to carry on a conversation while you're running. If you can't pass the talk test on most runs, you're running too quickly.

tapering   Reducing your mileage in the several days before an important race to gear up for a peak performance.

tempo run   A run of 20 to 40 minutes at your lactate threshold that you do to boost your performance in long races.

tights   Snug leggings for running in cold weather that don't restrict your freedom of movement.

trail running shoe   A training shoe with a heavily lugged outsole and other features designed for the special hazards of running on trails.

training log   A written record of your training that helps you to monitor your progress and learn from your mistakes.

training partner   A runner of similar ability with whom you run at least occasionally.

tune-up races   Short races run as part of your preparation for longer, more important races.

ultramarathon   A race that's longer than a marathon. The most common ultramarathon is 50 miles.

upper   The top part of a running shoe that holds the laces.

VO₂ max   Scientific shorthand for maximum oxygen uptake, a measure of how much of the oxygen you breathe while running that your body can use. The higher your VO_2 max, the faster you can run.

The Wall   What you crash into in a marathon, usually around 20 miles, when your body runs out of glycogen. When you hit The Wall, you have to slow down drastically.

warm-up   A short, easy jog before a race or hard run that prepares you for more intense activity.

wicking   The ability of a fiber to move moisture from your skin to the surface of a garment so that you stay more comfortable while running.

Runner's Pace Chart

Pace per mile	1 mile	2 miles	3 miles	5K (3.1 miles)	4 miles	5 miles	6 miles	10K (6.2 miles)
6:00	6:00	12:00	18:00	18:39	24:00	30:00	36:00	37:18
6:10	6:10	12:20	18:30	19:10	24:40	30:50	37:00	38:20
6:20	6:20	12:40	19:00	19:41	25:20	31:40	38:00	39:22
6:30	6:30	13:00	19:30	20:12	26:00	32:30	39:00	40:24
6:40	6:40	13:20	20:00	20:43	26:40	33:20	40:00	41:26
6:50	6:50	13:40	20:30	21:14	27:20	34:10	41:00	42:28
7:00	7:00	14:00	21:00	21:45	28:00	35:00	42:00	43:30
7:10	7:10	14:20	21:30	22:16	28:40	35:50	43:00	44:32
7:20	7:20	14:40	22:00	22:47	29:20	36:40	44:00	45:34
7:30	7:30	15:00	22:30	23:18	30:00	37:30	45:00	46:36
7:40	7:40	15:20	23:00	23:49	30:40	38:20	46:00	47:38
7:50	7:50	15:40	23:30	24:20	31:20	39:10	47:00	48:40
8:00	8:00	16:00	24:00	24:51	32:00	40:00	48:00	49:42
8:10	8:10	16:20	24:30	25:22	32:40	40:50	49:00	50:44
8:20	8:20	16:40	25:00	25:53	33:20	41:40	50:00	51:46
8:30	8:30	17:00	25:30	26:24	34:00	42:30	51:00	52:48
8:40	8:40	17:20	26:00	26:55	34:40	43:20	52:00	53:50
8:50	8:50	17:40	26:30	27:26	35:20	44:10	53:00	54:52
9:00	9:00	18:00	27:00	27:57	36:00	45:00	54:00	55:54
9:10	9:10	18:20	27:30	28:28	36:40	45:50	55:00	56:56
9:20	9:20	18:40	28:00	28:59	37:20	46:40	56:00	57:58
9:30	9:30	19:00	28:30	29:30	38:00	47:30	57:00	59:00
9:40	9:40	19:20	29:00	30:01	38:40	48:20	58:00	1:00:02
9:50	9:50	19:40	29:30	30:32	39:20	49:10	59:00	1:01:04
10:00	10:00	20:00	30:00	31:03	40:00	50:00	1:00:00	1:02:06

continues

continued

Pace per mile	1 mile	2 miles	3 miles	5K (3.1 miles)	4 miles	5 miles	6 miles	10K (6.2 miles)
10:10	10:10	20:20	30:30	31:34	40:40	50:50	1:01:00	1:03:08
10:20	10:20	20:40	31:00	32:05	41:20	51:40	1:02:00	1:04:10
10:30	10:30	21:00	31:30	32:36	42:00	52:30	1:03:00	1:05:12
10:40	10:40	21:20	32:00	33:07	42:40	53:20	1:04:00	1:06:14
10:50	10:50	21:40	32:30	33:38	43:20	54:10	1:05:00	1:07:16
11:00	11:00	22:00	33:00	34:09	44:00	55:00	1:06:00	1:08:18
11:10	11:10	22:20	33:30	34:40	44:40	55:50	1:07:00	1:09:20
11:20	11:20	22:40	34:00	35:11	45:20	56:40	1:08:00	1:10:22
11:30	11:30	23:00	34:30	35:42	46:00	57:30	1:09:00	1:11:24
11:40	11:40	23:20	35:00	36:13	46:40	58:20	1:10:00	1:12:26
11:50	11:50	23:40	35:30	36:44	47:20	59:10	1:11:00	1:13:28
12:00	12:00	24:00	36:00	37:15	48:00	1:00:00	1:12:00	1:15:30

Pace per mile	10 miles	Half-marathon (13.1 miles)	15 miles
6:00	1:00:00	1:18:39	1:30:00
6:10	1:01:40	1:20:50	1:32:30
6:20	1:03:20	1:23:01	1:35:00
6:30	1:05:00	1:25:13	1:37:30
6:40	1:06:40	1:27:23	1:40:00
6:50	1:08:20	1:29:34	1:42:30
7:00	1:10:00	1:31:32	1:45:00
7:10	1:11:40	1:33:57	1:47:30
7:20	1:13:20	1:36:08	1:50:00
7:30	1:15:00	1:38:20	1:52:30
7:40	1:16:40	1:40:30	1:55:00
7:50	1:18:20	1:42:42	1:57:30
8:00	1:20:00	1:44:52	2:00:00
8:10	1:21:40	1:47:02	2:02:30
8:20	1:23:20	1:49:15	2:05:00
8:30	1:25:00	1:51:25	2:07:30
8:40	1:26:40	1:53:07	2:10:00
8:50	1:28:20	1:55:18	2:12:30

Pace per mile	10 miles	Half-marathon (13.1 miles)	15 miles
9:00	1:30:00	1:58:00	2:15:00
9:10	1:31:40	2:00:11	2:17:30
9:20	1:33:20	2:02:22	2:20:00
9:30	1:35:00	2:04:33	2:22:30
9:40	1:36:40	2:06:44	2:25:00
9:50	1:38:20	2:08:55	2:27:30
10:00	1:40:00	2:11:07	2:30:00
10:10	1:41:40	2:13:17	2:32:30
10:20	1:43:20	2:15:28	2:35:00
10:30	1:45:00	2:17:40	2:37:30
10:40	1:46:40	2:19:50	2:40:00
10:50	1:48:20	2:22:01	2:42:30
11:00	1:50:00	2:24:12	2:45:00
11:10	1:51:40	2:26:23	2:47:30
11:20	1:53:20	2:28:34	2:50:00
11:30	1:55:00	2:30:45	2:52:30
11:40	1:56:40	2:32:56	2:55:00
11:50	1:58:20	2:35:08	2:57:30
12:00	2:00:00	2:37:19	3:00:00

Pace per mile	20 miles	Marathon (26.2 miles)
6:00	2:00:00	2:37:19
6:10	2:03:20	2:41:41
6:20	2:06:40	2:46:03
6:30	2:10:00	2:50:25
6:40	2:13:20	2:54:47
6:50	2:16:40	2:59:09
7:00	2:20:00	3:03:03
7:10	2:23:20	3:07:55
7:20	2:26:40	3:12:17
7:30	2:30:00	3:16:39

continues

continued

Pace per mile	20 miles	Marathon (26.2 miles)
7:40	2:33:20	3:21:01
7:50	2:36:40	3:25:23
8:00	2:40:00	3:29:45
8:10	2:43:20	3:34:07
8:20	2:46:40	3:38:29
8:30	2:50:00	3:42:51
8:40	2:53:20	3:47:13
8:50	2:56:40	3:51:35
9:00	3:00:00	3:56:00
9:10	3:03:20	4:00:19
9:20	3:06:40	4:04:41
9:30	3:10:00	4:09:03
9:40	3:13:20	4:13:25
9:50	3:16:40	4:17:50
10:00	3:20:00	4:22:12
10:10	3:23:20	4:26:34
10:20	3:26:40	4:30:56
10:30	3:30:00	4:35:19
10:40	3:33:20	4:39:40
10:50	3:36:40	4:44:02
11:00	3:40:00	4:48:24
11:10	3:43:20	4:52:46
11:20	3:46:40	4:57:08
11:30	3:50:00	5:01:30
11:40	3:53:20	5:05:52
11:50	3:56:40	5:10:15
12:00	4:00:00	5:14:38

Organizations

American College of Sports Medicine

www.acsm.org

The members of this professional organization are primarily sports medicine and exercise science professionals. This organization regularly disseminates information to the public on the latest in exercise science and nutrition based on the research of its members. It also publishes *Medicine & Science in Sports & Exercise*, a monthly, peer-reviewed publication of recent research.

American Running Association

www.americanrunning.org

This nonprofit, educational organization of athletes and sports medicine professionals distributes brochures and other information to the public about training, nutrition, and injury treatment and prevention. Members receive a monthly e-newsletter, *Running & FitNews*.

American Trail Running Association

www.trailrunner.com

This association promotes trail running in the United States.

Lifelong Fitness Alliance

www.50plus.org

This association provides information on matters such as how exercise lessens the effects of aging and special exercise considerations for older adults. The group also sponsors lectures and sporting events.

Road Runners Club of America
www.rrca.org

This nonprofit association consists of running club members. The national office provides services and information about running to local clubs and the general public. In addition to its quarterly magazine, *Footnotes*, it also produces brochures on children's running and other topics.

USA Track & Field
www.usatf.org

This organization is the national governing body for track and field, road racing, and racewalking in the United States. Its various committees and local associations administer running events and regulations. It also maintains race records, including age-group rankings.

Running-Related Charity Groups

Fred's Team
www.mskcc.org

Affiliated with the Memorial Sloan-Kettering Cancer Center, this group encourages runners and walkers to raise funds at events for cancer research. It's named in honor of Fred Lebow, who created the five-borough New York City Marathon and died of cancer.

Joints in Motion
www.arthritis.org/events/JointsinMotion

Affiliated with the Arthritis Foundation, Joints in Motion trains runners to participate in major marathons while raising funds for arthritis research.

Leukemia & Lymphoma Society Team in Training
www.teamintraining.org

Affiliated with the Leukemia & Lymphoma Society, Team in Training trains runners and walkers to participate in marathons and triathlons while raising money to support the society's research and programs.

Susan G. Komen Foundation
www.raceforthecure.com

The foundation organizes the national Race for the Cure series of 5K races, which raises money for breast cancer research.

Magazines and Newsletters

Marathon and Beyond
www.marathonandbeyond.com

This magazine offers detailed training information for races of the marathon and longer, and comprehensive stories about the history of the sport. It comes out six times a year. Each issue is the size of a small book.

National Masters News
www.nationalmastersnews.com

This is the official publication for masters (age 40 and over) in running, track and field, and racewalking. It primarily consists of competition results and event calendars.

Runner's World
www.runnersworld.com

This monthly magazine is the largest running publication in the world. It's aimed primarily at beginning and intermediate runners. It contains articles on low-key training, cross-training, nutrition, and weight loss.

Running Times
www.runningtimes.com

This magazine contains training, nutrition, and sports medicine advice and shoe and apparel reviews aimed to performance-oriented runners. It comes out 10 times a year. Bill Rodgers is a contributing editor, and co-author Scott Douglas is a senior editor.

Trail Runner Magazine
www.trailrunnermag.com

This magazine provides extensive information on trail running training, gear, and technique. It comes out every other month.

The Internet

www.active.com
This site includes an extensive nationwide calendar of events that accept online registration.

www.americanrunning.org
The home page of the American Running Association includes articles on training, sports medicine, nutrition, a listing of free running-related brochures, and help with choosing a running shoe.

www.coolrunning.com
Race results, stories, commentary, and race schedules are all available on this site.

www.marathonguide.com
This site contains information on and links to hundreds of marathons in the United States and abroad.

www.rrca.org
This site is the home page of the Road Runners Club of America.

www.runnersworld.com
This site provides news, race coverage, records, and training advice that's updated every working day.

www.runningnetwork.com
You can find lots of regional magazines and results on this site.

www.runningtimes.com
News, training articles, injury primers, and race reports are added daily to this site.

www.usatf.org
This site is the home page of USATF, the national federation for road racing, track and field, and racewalking in the United States. It features an extensive database of user-generated running routes throughout the United States.

Index

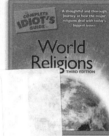

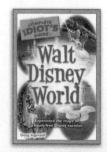